Zen of the Plains

Experiencing Wild Western Places

ZEN
OF THE PLAINS

Experiencing Wild Western Places

Tyra A. Olstad

Number 2 in the Southwestern Nature Writing Series

UNIVERSITY OF NORTH TEXAS PRESS
DENTON, TEXAS

10 9 8 7 6 5 4 3 2 1

Permissions:
University of North Texas Press
1155 Union Circle #311336
Denton, TX 76203-5017

The paper used in this book meets the minimum requirements of the
American National Standard for Permanence of Paper for Printed Library
Materials, z39.48.1984. Binding materials have been chosen for durability.

Library of Congress Cataloging-in-Publication Data

Olstad, Tyra.
Zen of the plains : experiencing wild Western places / by Tyra A.
Olstad.
    pages cm -- (Number 2 in the Southwestern nature writing series)
Includes bibliographical references.
  ISBN 978-1-57441-552-0 (cloth : alk. paper) -- ISBN 978-1-57441-562-9
(ebook)
1. Wilderness areas--West (U.S.)--Philosophy. 2. Wilderness
areas--West (U.S.)--Pictorial works. 3. Plains--West (U.S.)--Philosophy.
4. Plains--West (U.S.)--Pictorial works. 5. Grasslands--West
(U.S.)--Philosophy. 6. Grasslands--West (U.S.)--Pictorial works. 7.
Natural history--West (U.S.) 8. Zen Buddhism. 9. West (U.S.)--Pictorial
works. I. Title. II. Series: Southwestern nature writing series ; no. 2.
F591.O635 2014
978--dc23
                    2014001194

Book design by Mark Lerner

Zen of the Plains: Experiencing Wild Western Places is Number 2 in the
Southwestern Nature Writing Series

The electronic edition of this book was made possible by the support of the
Vick Family Foundation.

Dedication

For Jon C. Olstad, who has given me a sense of freedom and curiosity and encouraged me to live life as an adventure; and Jane L. Olstad, who has been my rock, my map, my guide back to the world every time I've ventured too far.

Contents

List of Illustrations   ix

Acknowledgments   xiii

Prologue: Flyover Country; Scottsbluff, NE   1

Chapter 1: Shortgrass / Semi-Desert Shrub-Steppe   9

1.1 Terra Incognita: Petrified Forest National Park, AZ   9

1.2 Can't Get Lost: Painted Desert Wilderness Area, AZ   16

1.3 Blank: Painted Desert Wilderness Area, AZ   24

Interim: Highway 36; Northwestern KS   32

1.4 Slow Down!; Petrified Forest National Park, AZ   37

1.5 Rhythms, Cycles, Spirals; Petrified Forest National Park, AZ   51

    Part I: Sun-Sitting   51

    Part II: A Day   60

Interim: Sense of Place; The Red Desert, WY   78

1.6 The Quest; Pilot Rock, Painted Desert Wilderness Area, AZ   93

Interim: Dream of Place; Laramie, Wyoming and the Painted
    Desert, AZ   124

1.7 Beauty and Desire, Beauty and Despair; Petrified Forest National
    Park, AZ   130

Chapter 2: Mixedgrass 137

2.1 Wonderlands; Badlands National Park, SD 137

2.2 National Grasslands; Buffalo Gap and Comanche Nat'l
    Grasslands, SD and CO 146

2.3 Animal Encounters; Badlands National Park, SD 155
    Part I: The Theory of Birds 155
    Part II: Rewildling **161**

Interim: Medora to Marmarth (With Some Dinosaur Statues in
    Between); SD, ND, MT, and WY **166**

2.4 Interpretation and Inspiration; Badlands National Park, SD **176**

Chapter 3: Tallgrass 183

3.1 Experiment and Experience, Or, How I Tried to Like a Prairie;
    Konza Prairie Preserve, KS **183**

Interim: In Which I Discover an Island and Fall in Love with a
    Forest; Tongass Nat'l Forest, AK **196**

3.2 Conversations with Konza; Konza Prairie Preserve, KS **206**

Chapter 4: Shortgrass / Semi-Desert Shrub-Steppe 219

4.1 The Return to the Plains; Fossil Butte National Monument,
    WY **219**

Interim: The Mapmaker's Discipline; Fossil Butte, WY and Petrified
    Forest, AZ **222**

4.2 Winter; Fossil Butte National Monument, WY **227**

**Conclusion: A Brief Meditation on Expectation and
Emptiness** 235

Notes **237**
Bibliography **255**
Index **267**

Maps, Illustrations, and Diagrams

List of Maps

Map 1: Journeys through parks and prairies

Map 2: Painted Desert Wilderness Area

Map 3: Northern half of Petrified Forest National Park

Map 4: Headquarters area, Badlands National Park

Map 5: Konza Prairie Preserve

List of Illustrations

01: The Painted Desert Wilderness Area – clay and sage crouching
    under the silhouette of Pilot Rock

02: Beautiful! Beautiful! Magnificent desolation!

03: Lithodendron Wash

04: Following the bobcat

05: View from Pintado Point

06: Agate Fossil Beds National Monument, Nebraska

07: Petroglyph panel on the bank of Lithodendron Wash

08: Self-portrait with sun

09: Tawa Point, dawn

10: Clay, rock, and horizon baking in the midday sun

11: Sacred datura, opening for a storm

12: Old Route 66, the morning after a monsoon

35: Triticum—a wild wheat

14: Enchantment

15: Night sweeps over the Painted Desert Inn Cabins

16: Pilot Rock, summer noon

17: Mural by Fred Kabotie, dining room, Painted Desert Inn
    Museum

18: Pilot Rock, evening storm

19: Foxtail barley, Hordeum jubatum

20: Sunset in the Wonderlands

21: Boundary between Badlands and Buffalo Gap

22: Ah, Matsuo Basho, how much I too desire!: "Inside my little
    satchel, / the moon, and flowers"

23: Marmarth station

24: Trail, Konza Prairie Preserve

25: Post-burn puddle

26: My little island, off the coast of a larger island off the coast of
    southeast Alaska

27: Celastrina (neglecta?)—an azure butterfly, one of many little
    prairie wonders

28: Mooless Konza cattle

29: Trail in winter

30: Life bursting forth after burn

31: Grasses grow back; I leave

32: Fossil Butte, Wyoming

33: Road alongside Fossil Butte; autumn sky rolling in

36: The first blizzard sweeps in, with 30 mph winds, dangerously
    bitter temperatures, and breathtakingly beautiful skies

35: Winter comes to Fossil Butte

35: Winter on the plains

36: Dawn at -5 degrees; air raw with light

37: Sparkling world of snow, sky, and rabbit

38: Post-blizzard stillness

39: Train cutting through the late morning canvas

40: Zen

List of Diagrams

1: Dimensions of Place

Acknowledgments

Although this work mentions few people by name, I could not have completed it without the support and inspiration of friends and colleagues I've been fortunate enough to meet and work with over the years. A heartfelt thank you to enthusiastic, dedicated, and caring personnel at Petrified Forest National Park, Badlands National Park, and Fossil Butte National Monument as well as professors and fellow students at Dartmouth College, the University of Wyoming, and Kansas State University. Special thanks to Kevin Blake, John Harrington, Jr., Lisa Harrington, Elizabeth Dodd, and Wendy Ornelas.

Journeys through parks and prairies

Therefore, take yourself and observe yourself.
Take the world and observe the world.

— Lao Tzu, *Tao Te Ching*

Flyover Country

Scottsbluff, Nebraska

[W]hile I know the standard claim is that Yosemite, Niagara Falls, the
upper Yellowstone and the like, afford the greatest natural shows, I am not
so sure but the prairies and plains, while less stunning at first sight, last
longer, fill the esthetic sense fuller, and precede all the rest . . . what most
impress'd me, and will longest remain with me, are these same prairies.

—Walt Whitman, *Specimen Days,*
America's Characteristic Landscape[1]

Hot. Hazy. The June sun was glaring down on the dusty brown earth and
distant black cattle and my father and me, sitting in a Piper Cherokee,
slowly buzzing our way west.

It was our fourth day in that little plane. We had begun the trip full of
enthusiasm, lifting off from the Niagara Falls International Airport into a
sun-pierced sky and skimming over islands of light on Lake Erie. The next
day, we slipped between tidy white puffs and their neatly spaced shadows

on checkerboard fields below. Ohio, Indiana, Illinois, Wisconsin, then past the muddy meanders of the Mississippi (the Mississippi! I'd never seen the Mississippi!). The land began flattening out, drying brown, browner, beige. Thin strips of road cut indomitably straight lines toward the horizon, occasionally intersecting in sharp, desperate 90-degree angles. Tiny bovine dots clustered just as desperately at infrequent watering holes while bzzzz the engine droned on above them, were we actually moving or just hovering, suspended in time and space? It was hard to tell.

We were on our way to Colorado (Colorado!)—Rocky Mountain National Park. I had never been to Colorado, or even west of the Mississippi. Aside from a few trips to visit family in North Carolina, Ohio, and Albany, I had rarely ventured far from the same house on the same street in the same semi-rural community in Western New York. When my parents offered to take me on a trip for a high school graduation present, *Colorado!*, I told them, I want to go to that legendary place called *Colorado!* To see *mountains!* Real, high, rocky *mountains!* (I think I'd seen a generic Western landscape photo in a calendar in third or fourth grade, dreamed of the Rockies ever since?)

Of course, to get to Colorado from Western New York, we had to cross the Great Plains—that sparse, dull, desolate stretch of grass and dirt that yawns across the middle of the continent. An Empty Quarter. The Great American Desert. Flyover Country.

The thought of flying over anywhere intrigues my father, who is a recreational pilot. He suggested that instead of taking a commercial flight, we could borrow a single-engine Piper Cherokee and fly ourselves. That way, as he put it, we could see a bit of the country along the way, go wherever our whims and the weather led us. At that point in my life, I couldn't comprehend how much distance, how much land, how much *space* stretched between New York and the Rocky Mountains, so I agreed to pack up a tent, boots, and aviation charts and fly west.

We made it to Lima, Ohio, the first night. At the airport there, another pilot heard we were bound for Colorado and suggested aiming
for Loveland. *There's a national park nearby*, he said. *Okay*, we replied,
happy to have a destination. In Prairie du Chien, Wisconsin, the next
night, we ate fried catfish and watched the Mississippi meander by—a
grand, muddy threshold to the West. By Yankton, South Dakota, though,
I was beginning to suspect that some of my universal concepts—"space,"
"time," "travel"—might need to be rethought. On the fourth afternoon—
one of the longest afternoons of my life, hours and hours in that loud
stuffy cockpit, headset so tight on my brain, land and sky, land and sky,
so harsh on my eyes, land and sky—I was tired. Thirsty. Had a headache.
Ate an apple. Nearly a century after Willa Cather wrote *My Ántonia*, as
yet, "the only thing very noticeable about Nebraska was that it was still,
all day long, Nebraska."[2]

When the light began to stretch toward shades of early evening, Dad
and I gave up hope of seeing mountains on the horizon and radioed in to
KBFF—the Western Nebraska Regional Airport in Scottsbluff, Nebraska.
As usual, we knew nothing about the town where we happened to land.
Where should we eat dinner?, we asked the man who refueled the gas
tanks, *where should we stay, anything in particular we should see or do?*

Well, there's the actual Bluff, he replied, *you could go see that. It's the
main touristy thing here.*

We borrowed the airport's courtesy car and drove out to the landmark.
There might have been an entrance sign, a visitor center, something telling us we were in a national monument (established 1919, please stay on
the trail, don't harass the wildlife?), but really I don't remember a thing
about the place—nothing about geology, ecology, any cultural and historic
significance. I only remember the *feel*—the air, cooling comfortably; the
light, lingering softly; the space, so much *space*! We had just enough
time to walk to the bluff, touch the earth, breathe the sky, before the
purple-periwinkle dusk descended and there we were, out on the plains.

The sun touched the southwestern horizon. We stopped whatever we were doing and faced it.

"Every night we go through this," Devin said without breaking eye contact with the sunset. "Everything's going to be different here. In thirty seconds."

. . . As the sun shrank, the light turned tepid. Devin pointed straight at the bright, sinking knob, saying, "Watch it. It doesn't even pause. This whole thing is wound around us, some kind of great machine that's about to close us out. There it goes. There . . . there . . ." He inhaled when it happened. The light flashed out.

"Done," he said. He turned to me. His voice was softer now, a little crazy. "Now, here we are."

—Craig Childs, *Soul of Nowhere*[3]

When European and Euro-American soldiers, missionaries, fur traders, and emigrants made their first tentative tracks into the interior of the North American continent, they encountered a wasteland—a stark, desolate, uninhabitable, seemingly interminable stretch of land. The environment was so unfamiliar that people didn't even know what noun to use to describe it at first: French fur traders borrowed a term for "woodland meadow"—*une prairie*—to try to describe a grassy gap, but the word failed to encompass the prairie's dominant feature—the sky. In 1820, Major Stephen Long put the label "Great Desert" on a map, suggesting that the area was, in the words of rhetoricist Thomas Scanlan, "a sterile, barren, Godforsaken place, boring, monotonous, violent, and closed off from possibilities . . . beyond redemption."[4] The reality—stretches of tall, dense grass and/or scraggly brush—is something in between woodland meadow and true desert; ecologists today use the terms "grassland" and "steppe."[5]

The terrain, meanwhile, often consists of rolling hills, ridges and ravines, wide rivers and thin washes, but is most often thought of as flat—purely, relentlessly, pancake-pan flat. Thus another, not-quite-synonymous term:

"plain." Plain old planes—two-dimensional expanses that generally lack landscape features. The pejorative "Plain" was upgraded to ambivalent "Great-"ness by Alexander Henry the Elder in 1776, but not formalized until 1848, when John Fremont's cartographer included it on a map; William Gilpin enthusiastically repeated and geographically expanded the "Great Plains" soon thereafter.[6]

Great or Plain, names mattered little to mid-nineteenth-century emigrants who knew they faced a long haul across harsh, exposed stretches of country that separated them from their far western promised lands. After weeks of dirt, grass, and sky, travelers on the Oregon Trail welcomed the sight of Scottsbluff not least for the visual relief of vertical topography. Plains territories enjoyed a glowing if brief perceptual and demographic boom in the mid- to late-1800s when political, promotional, and climatic factors (passage of the Homestead Act of 1862, publication of numerous brochures depicting the Great Plains as an Edenic garden, and a multi-year stretch of slightly wetter weather) convinced thousands of settlers to try claiming their own 160 acres in the heart of the continent. Eager homesteaders rapidly privatized and plowed under the easternmost tall- and mixed-grass prairies, but realized that they would need to own and/ or use larger tracts of land in order to survive on the short-grass prairies and semi-desert shrub-steppes of the western Great Plains, Great Basin, and Southwest—drier, rockier terrain that would barely support livestock. Though the federal government expanded available range parcels to 640 acres through the Desert Land Act of 1877 and Stock Raising Homestead Act of 1916, no amount of legislation could overcome the stark reality of harsh climates and rocky soil. When the Dust Bowl blew through, many settlers wearily conceded, as anthropologist and essayist Loren Eiseley expressed it, "[w]e were mad to settle the West in [this] fashion . . . You cannot fight the sky."[7]

At the same time that farmers and ranchers were trying to scratch a living out of the dusty soil and volatile seasons, wealthy Easterners were speeding across the plains in search of sublime scenery. Imaginations ignited by late-nineteenth and early-twentieth century promotional materials (travelogues, newspaper articles, landscape paintings, and, soon enough, photographs), more and more Americans headed West to see their new national parks and monuments. Before reaching the rugged mountains, shadowed forests, and sparkling waters (as well as the luxurious resorts) promised by the railroad industry's "See America First" campaign, however, tourists had to get across that unimaginable "immensity of open space," notable only for its "overpowering sense of vastness . . . indescribable feeling of solitude, [and] mighty loneliness," as Walter Marshall described it in his 1882 travelogue *Through America; Or, Nine Months in the United States.*[8] According to historian Jean Retzinger, who analyzed a half-century's (1866–1906) worth of advertisements and first-hand accounts of railway journeys across Nebraska, "for many [early tourists], the landscape possessed even fewer distinguishing characteristics; emptiness and absence seemed its most noticeable attributes."[9] So much open land, Kathleen Norris adds in her spiritual geography *Dakota*, "evokes in many people a panicked desire to get through it as quickly as possible."[10]

Scorn for emptiness and absence—amplified by loneliness, sadness, and panic—continued to plague prairies during early- and mid-twentieth century tourism booms in America. Enabled by a growing road system and increasingly affordable personal automobiles, citizens went in search of the "sublime, picturesque, and uncanny" landscapes preserved in National Parks and reproduced in the rugged photographs of Ansel Adams and romantic paintings of Albert Bierstadt and Thomas Moran. Relatively flat, featureless grasslands could hardly compare. According to standards of landscape design, prairie lines are too simple, their form too flat, colors and textures too bland to be beautiful; "[n]othing is there," scenic management specialist Neil Evernden explains the woes of wide horizons, "no things to measure or enjoy . . . nothing to possess."[11] Even

Aldo Leopold, that giant of environmental ethics, realizes: "When hoping if not expecting to be entertained by the grand, amusing, and spectacular parts of nature (such as in national parks), we find the . . . plains 'tedious' and the prairies . . . boring." ("A plain exterior often conceals hidden riches"! he promises.)[12]

Feedback between artistic interpretation, environmental preservation, and increased visitation has amplified the gap between scenic parks and the seemingly dull, desolate plain planar Plains. Now, more than ever, westbound travelers have, in the words of geographer Kevin Blake, "little inclination to take the time needed to understand the simpler and smaller beauties of the plains. They want mountains."[13]

Oh, right. Mountains.

Mountains are revered in many cultures—they are the homes of gods, the sites of temples, the dwelling place of gurus, found at both the center and the farthest corners of spiritual landscapes. Visible for vast distances, they provide a reliable anchor for tales and an omnipresent waypoint for journeys. Truth-seekers make pilgrimages to the tops of peaks, or, out of even greater deference and respect, circumambulate their bases—around and around and around, bowing, bending down then lifting up, moving forward, standing still.

I grew up in a place with no mountains and no monuments, no parks and definitely no plains—a relatively comfortable, happy childhood in a relatively comfortable, pleasant place. I didn't know it yet, but I was looking for something bigger, deeper, wilder. This trip marked the beginning of a long pilgrimage around and over and into "flat," "desolate," "empty" places, some of which changed me and some of which did not.

Rocky Mountain National Park? Nice enough. Dad and I, along with hordes of other tourists, blithely claimed a campsite, headed to Estes for dinner, drove the scenic routes (parking our rental SUV in the middle of the road to snap photos of elk, need be), and, of course, tried to summit Longs Peak. (It was a little higher than we'd expected.) Ten years and Arizona, South Dakota, Kansas, Alaska, and Wyoming later, memories from that part of the journey have dimmed. No, what I remember best is the feel of *space* in Scottsbluff—the simple sweep of the horizon; the rich color of the air. My first glimpse of Zen out on the plains.

CHAPTER 1

Shortgrass / Semi-Desert Shrub-Steppe

1.1 Terra Incognita
Petrified Forest National Park, Arizona

Before desire and before knowing, how can I say I am? Consider.
Dissolve in the beauty.

—The 72nd of Shiva's 112 ways to open the invisible door of
consciousness, trans. by Paul Reps[1]

The wind was whipping fiercely. Grey clouds hung low over a rugged
expanse of scraggly sagebrush, sandy arroyos, and the occasional tumbleweed or dust devil or raven swooping by. Because I didn't yet have the
words for "sagebrush" or "arroyo" or "raven" on that cold November
morning, I was left with nothing but an empty horizon and big black
birds.

I had been driving for hours, following Interstate 40 into northern
Arizona, where I was to report for an internship at Petrified Forest
National Park. Although I sought a bit of adventure—anything other than

another long cold winter at college in New Hampshire—I was beginning to wonder just what I was doing, where I was going, how I could possibly pass the next four months in such a place. (Such a place! Were there *any* people here? What *were* those birds?) Having spent my life comfortably surrounded by roads and rivers, trees and buildings, I was both intrigued and terrified by the yawning desolation of the landscape—what was out there but cold, windy, open space?

Space.

When I finally saw the big brown sign for Exit 311, I pulled off the Interstate and slowed from 70 miles per hour to 30, then 10. The slower I went, the more ragged, dusty, and bleak the place looked. Interpretive displays at the visitor center tried to convince me that the semi-desert shrub-steppe brims with wonders, but a few paragraphs of text and a few minutes' worth of introductory film hardly gave me time to internalize information. (Antiquities Act? *Artemisia*? *Aur-o-car-i-ox-y*-what?) My mind was whirling as I got back into my car and started to drive down the park's twenty-odd miles of neatly paved road.

Then it happened. A half-mile or so later, just before the first scenic overlook, I came around a curve and the earth dropped away or the sky lifted up and I felt the delicious, dizzy onset of agoraphilia.

There it was: the Painted Desert.

The Painted Desert is a land of rusty clay hills, sharp sandstone ledges, winding washes and pockets of grass that stretches in a polychromatic arc across northeastern Arizona. By formal classification standards, the region is not technically a "desert" but rather a shrub-steppe or shortgrass prairie, marked by an arid climate and predominance of low, woody vegetation. Long before ecological equations and regional maps could inform the public of this fact, Spanish explorers affixed the term "desierto"—"El Desierto Pintado"—to the barren but beautiful land they encountered on their quest to locate the

Painted Desert Wilderness Area—clay and sage crouching under the silhouette of Pilot Rock

Seven Cities of Gold for Francisco Vasquez de Coronado. Lieutenant Joseph Christmas Ives and his Colorado River Exploring Expedition formalized use of the toponym "Painted Desert" in 1858—five years after Lieutenant Amiel Weeks Whipple wrote about "quite a forest of petrified trees" he had discovered while surveying the 35th parallel.

By the turn of the twentieth century, these fossil forests had become an attraction for railway travelers. An increasing number of early visitors were so intrigued and delighted by the colorful crystalline wood that they arranged to cart large chunks back home. Afraid that the dwindling deposits might disappear altogether, local enthusiasts—including John

Muir, who spent several years in the area—urged President Theodore Roosevelt to exercise the power granted to him by Antiquities Act of 1906 to preserve sites of superlative cultural and/or geologic merit for all present and future generations of American citizens. Thus Petrified Forest National Monument—one of America's first national monuments—was born. Congress conferred National Park status in 1962, protecting the jumble of geologic curiosities as well as a diverse array of other significant resources: fossils dating to the dawn of the dinosaurs, artifacts from eras of Native American inhabitation, intact tracts of shortgrass-steppe, and, encompassing it all, breathtakingly beautiful scenery.

The Painted Desert. To the Diné, or Navajo people, the southwestern swath of their reservation is not a noun but a clause: *Hal chiitah*, "amidst the colors." Hopi and Zuni descendants of earlier inhabitants—the Ancestral Puebloans—consider the region *Assam unda*, or the "country of departed spirits." Meanwhile, if you look at a park map today, you'll see not just "Petrified Forest" or "Painted Desert" but two units of capital-"W" Wilderness, established "for the permanent good of the whole people" by Congress and National Park Service officials on 23 October 1970.[2]

Shrub-steppes and Spaniards; spirits and skeletons; Wilderness. That's what I was looking at on that Novembery morning—Wilderness. Wildness. I knew no names, nothing about attributes or management plans or preconceptions of "place," just tangled-earth, stormy-skied, meaningless, memory-less space.

Space.

Of course, there's no such thing as "wilderness" or "empty space," no terra incognita wholly unknown to and unaffected by man. Scientists and surveyors, settlers and travelers have traipsed about if not tried to live on nearly every inch of the earth's surface, including the Painted Desert.

If the long legacy of place-names isn't proof enough that people have known the area for ages, it's open for public consumption in professional journals and postcard booklets, photo albums and travelogues, satellite images and a 1:24000, 7.5 minute topographic map, available for purchase at the Painted Desert Visitor Center. Moreover, the land itself is riddled with physical traces of inhabitation and use—petroglyphs and pottery sherds, stone tools and building blocks, railroad tracks and Route 66, roads and buildings and bridges. The Painted Desert is not a geographic unknown. But it was unknown to me.

Geographer J. K. Wright happily champions the place of the imagination: "[w]hether or not a particular area may be called 'unknown' depends both on whose knowledge and what kind of knowledge is taken into account."[3] Observed or derived, physical or abstract, personal or cultural, what do people "know" of their backyards much less the entire globe? Society in general may be aware of the existence of a place called the Painted Desert, but that doesn't mean everyone can locate it on a map; scientists may be able to list species and soil types, but will never be able to identify and explain all of the phenomena that make up the smallest patch of prairie. I could spend the rest of my life exploring the northern wilderness unit's 43,020 acres, hiking every wash, touching every rock, greeting every bird every bush every rare and beautiful raindrop and there would always be more to see, to learn, to know, to feel.

Feeling is believing; philosopher-geographer Edmunds Bunkše plays with a multiplicity of "feelings": "feeling" as the sensory process by which a person experiences the external environment and "feeling" as the emotional expression of an individual's inner way of being. Emotions are tactile, he suggests—based in real-world phenomena.[4]

I agree. When first I stood at Tiponi Point, awed by the spare, rugged beauty of the landscape—a low sky, a labyrinth of color, and a big black knoll defining and dominating the border between the two—something caught in my heart. The lines? The textures? The allure of unexplored terrain? I wasn't expecting, much less aspiring, to fall in love with the Painted Desert—to return to it again and again; to have it haunt my dreams. Had I stayed up at the overlook, merely ogling the scene from above and afar, I may not have. The place couldn't become part of me until I touched it; felt it; knew it in my bones.

Visitors can access the northern wilderness unit via a trail starting just west of the Painted Desert Inn Museum, about two miles into the park. "Beware of rattlesnakes," reads the informational / warning sign located at the trailhead, "Never reach where you can't see. Wear sturdy boots," and, in bold, "**you must be prepared.**" Taking the

Beautiful! Beautiful! Magnificent desolation!

advice to heart, I filled my water bottle, laced up my boots, zipped on my windbreaker, and slipped off the edge of the flat, shrubby plains. The path switchbacked me down through dark outcrops of basalt, pale ledges of sandstone, and crumbles of rust-red clay; down past clumps of grass and brush and three lonely piñon pines; down from the breathtaking plains panorama to a narrow V-shaped drainage, nothing to see but elephant-skin walls of bentonite. Nothing, that is, but mud and stones; petrified wood and weeds and wildflowers. Ten thousand nameless wonders.

I meandered along, marveling at the texture of the clay and the crunch of cobbles—the secrets that each twist revealed. But then I turned a corner and *Whoosh!* a cold dry wind tore the breath from my lungs. (Couldn't breathe. Breathtaking.) I had popped out of the safe, sheltered channel and stood at the edge of a giant field—nothing but rocks and bushes, cliffs of clay; above them sky. A huge, grey sky. ("And the SKY," Georgia O'Keeffe once wrote a friend, "Anita you have never seen SKY.")

No more trail—just an unmaintained social path, a trace of trampled dirt and a few cairn-like piles. No more landmarks, at least none that I could recognize in that jumble of wildness. Nothing but me and that space. Was I supposed to step out into *that*? In my thin red windbreaker, my scuffed and broken boots? I might as well have stepped off into the ocean. Too much. Sensory overload. Cognitive dissonance. (Utter fear.)

Retreat! I turned around, huddled into the drainage, raced back up the trail. Returned to my car, my safe familiar shell from which I could see the remaining twenty-six miles of scenery.

It was magnificent.

Beautiful! Beautiful! Magnificent desolation!

— Buzz Aldrin, the moon

1.2 Can't Get Lost
Painted Desert Wilderness Area, Arizona

Ours is largely a two-dimensional world.
We are not creatures who look up often.

—Barry Lopez, *Arctic Dreams*[5]

"You can't get lost," the ranger chortled at my naïveté, "you can see where you came from."

True, perhaps. With low vegetation and undulating topography, prairies afford a clear view of the horizon—no need to worry about trees or mountains obfuscating the view. Then again, external sensory cues are crucial for navigation. When in unfamiliar space or when returning to remembered places, people need landmarks or focal points by which we can orient ourselves. Without some sort of geographic marker to tell us where we are—a road, a slight rise, the sun arcing through the sky—we wander aimlessly in circles. (Literally. Psychologists have documented people's tendency to move in loops when blindfolded and clueless.[6]) Unabashedly stark, unforgivingly horizontal, indistinguishably landmarkless plains evoke panic in people who find themselves stranded between infinite empties of grass and sky.[7]

But in the badlands and steppe of the Painted Desert Unit of the Petrified Forest National Wilderness Area, you can't get lost. If you're not sure where you are, the ranger explained, just find the nearest little knoll and look around. The Painted Desert Inn Museum sits atop a large mesa, marking the start of the access trail; you can always see where you came from.

As for where you're going? That's another story.

Looking back, I have to laugh at myself too—at my first timid forays into the wilderness. Was there really a time when I was hesitant to step off the trail? Was there really a time when I couldn't distinguish the tidy rooflines of the Painted Desert Inn Museum from the hodgepodge of hills below? Was there really a time when Pilot Rock—that big, dark, mound on the horizon, Pilot Rock, Pilot Rock—didn't anchor the farthest corner of my geographic self?

Yes.

The second time I went hiking in Petrified Forest's Wilderness, I was armed with a topographic map, a list of destinations, and descriptions of routes out and back. I traversed the first mile with confidence, following the social trail as it clung to the base of the mesa then terminated near the edge of a wide dry riverbed. Aha!, I consulted the map, "Lithodendron Wash"—the "stone tree wash"—an appropriate name for an intermittent waterway winding through a land of petrified logs.

Also, I noted, squinting at the paper in my hand, the only named feature within miles. "Chinde Mesa" sat on the park's northern border, five or six miles away; "Pilot Rock" was even farther, seven or eight miles as the raven flies. Somewhere out there, according to another ranger—a desert rat whose bleached blue eyes had crinkled with delight when I'd asked for hiking recommendations—there were also places called "Angels Garden" and "Black Forest"—wondrous concentrations of heavenly hoodoos and scatters of dark stone trunks. I was aiming for "Onyx Bridge," only two miles out, he'd promised, putting a neat "x" on the map near the second? no, third twist of Lithodendron Wash. For the most part, though, the forty-three-thousand-odd acres of the Painted Desert Unit were depicted as an unnamed tangle of topographic lines. (At a scale of 1:50,000 and contour interval of 10 meters, undulating expanses and tight ridges are rendered illegible.)

Looking up from the map, I realized that the terrain was also illegible at a scale of 1:1. Before me was the indubitable wash. Beyond it? A rise of clay capped with tumbles of sandstone; a stretch of mud clumped with shrubs. Wind, then, beginning to stir swirls of red earth. Clouds closing in, sky sitting down. My faith in names and charts faltered. Almost involuntarily, I turned back to see where I'd come from. True to form, the Painted Desert Inn Museum stood out, a beacon of safety and civilization crowning the switchbacks of the access trail. I looked up at it, then out across the wash; back, out; back, out, around, and—retreat!—followed the social path along the bottom row of clay hills, through a drainage, and up the side of the mesa, grateful for every tiny little cairn.

Once I reached the trailhead and caught my breath, I paused to consult the access trail sign with its bold "**be prepared**" and optimistic "Use landmarks for direction." In so doing, I realized that, according to official designations, I hadn't even stepped foot in Wilderness. The path is in "backcountry"; true Wilderness starts on the other side of the Lithodendron Wash.

Lithodendron Wash

"Maps are geocentric," write cognitive scientists Ranxiao Wang and Elizabeth Spelke, "but the representations that underlie place recognition are egocentric: they specify the appearance of landmarks from the vantage point of the navigating animal."[8] In other words, we live and move with*in* the spatial environment and cannot experience it as if it were a satellite image or geometric chart. Animals' brains are wired to process sensory cues—sights, sounds, and smells, in particular—to determine our location and orientation relative to our environment. We are not meant to live between two-dimensional squiggles on a thin sheet of paper.

Beyond our automatic biophysical response to space, we also engage elements of consciousness—"non-sensory factors such as goals, expectations, and stored representations of the local environment," psychologists John Philbeck and Sean O'Leary call them[9]—to process interpretations of place. Goals, expectations, stored representations: what do people want from a place; what do we think we will find; how do we remember, recall, and recreate our presence in time and space?

In 1975, geographer Jay Appleton revolutionized the field of landscape perception with his "prospect-refuge" theory, which suggests that the minds of modern *Homo sapiens* contain vestiges of early hominids' evolution on African savannas. We desire, he wrote, to experience "environmental conditions favourable to biological survival," namely a balance between the ability to see (to have a *prospect*) without being seen (to hide, or take *refuge*).[10]

Elaborating upon this hypothesis, psychophysicist Stephen Kaplan identified a number of qualities that people seek in a landscape: *complexity*, for example, along with *mystery*—allure of the anticipated unknown. Kaplan is careful to distinguish, though, between complexity and incoherence, mystery and surprise. People want and need to be able to recognize some sort of spatial structure in a landscape, he claims; the ease with which a person can interpret a particular space, find their way, and, "not trivially," find their way back determines affective response. According to his research, *legibility*—"the inference that being able to predict and maintain orientation will be possible as one wanders more deeply into the scene"—trumps interest.[11]

The Painted Desert is interesting but illegible. It hovers at perceptual extremes: look one way, you see a vast plain completely void of any distinguishing feature; turn, and see nothing but a jumble of rock and brush. Too simple, too complex. Too boring, too mysterious. What can one ask for, hope for in such an ambivalent landscape? Kaplan offers hope: "As one increases one's skill at knowing what to look for, an environment that might have been confusing, or boring, even, becomes transformed into one rich in things to see, explore, and think about." Thus "stored representations"—memories, meanings, cognitive maps—help us to comprehend and appreciate otherwise undifferentiated, meaningless space.

Space.

In my first attempt to explore the Painted Desert, I descended from the comfortable vantage of the "scenic view," stepped out of a sheltered drainage, and realized that my windbreaker was like paper against a prairie wind. Take two: I made it to banks of the Lithodendron Wash, clutched a map, and realized that I knew nothing of the real red grey blue world. After that—my third, fourth, fifthsixthseventh expeditions— I hiked ever farther, wider, following the mud-cracked meanders of the main wash to the northeast, to the southwest, on cold overcast days and, more often, under the uncompromising glare of a wintry desert sun. During workdays, when I wasn't out pacing the park's established trails or helping catalogue 220-million-year-old bivalves, I studied the desert-steppe-backcountry-wilderness from the picture windows of the Inn, trying to correlate the map's lines and x-es with the world of rock and clay below. Every weekend, though, when I laced up my hiking boots, headed down the access trail, and entered into the landscape, all thoughts of glorious exploration would collapse and I'd find myself trudging out and back along the safe, familiar bends of Lithodendron boulevard, too timid to stray far from the safe, legible known.

Then one day—a pale, sunny day, unseasonably warm for January—I aimed for the field of petrified stumps that supposedly stood about four miles and five twists alongside the Litho. After an hour or two of hiking, I had to admit that I'd gone too far north, too far east, too far . . . I had no idea. No idea where I was, much less where I was going. As usual. I stopped to consult the map. Was I at this turn, near this rise? Had I passed these lines, did those represent the lumps in front of me? The hills were whitish, capped with gritty swirls of sandstone. The sky was blue, etched with sweeping horsetails. The sun was bright, shadows short, how did that help me know where I was—where was I?

Before turning around (retreat!), I took one last look at the northern horizon. There was Chinde Mesa, closer than I'd ever seen it—so close that I could pick out green splotches of cedar growing in pockets on the striped wall. Pilot Rock, too, loomed larger, darker, even more imposing than before. And there . . . *what is that?*, my eye snagged on a curious line, *a vertical?*

Mystery! What little thing would be so bold as to stand up tall in a land of horizontals? How could such a slight mark look so prominent in the expanse of unnamed unknowns? What *was* that slender dash daring to point toward the great prairie sky? I reset my internal compass and stepped out of the wash. Curious. No idea what to expect. No expectations, no desires.

Two hours later, I would write if my goal was to describe cross-country travel in the semi-desert shrub-steppe, *my calves were sore from traversing a deceptively wide stretch of sandy rises and blow-outs; my knees and elbows were bruised and scratched from tumbly attempts to climb bentonite hills.*

Know, I would continue, sharing hard-earned advice, *that walking on desert pavement and clay "popcorn" is like walking on marbles. Know that sage catches sand. Know that maps are meaningless.*

Everything, I should conclude, *is farther away than it looks.* Then a quote from William Least Heat-Moon's *PrairyErth*: "There are several ways not to walk in the prairie, and one of them is with your eye on a far goal, because you then begin to believe you're not closing the distance any more than you would with a mirage . . . On the prairie, distance and the miles of air turn movement to stasis."[12]

But none of that matters—distance, description, conclusion. Only the tree matters—the old dead juniper.

Trees have always commanded respect in open landscapes, perhaps because they're such singular wonders. Kaplan and colleagues insist vertical features provide focus and structure to a scene, giving onlookers the chance to gauge depth and distance. To Appleton, trees signal a touch of refuge—relief from the relentless sun and omnipresent wind. Organizers of the "Lone Tree Exhibit"—a series of photographs featuring a tree from each of the national grasslands—agree, "for those who feel vulnerable and exposed the lone tree can bring comfort to the soul and relief to the eye in the vastness of the landscape."[13]

Indeed, when early settlers found themselves feeling vulnerable and exposed, they tried to fill the plains with as many trees, windmills, even fenceposts as possible. Today, photographers like Jessica Reichman use these "vertical intrusions" to "draw the viewer's attention while reinforcing the landscape's solitude and contemplative characteristics" against the dominant sweep of "a vast and awe inspiring sky."[14] Even authors and philosophers such as Jerry Sheppard and Laurence Ricou "need vertical landmarks on which their characters can fix" and seek fellow upright figures to ease the "existential dilemma of finding meaning in an indifferent, even hostile universe."[15] When faced with "too much sky . . . too much horizontal, too many lines without stops," writes Wright Morris in *The Home Place*, people want to—*have* to—believe that "the exclamation, the perpendicular, ha[s] to come. . .

"It's a problem of being. Of knowing you are there."[16]

Being. There. Where?

One day—a pale, sunny, otherwise unremarkable day—I found myself at the edge of a precipice, rock underfoot, sky overhead, long featureless horizon so far away and only the strong, silvery trunk of an old dead juniper to which to cling.

The old dead juniper was smooth as driftwood—desert driftwood, washed securely into place. Its roots gnarled up out of the stone, twisting and flowing, feeling their way into the open air. Its branches were weathering away—splintering, shimmering, as the ground exhaled waves of winter warmth. Who knows for how long it had been dead, the old juniper, had it ever been alive?

I can still feel my hand on the trunk. That's the most indelible memory I have of the old dead juniper—my chapped knuckles and scraped palms on the warm, silky trunk. I can see, too, the lower branch lifting toward Pilot Rock; another, slightly higher, pointing back at the Painted Desert Inn; and the top, too high to touch, yawning out, stretching up, reaching for clouds, channeling light from the sun into the rock and my attention from the earth into the sky.

This tree—this vertical—was not a hopeful comrade or lonely sentinel or existential cue; it would offer neither shade nor solace. But that wasn't what I was seeking. I simply wanted to touch it—to believe, if only for a moment, that we were both real.

1.3 Blank
Painted Desert Wilderness Area, Arizona

When I found my tracks in the snow / I followed, thinking that they might /
lead me back to where I was. But / they turned the wrong way and went on.

— Jim Harrison and Ted Kooser, *Braided Creek*[17]

After discovering the old dead juniper, my relationship with the wilderness changed. Something opened up—a whole world beyond that which maps depict and senses perceive. I was no longer tied to the Lithodendron Wash, no longer planned what I wanted much less expected to see, but rather was happy to let my feet find their own destinations. Onyx Bridge?

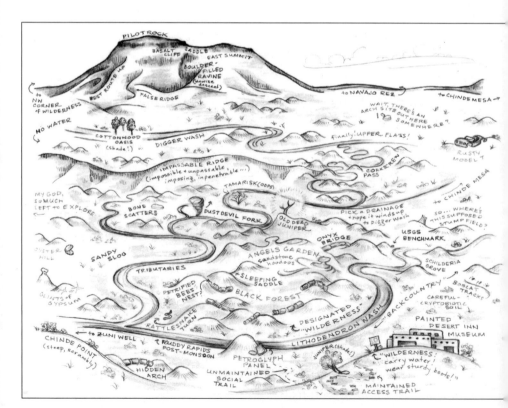

Painted Desert Wilderness Area

Pilot Rock? No, where did the coyote go, how did the wind howl? I ran, I crawled, I stammered, I skipped my way across fields and through sagebrush flats; up ridges and along ravines. I built understanding and deepened appreciation, recognized coherence and courted mystery. I became a wanderer.

Wandering is a little-known art, a seldom-sought skill. John Muir sauntered; Henry David Thoreau ruminated; according to philosopher Thomas Heyd, seventeenth-century Zen poet Basho "perfected an aesthetics of wandering"—an intention to walk with heightened consciousness of self and place; an ability to walk with a mind as open as the landscape.[18]

It's an "old business," according to Barry Lopez, this practice of "walking slowly over the land with an appreciation of its immediacy to the senses and in anticipation of what lies hidden in it."[19] In *Arctic Dreams*, he writes of a wise friend who "listen[s] . . . to what the land is saying"—who "walk[s] around in it and strain[s his] senses in appreciation of it for a long time" with the belief that "the land would open to him."[20] Similarly, in *House of Rain*, Craig Childs writes of an acquaintance who "reads a place" by "walk[ing] in a halting sort of way . . . stopping, hands hanging limp but open, as if he were feeling the air . . . sometimes walking back on himself before turning around again, or pausing for long minutes without moving."[21] Although I tried to listen and pause during my first season at Petrified Forest, my style was more of what humanist geographer Yi-Fu Tuan would call an "unstructured field trip"—venturing forth "just to see what's out there, with no prior questions in mind."[22] No questions. No desires.

Amazing!, the things one can find if one stops looking for things to find. I became enamored of sweeps of sandstone and cracks in mudstone, first for the elegance of their abstract patterns then for the geological processes that shaped them. I began recognizing different fossils entombed in the iron-rich claystones and mudstones of the Chinle Formation: the famous trees—giant, agatized *Aurocaryoxylon arizonicum,* pock-marked

Woodworthia, and radiant *Schilderia*—as well as the purpley-cream, sometimes pearlescent sheen of bone—remains of lizard- and salamander-like archosaurs that slithered and stomped through fluvial floodplains alongside the earliest dinosaurs. So too my eye picked up patterns chipped into dark, "varnished" sandstone slabs—petroglyphs, or "stone symbos," in the shape of elaborately carved lizards or lewd anthropomorphs, or squiggles and spirals; sometimes, just a lonely hand or sheep. A few times, I even found pottery sherds—black on white, red-slip, corrugated—tangible traces of those who came before.

Most shockingly, one day when I was out traipsing aimlessly around those 43,020 acres of sandstone and clay, juniper and sage, 220-million-year-old phytosaurs and thirteenth-century pottery sherds, I tripped over a three-inch wide metal disc pummeled into the earth. The words "US GEOLOGICAL SURVEY BENCHMARK" and, in smaller lettering, "$250 FINE OR IMPRISONMENT FOR DISTURBING THIS MARK" were stamped into its surface. So much for the imprints of man's work remaining substantially unnoticeable; the scientific need to map and measure territory trumps the romantic mystery of dusty time and unknown space.

By the end of February, I thought I knew the wilderness. I had spent months learning, exploring, and explaining its geological, paleontological, archaeological, biological, ecological, and generally logical-ological attributes. Every weekend, I was out hiking, sketching, prowling its hills and hollows, cliffs and caves, flats and shadows. I knew the stone trees and fossilized reptiles, the sandstone swirls and ashy piles, the iron and manganese, the rock. I knew what routes to take to get to the old dead juniper and to particular petroglyph panels; to villages of hoodoos, to valleys of bone. I knew where the earth and sky collided, and where they opened up. I knew the Painted Desert.

Then one of my last weekends, I headed up to the trailhead eager to wander, stepped to the edge of the mesa, and found that the desert had disappeared. The landscape had been erased. Blank. Reds oranges purples blacks? The bones the glyphs the odd metal markers? All buried in white. Overnight, while I had been sleeping, dreaming, the sky had cracked open and fallen in soft crystalline flakes. It had . . . snowed?

The Wilderness was a giant mirror: blue-white sky reflecting the earth, white-blue earth reflecting the sky. I stood between the two, blinking, blinded, until I mustered the resolve to go ahead and hike anyway (*not much time left*, I feared). Down I slipped and skidded—down the icy switchbacks, into the frozen drainage, across the snowy expanse, hoping to find some trace of my desert still there, underneath. But the contours were unrecognizable—white lumps, sleeping giants—where *was* I, lost? Lost *again* in this blank, empty space?

"Space," the United States Department of the Interior's Bureau of Land Management declares in its *Visual Resource Inventory* Handbook H-8401, is a landscape's "three-dimensional arrangement of objects and voids."[23]

"Space," neurobiologists Oliva et al. conclude, "is composed of structural and semantic properties . . . [A] space has a function, a purpose, a typical view, and a geometrical shape. The shape of space stands as an entity that, like the shape of an object or a face, can be described by its contours and surface properties."[24]

"Space," geographer/philosopher Edward Casey begins, is the "volumetric void in which things are positioned."

"There is no landscape of space," he continues:

Phrases such as "wide open spaces" that we apply unthinkingly to landscape only confuse the issue . . . [A]n open landscape does not fade into space. A landscape may indeed be vast . . . it will never *become* space . . . No matter how capacious a landscape may be, it remains a composition of places, their intertangled skein.[25]

Space, say the experts, has no materiality, no physicality, no thingness. Unlike sensual, experiential, knowable "place," space is an abstract concept—a reference to absolute geographical measurements devoid of sociocultural, political, and/or personal meaning. People live in places and dream of space.

Yet, Gary Treddinick muses in *The Land's Wild Music*, even if "space is abstract, immaterial, and voluminous distance" and "*a place* [is] a locale, the land *here*, the enfolded natural and cultural histories,. . ."

> [A] place will possess, among other things, a characteristic space or amplitude . . . Its space is the way the light sits and the winds move, the way sounds travel. Its space is the quality of the intervals between its many pieces, between the great horned owl and the jackrabbit, between the notes of the raven's song, right down to the vibrant voids between the atoms in the grains of its sandstones or its granites. Its space is . . . what holds a place's pieces apart. It is the tone of its millions of interrelationships.[26]

Space.

To those who claim that there is no such thing as experiential space— that the individual is always doomed to be in what scholars call geographical place—I invite you to walk in the snow-covered steppe. Venture into a blank, wide wilderness. Experience the Painted Desert painted white. It's not a matter of gauging distance or filling emptiness—historian Robert Thacker's "struggle to understand the prairie and figure out what to make of it intellectually and artistically"[27]—but rather a full, rich, sensual, deliriously delightful disembodiment. Dis-place-ment.

I have no idea how far or for how long I walked in the bright, white, blue-white world before a pattern—a line, a series of shadowed pawprints—startled me out of my placeless, timeless curiosity: coyote.

Yes, coyote—that ubiquitous symbol of the Southwest; that trickster who trots through cartoons and legends; that spirit evoked in fetishes and knickknacks; that singer, that scavenger, that emblem of the wiliest of wild creatures. People know coyote for his howl (transient, lingering in the air, adding dimension to moonlight), his tawny tail (bushy, tattered, dusted with sage and sand), and, especially, for his sly, happy grin, but saw only his tracks. His signature, left in snow and mud, laughing, *I was here. I am here.* They dance onward across stone and between juniper. They led me off into the snow-covered plains, promising, Come *here*: Wander! Wonders!

Coyote as trickster: he might have been laughing at me, trying to get me lost, to lead me astray? But I read in his tracks an indomitable spirit, a wise wanderer, a happy scribe. Moreover, coyote was not the only print-maker out that morning: rabbit had romped with fellow rabbit; birds had landed and fluttered in giddy little circles; pronghorn had grazed idly through, weaving meanders of two-toed tracks. Signatures, prints, traces of animals, birds, plants. A veritable zoo, a jungle. A desert of life.

I took a step—one tentative little shuffle into the blank world of wild creatures. The snow rustled, whispered, and sighed beneath my boot. Another step. It crackled, crunched, chortled . . . and I was off, running, skipping, leaping without path or purpose beyond the symphony beneath my feet. Up and on and forward I went until I fell gasping in a great noisy field of sparkles. Snowflakes tingled on the back of my neck and into the wrists of my coat, then melted into little rivulets and ran into my sweater and my mittens. I stretched out, sweeping my arms and legs in angelic arcs, then rolled over, nose to the snow, and considered its close blue shimmer, its frozen light.

When I started shivering, I stood up, a little dazed, a little woozy, and looked back to see where I had come from. Lithodendron Wash? No. Access trail? Somewhere. Painted Desert Inn, at least, the Painted Desert Inn? I was blinded by the sunlight shining off sky and snow. All I could see was an odd line of splotches—daubs of shadow, crookedly careening through the otherwise clean, smooth field of white. Had *I* left those blemishes? Surely not *mine*, those abstract expressionist prints.

Yes they were mine. Mine, mine—I wanted to claim the big blank desert as mine. I turned away from the access trail and out toward Chinde Mesa, Pilot Rock, and an empty white expanse. Stepping forward, purposefully swinging my leg out to the side, I carved a crescent-shaped swath in the snow. Pleased, I swept an arc with my other leg. And again, again. Steps. Footprints, tracks, strokes. Backwards, forwards, one-footed; rolling, cartwheeling, onward into the blank white desert, onward onto the great white plane, personalizing it with swishes and swooshes, swirls in snow.

I'm here too! I sang with coyote, scribed, I'm here!

Southern Arizona writer Charles Bowden's rules for being in the desert, which came to him "in a white flash of light":

"1. You are in the right place.

"2. You do not belong here.

"3. Deal with this fact.

"4. Time's up."[28]

The sun was warm and the ground thirsty. By noon, great hot spots had started to melt out of the snow, slowly and surreptitiously at first, then spreading hungrily like flames through a canvas. Hilltops peeked out from under their wintry blanket; streamlets trickled down crevasses; pawprints and footprints alike turned mud red, wet-rusty-earth red, boot-sucking red.

Euphoria broken and reality resuming, I began looping back toward the Litho and, beyond that, the access trail and civilization. Just in time. I barely made it back across the Wash, which was, of course, flowing. I should have known—all of that snow! Of course it would melt, and when it melted, it would have to go somewhere. Of course it would follow the

Wash, tracing the edge of the wilderness. I should have known. (Ah, but that's the mistake. Just when you think you know a place, discovered the last of its little secrets, claimed and commanded your presence, that's when ten thousand nameless wonders will fall from the sky and melt into the ground, magic.)

Following the bobcat

As late afternoon's deep glow buoyed up into the winter sky, I paused at the top of the trail to catch my breath and look back across the Painted Desert. The land was sweating and steaming; colors lay rich and moist in thick layers of red, orange, and purple. Snow persisted in a few shadowy pockets, but for the most part, the place was back: there were the sinuous bends of Lithodendron Wash; there the hills of the Black Forest; Chinde Mesa ever on the horizon; and Pilot Rock, always Pilot Rock dominating the farthest corner of the wilderness.

My footprints? Gone, forgotten.

Interim: Highway 36
Northwestern Kansas

Yet, not all unscenic parts of nature are dangerous or disgusting; some are merely boring. I gather that driving across Kansas does not, for most people, afford a positive aesthetic experience.

—Robert Fudge, "Imagination and the Science-Based Aesthetic Appreciation of Unscenic Nature"[29]

What's with all of the *trees?* I whined after my internship ended and I returned to safe, comfortable routines back East; worse yet, *buildings,* where's the *sky?* How do you *breathe?* A mere four months at Petrified Forest had made the previous twenty years of my life feel foreign and faded, tamed and trammeled. I bored family and friends with tales of adventures; I surrounded myself with photographs of rocks and clouds; I tacked a rather tattered topographic map to my bedroom wall and let its squiggles and squirms and scrunches of lines seep into my dreams. I researched wilderness and Wilderness, wrote of junipers and snow, and in many ways reimagined my relationship with the place from a geographic and temporal distance. Then, a year and a half after I had packed my car, bid friends and colleagues farewell, and whispered *good-bye*—that's it, once, quietly, *good-bye* to the sage, to the rabbits, to the Lithodendron Wash and to Pilot Rock—I unexpectedly found myself heading west (West again! Thoreau: Westward I go free!) to another internship at the park.

My mother offered to join me for part of the long drive. I welcomed the company, rightly suspecting that the Midwest would feel even bigger, slower, and more exposed when seen by car than it had by airplane four years earlier. We tried to break up the trip a little—swung through Indiana Dunes, skirted Chicago, stopped for chocolate cake somewhere past Des Moines—but I didn't really pay attention until we reached Nebraska and the ground began to unfurl and assert itself against a sky of bright, billowy puffs. Nebraska! Back in Nebraska! Aiming for Red Cloud—the home of Willa Cather.

I can't honestly say I'd always been moved by Willa Cather's work. While in high school, I'd found a copy of *My Ántonia* on the bookshelves at home—a dusty paperback sitting alongside Robert Louis Stevenson ("[the Plains are] a world almost without feature; an empty sky, an empty earth, front and back"), Charles Dickens ("the great blank" is "oppressive in its barren monotony"), and William Faulkner ("Wonder. Go on and wonder"). Once I began reading it, I thought it interesting enough to continue and finish, but didn't remember much more than the cover painting and a side plot involving wolves. Sometime, though, between those wide, dusky hours at Scotts Bluff and those wild, wondrous months at Petrified Forest, I came to understand and deeply appreciate Cather's oft-quoted lines from *Death Comes for the Archbishop*:

> The plain was there, under one's feet, but what one saw when one looked about was that brilliant blue world of stinging air and moving clouds . . . Elsewhere the sky is the roof of the world; but here the earth was the floor of the sky. The landscape one longed for when one was far away, the thing all about one, the world one actually lived in, was the sky, the sky![30]

Stinging air! Moving clouds! What place had birthed such beautiful words? I wanted to experience Cather's world of sky, so convinced Mom to veer from state highways onto county routes, pausing only in Beatrice for Homestead National Monument and the local Dairy Queen. It was August. Hot. Hazy. . .

This, of course, is when I'm supposed to describe the scene as we rolled into Red Cloud—the time of day, the season, the color of the air, the feel of the earth, our first glimpse of brick buildings lining Main Street, proudly defying the immensity of the surrounding country.

But memory works in funny ways.

What you stick to counts less than what sticks to you, like burrs and por-
cupine quills
                                        — Robert Frost, *The Collected Notebooks*[31]

My mother and I were on vacation—an unstructured, unscrutinized, unabashed diversion "from the boredom and meaninglessness of routine, everyday existence," as sociologist Erik Cohen puts it.[32] We weren't about to go on any arduous treks or take notes for travelogues—we just wanted the tires to roll smoothly down back roads under Cather's brilliant blue sky, leaving us free to enjoy the day. Our willingness to slow down, encounter "authentic" details, and enhance our understanding of cultural and literary history put us a step up from "Recreational" on Cohen's rubric of touristic experiences, but unlike the journal-keeping, souvenir-collecting, and photograph-taking sightseer that many researchers describe and psychoanalyze, I wasn't recording my impressions along the way. My memory was on vacation too. Red Cloud, Nebraska? Forgotten, along with Indiana, Illinois, and Iowa.

Instead of Red Cloud, I remember a placeless moment, a random road, a smooth, beautiful stretch somewhere in northwestern Kansas. We were cutting diagonally across a corner of the state in an attempt to get back on track, post-Cather detour. I was behind the wheel, sporadically swerving to avoid sparrows that kept flitting out from eye-high patches of sunflowers. Sunset was lingering in soft, sleepy pastels; fresh, cool air filtered through our open windows along with meadowlarks' bright trills. Out of nowhere—or out of everywhere—a deep, unexpected happiness rose in me. I was happy for the hills, happy for the breeze, happy for the magic light of dusk and even for those darn little sparrows. Such *wildness!*, I inhaled, happy to be back in the plains after more than a year's exile in tight, loud locations back East; such *space!* Such ineffable *beauty*, there, then, out on the purpley-beige plains of western Kansas.

I also remember thinking how curious it was that Mom—my very own mother, sitting right next to me, looking at the very same landscape and breathing the very same air—did not share my enthusiasm for western Kansas. Yes, she agreed, it was pretty, but good god, couldn't I just stop somewhere, find a motel, wasn't there *any*where, any*thing* in these empty, godforsaken plains?

Such difference in landscape perception and preference could be attributed to differences in personality; maybe I was more like plains writers Dan O'Brien, William Least Heat-Moon, and Paul Gruchow—"a prairie person,"[33] a "fellow [/ gal] of the grasslands,"[34] happy to have returned to a place where I get my sense of distance back[35]—than my mother was. Or perhaps I was not, in fact, a tourist, but actually a traveler—a whole different breed. "Travellers." Edmunds Bunkše differentiates between the recreational character and those who want more intense, meaningful experiences, "seek *epiphanies*—moments of sudden expansion of consciousness and transformation during which the traveller sees herself or himself in some wider frame of reference."[36]

That sounds right. I definitely saw myself in some wider frame of reference—that great big sky, that great big earth, that strip of road, those spirited birds darting into and out of my consciouness—but how could one *not* see oneself in a wider frame of reference when crossing the open prairie? With all of the descriptions of crushing loneliness, palpable sadness, and infinite boredom attributed to plains landscapes, one would "expect to find utter emptiness," as Craig Childs writes of the similarly disparaged desert southwest, "There should be nothing but the barren end of the world here." Instead, such seemingly empty landscapes are filled with "an inalienable, voracious presence" —a Soul of Nowhere.[37]

Some explorers, homesteaders, emigrants, and, yes, travelers have tried to express a sense of transcendence: nineteenth-century tourist Henry Sienkiewicz glowed: "Not only one's sight but even one's soul and thoughts lose themselves in the prairie. The soul abandons familiar paths, forgets its own identity, merges with the environment, and soon ceases to be a thing apart, having been absorbed by the powerful presence of the prairie like a drop of water in the sea."[38] For others, though, prairies offer a bewildering juxtaposition, or what rhetoricist Tom Scanlan characterizes as a problem for the imagination: "What sort of reaction can one have to a land that both dwarfs one with its scale and at the same time concentrates the psyche on the only point of reference, the self?" he asks.[39]

I reacted with delight; Mom with disinterest. *What does that mean?*, I wondered then and wonder still, *why doesn't* everyone *long to be absorbed by the prairie; why doesn't* everyone *want to feel more existent?* ("'[W]hy should the light of sunrise and sunset be more poignant than that of the noon?'" asks Appleton in *The Experience of Landscape*.[40])

Two factors to take into account: firstly, my mother had already driven back and forth across the Plains before; they weren't new—an opening, a revelation—to her. Secondly, and perhaps more importantly, she had a migraine, likely exacerbated as much by my bursts of admiration ("The *sunflowers! The sunset!* Isn't it *gorgeous!*") as the ups and downs of the road. "What one thinks of in any region, while traveling through," to heed the words of Barry Lopez, "is the result of at least three things: what one knows, what one imagines, and how one is disposed."[41]

What did I know?

Nothing.

I had no idea where I was or what I was doing there.

Driving. Dusk.

The texture of the road against the tires made a sound like the singing of whales.

What did I imagine?

Nothing. Maybe everything.

How was I disposed?

Kensho, to borrow a Buddhist term: a brief glimpse of enlightenment. Euphoria.

I was back on the plains.

1.4 Slow down!
Petrified Forest National Park, Arizona

Look for it, it cannot be seen. / It is called the distant.
Listen for it, it cannot be heard. / It is called the rare.
Reach for it, it cannot be gotten. / It is called the subtle. . .
Thus, it is called the formless form, / The image of no-thing

—Lao Tzu, *Tao Te Ching*[42]

Pedal pedal pedal, breathe. Breathe, try to make it up the hill—the long, slow hill.

Yes, there are hills in the plains. Even in places without pronounced mesas and buttes or ridges and ravines, there are hills and valleys— slight undulations, swelling and sinking leisurely across great stretches of space. The slopes are so smooth and so gradual that, while driving, you may not notice your toes pressing lightly on the accelerator or relaxing onto the brakes; while walking, you may shorten or release your stride imperceptibly. But bicycling? Up a hill? Kinesthesia kicks in: shift down a gear; pedal and breathe.

I knew this hill. I hadn't noticed it during my first internship at Petrified Forest (there had been so many other things to see and learn! And it had been winter. And I hadn't had a bike), but when I returned in August with a bike, I was out riding as often as possible—experiencing the place from a different perspective and at a different pace. Every time I went for a ride, morning or evening, weekday or weekend, I had to come back up this hill: pedal and breathe.

I somehow forgot about it, though, whenever I decided to roll away from my housing near headquarters and onto the park road. The scenic drive leads northward for a few miles, passing a number of overlooks: Tiponi Point, named for figurines Hopi people use to represent a corn goddess; Tawa, the Hopi sun spirit; Kachina, Puebloan people's term for supernatural life forms as well as the dancers and dolls that assume their spirits (also the location of the Painted Desert Inn); Chinde, as with the distant Mesa, a Navajo reference to malevolent ghosts; and, ultimately, Pintado. Once called 350-Degree Point, Pintado perches high atop basalt outcrops, affording a nearly full panoramic view of the colorfully "painted" hills and sage-mottled plains below. From there, the road turns south and begins to lose elevation, passing three more scenic pull-outs all clumped together along a steep ledge where dusty, open prairie drops into barren, tangled badlands: Nizhoni, a Navajo word that can be translated as "beautiful," but carries the richer connotation of "beauty and wholeness"; Whipple, named for Lt. Amiel Weeks Whipple; and Lacey, in honor of Congressman John Fletcher Lacey, who drafted and campaigned for the Antiquities Act of 1906. After those, there's a quick hop over the Interstate then nothing but low bushes, grasses, and the occasional tumbleweed or pronghorn or jackrabbit until a lone cottonwood, a bridge over the Burlington Northern Santa Fe railroad, and, finally, some seven miles later, the mighty Puerco River trickles by.

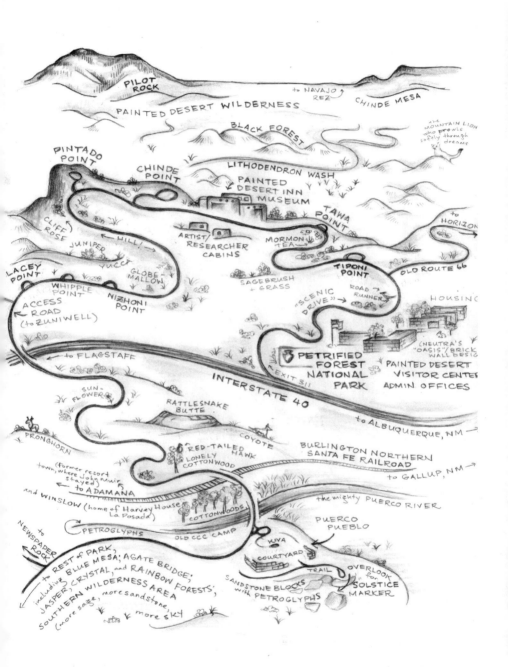

Northern half of Petrified Forest National Park

("Puerco" is Spanish for "pig" as well as "muddy," though even the latter would imply a generous amount of moisture for the mostly subsurface channel.) As the most significant, semi-permanent waterway in the area, the river was an important resource for Ancestral Puebloan people several centuries earlier. Remnants from a hundred-plus-room city—what Euro-Americans dub "Puerco Pueblo"—still sit within easy walking distance of the river and tens of dozens of enigmatic petroglyph panels, including a "Newspaper Rock" rivaling any others in the Southwest, line the banks.

I had a tendency to glide happily all the way down from Pintado to Puerco, pedaling easily despite unpredictable gusts of wind. As soon as the brush-studded horizon smoothed out, crimping only for Twin Buttes far to the west and Black Knoll far to the east, I could sit up, relax, and let my legs whirl in pace with the wheels while my mind drifted or skittered along with the clouds. Floating through such an expansive landscape, sage-scented air whooshing past my ears and into my lungs, I felt even the infinite was possible: *Aah,* I would exhale, practically fly, *why not keep going?* Why not bike all the way to the Rainbow Forest Museum, another 15 miles beyond the Pueblo? Or to Holbrook, the nearest town, another 19 or 20? The Mogollon Rim! Tucson! Mexico! The edge of the earth, how far was that?

This was my favorite stretch of space.

Space again—stillness and motion; distance and possibility. "Space," Terry Tempest Williams writes in *Ode to Slowness*, "is the twin sister of time. If we have open space then we have open time to breathe, to dream, to dare, to play, to pray to move freely, so freely, in a world our minds have forgotten, but our bodies remember. Time and space."[43]

Ahh, the other variable: time. That's the problem with plains, many argue—it takes so much time to appreciate them. Residents understand the complexity and integrity of the ecosystem and appreciate the rhythms and cycles of days and seasons, but travelers and newcomers accustomed to trees and mountains or buildings and roads see nothing but that flat, far horizon. Unless they happen to be there at a particularly moving moment—towering thundercloud! Whirling dust devil! Great crane migration!—well, then, either people need to be told to stop, sit, and contemplate the rocks, the flowers, and the starry night sky or else they need to return again and again, sunrise, sunset, season after season in order to appreciate the subtle joyousness of wide open spaces, right?

"Much of the grassland flora and fauna is too subtle to be seen from a passing car," a bulletin at Tallgrass Prairie National Preserve proclaims, adding, "but careful scrutiny reveals the special beauty, wonder, and complexity of the prairie."[44] It's not just a matter of scrutiny: a brochure for Tallgrass Prairie Parkway Wildlife and Natural Heritage Trail Guide avers, "this land is best enjoyed when experienced in every season, in many different ways,"[45] while Nebraska's Sandhills Journey Scenic Byway advises travelers to "take all the time you need . . . Luxuriate in the scenic wonders [such as] majestic cottonwoods . . . glimpses of wildlife, large cattle drives, historic markers with remembrances of early settlers, and more stars than you have ever seen . . ."[46] Don't forget the Breathtaking Sunsets! The historic windmills! And, of course, the large flock of wild turkeys that wanders back and forth across Highway 2 to reach the football field in Dunning each day.

Can brochures and byways teach people to slow down? It's a matter of ethics as well as aesthetics, according to Rex Funk, Superintendent of the Open Space Division for the city of Albuquerque, New Mexico: people need to learn a certain set of skills, perspectives, and attitudes to see and understand the unique beauty and diversity of seemingly barren places. Yes, conscious appreciation for "Art in the Landscape"—elements of design such as line, pattern, color, contrast, and motion—is part of perception, but so is recognition for less formal and far less permanent attributes such as "Processes and Cycles" and "Continuity and Change." (You can't see those from a car.) For the most part, Funk finds, it's a matter of "Scale" and "Tempo": "In crossing great spaces the temptation is to move faster," he warns, with the admonishment, "[b]y moving faster, one sees less . . . In order to appreciate this landscape, take time and get closer."[47]

Take time—take, take, it's always "take," as if time is something you need to steal or squirrel away in order to "get" closer. Instead of taking and getting, what about simply being—realizing it *is* time. It's time "to drop out of the fast lane," Candace Savage introduces her *Prairie: A Natural History*—time to slow down "and give the prairies, our prairies, a second, loving look."[48]

That's even better: to *give*.

Pedaling back up that long, slow hill at Petrified Forest, I certainly dropped out of the fast lane, but can't say I gave the plains a loving look. I paid vague attention to particular patches of globemallow and little brown mile markers alongside the road (10. . .9. . .8, feeling increasingly far apart) just to confirm that I actually kept moving. Other than that, I spent most of the ride hunched over the handlebars, cursing the wind. (And myself, for not remembering just how far it was back to quarters.)

I want to advocate slowing down—*slow down!*—to insist that in order to see any place, particularly the prairie, even more so the semi-desert sagebrush-steppe, you have to SLOW DOWN. GET OUT OF YOUR CAR. Get on your bicycle or put on your boots. Grab a field guide. And binoculars. Bike or walk or crawl until you feel like you are in the middle of nowhere—the very heart of nowhere—the center of everywhere— then sit. Sit like a rabbit or a rock. Breathe. *Zazen*, it's called in Zen Buddhism—sitting meditation.

Sit; meditate, I want to say, on time and space. But is that something that can be taught, told, or taken?

This is how it goes: you are pedaling up a strip of hot, dark, chip-sealed pavement lined with faded strips of white and double-yellow.

Grasses—wheatgrass, ryegrass, cheatgrass—bob alongside the road; beyond that, brush and a desert rose or two are tucked in basalt-lined crevices. Maybe you pass a snake or toad, splattered near the sign reading "Speed Limit: 35."

You have made it through the longest, emptiest stretch of prairie, over the Interstate, around past Lacey, Whipple, Nizhoni, and have only the steepest section left. By now, though, your thighs are burning, your shoulders aching, the gears are making funny noises, and overhead, ravens are laughing at you—cackling, gurgling, *you'll never make it, craw! craw!*

That's what it's really like—the prairie, experienced at a slower pace. No matter how often you go out—morning or evening, August, September, as the weather permits, into October, deep fall—it's bigger than you think, uphill. (Does that make you want to slow down? Do you feel like getting out of your car and onto a bike?)

How about this, then: just as you're ready to believe the birds—to get off and walk the rest of the way, stop pedaling and breathe—you come up over a little rise and, *gasp!* Wilderness! Wildness! The Painted Desert, that desolate empty basin; those reds and browns and purples, those mesas and buttes and ridges! Oh, Pilot Rock! Every single time: El Desierto Pintado.

Pintado Point is Petrified Forest's version of what other parks call "Panorama Point" or "Artists Palette" or "Kodachrome Basin." Really, though, what name could describe such a sweeping view? The entirety of the Wilderness Area and beyond: north, the Navajo Reservation and the basalt necks of the Hopi Buttes; south, the park road and desert grasslands all the way to the White Mountains, 40-odd miles away; west, the railroad, the Interstate, stretching clear to Flagstaff and the San Francisco Peaks' pale, hazy shadows; and east, dawn. If you tried to calculate the amount of space you can see from Pintado Point—[30 miles north + say 45 miles south] x [120 miles west + ...]—you would have to figure in the distance

View from Pintado Point

to the sun. (And properly weight the 43,020 acres of Wilderness.) (And
Pilot Rock—it's like a vortex for sky; how does that fit into the equation?)

By any calculation, I earned that view. Especially after biking up, tired
and sweaty, I would pull into the parking area, unclip my shoes, lean my
bike against the low stone wall, walk up to the interpretive sign, and sit.
Sit and stare; listen and breathe. ("Simply by looking into the blue sky
beyond clouds, *the serenity*," Paul Reps translates the Vigyan Bhairava
Tantra.[49])

The interpretive sign at Pintado Point says something banal about the
amazing view, but what it really wants to talk about is air quality: "vistas
of remarkable clarity extend far beyond park boundaries because the air
quality in and surrounding Petrified Forest is among the purest. . ." To
prove the point, it includes a panorama labeled with mileage to distant
landscape features: Pilot Rock—7; San Francisco Peaks—120. One hundred twenty! When visitors pull into the parking area, get out of their cars
or RVs or off their motorcycles, and walk up to the wayside, invariably
someone exclaims, *120 miles! Wow! Is it really that far?*

Yes, it really is that far, I always wanted to exclaim back, *Space! Space!* I could have quoted Cather at them: in plains, the "great rock mesas . . . [a]re not crowded together in disorder, but placed in wide spaces, long vistas between."[50] Or I could have cited psychologists Oliva et al.: "[b]eyond a few tens of meters is vista space, where observers perception of distances to and between surfaces can become greatly inaccurate, with a dramatic accelerating foreshortening of space perception with distances over 100 meters."[51] William Least Heat-Moon: "good god, look at all this air!"[52] But I stayed silent; smiled; nodded. (I was normally thinking about Pilot Rock, anyway—so far to Pilot Rock!)

Likewise when anyone marveled *How beautiful!* I wanted to leap up and shout, *Yes!* "*This,*" to quote Edward Abbey's opening to *Desert Solitaire,* "is the most beautiful place on earth"! *Look* —the Lithodendron Wash! *Look* —Chinde Mesa! *Look* —Black Forest, Angels Garden, Devils Playground! *Look!*

No one wants to be assaulted by exclamation points. I stayed on my little stone perch, nodding, knowing that "beautiful" doesn't describe it; such landscapes are ineffable, especially when imbued with both memory and meaning.

Then the inevitable: I'd be sitting there, a spandex-clad gargoyle, glowing with pride, as though I personally had stretched this skin of brush and buttes wide across the skeleton of the earth, when a tourist would turn to their friend or spouse or child and say, *did you bring the camera / stand over there / smile!* Whrrr, click! That's all it takes—*whrrr* silence shattered; *click,* beauty trapped. *Whrrr, click,* then move on—turn around and walk away, get back in the car, race through the park, reach the next town, continue on to the final destination, someday download or develop memories and nod, hmm, pretty, where was I?

Maybe I should give people more credit. Maybe visitors remember where they were when they took their pictures. (Especially if they snap photos of the sign with its neatly labeled landmarks.) After all, as Michael Crang argues in "Picturing Practices: Research through the Tourist Gaze," photos are a sort of mnemotechnology, "providing visual prompts and locations for memories and stories."[53] Citing William Henry Fox Talbot, who "believed the photograph to be a copy of the memory of light, nothing more," photographer Peter Goin asks "[c]an we truly understand a sense of place without thinking about light memory?"[54]

Light memory. Memory, lite. The problem, cultural historian Don Gifford points out, is that "the camera offers another insidious possibility: I'll snap a picture of it now and really look at it later."[55] When people take pictures (there it is again—*take, steal*, like sucking the soul from a place), we literally lose touch with the few precious minutes we have there, focusing on the visual display as artificially framed in a flat screen and separating ourselves from the tangible experience—the sounds, the smells, and the wind, none of which can be later (re)captured or recalled in small, static pixels or print.

That might be part of the point. It can be construed as a matter of human instinct, survival even, enabled by modern technology: when we feel disoriented or bewildered by a bombardment of stimuli, we need merely "take out our cameras and drastically reduce the flood of sensations and impressions by looking at a framed landscape through a tiny hole," Yi-Fu Tuan wryly observes.[56] Wilderness, in particular—that cacophony of ridges and washes; those frighteningly exposed stretches of sage—can "'be tamed and rendered visibly manageable,'" writes Anne-Marie Willis, through the careful composition of a photograph.[57]

This is especially true for tourists—people on break from their daily lives, simply hoping to relax and see new places. Vacation is for leaving the noise and bustle of the everyday world behind; with a *whrrr* and a *click*, it can be safely confronted later, from a temporal and spatial distance. "Tourism in general and photography in particular," according to John

Urry, "serve to organize one's experience of time and space." In his seminal book *The Tourist Gaze*, Urry writes of a "'way of seeing' the world that is enforced on tourists and essentially conditioned by the imagery created for tourism destinations by the tourism industry."[58] People see a pretty image and are inspired to go visit a place. There, they stop at a "scenic viewpoint," which has been carefully designated to optimize distance and viewing angle so as to facilitate aesthetic appreciation. To perpetuate the orderly ideal and, later, prove they had, in fact, been there, the tourist takes a pretty picture. Then they leave.[59]

Is this but "an essential aspect of tourism," as Bunkše forgives those who seek to collect places, artifacts, souvenirs, videos, and photographs?[60] Or, to use Rod Giblett's expression, is it "ubiquitous touristic landscape pornography"?[61] What can visitors possibly remember of the few seconds or minutes they spent at Pintado Point if all they did was look at the place as filtered through the tiny lens or screen of a camera? And what can the resulting images possibly mean to those who took them and those who later ogle them? (How can I dare to ask these questions when I'm just as guilty as the rest? "Somewhere in west Texas," I label pictures; "somewhere, Arizona," "somewhere, Oklahoma," "somewhere, Colorado," somewhereKansas, somewhere, where, where?)

"The prairie," Minnesotan Paul Gruchow attests, "is one of those plainly visible things that you can't photograph. No camera lens can take in a big enough piece of it. The prairie landscape embraces the whole of the sky . . . Any undistorted image is too flat to represent the impression of immersion that is central to being on the prairie."[62] In other words, not only is it difficult to inspire people to take the time to really see grasslands when the main medium of communication and inspiration (the photograph) fails to convey grasslands' main feature (space), but if, by

some chance, tourists do choose to visit a prairie park, their main tool
for comprehension (the camera) cannot take in, much less organize that
space. It is a waste of time, a lost opportunity, a loss of presence to try to
take a small, static photograph of huge, featureless scenery.

Scenery. Scene. Obscene. Meaningless space, wasted time. ?

Agate Fossil Beds National Monument, Nebraska

I know most people don't have the luxury of living in a national park. I know most Americans live in cities and suburbs, at best visit the wilderness but do not remain. I know people have likes and dislikes, goals and priorities, somewhere to be other than Pintado Point. I know I should be happy that visitors are even willing to stop, get out of their car, walk to the overlook, read the sign, and take a photo before going on to other, more important things. But *please*, I want to throw their cameras off the cliff, *sit! Stay! LOOK, will you **LOOK**.* Oh, Ed Abbey, the more I biked the road, the more I sat on that stone wall at Pintado Point, the more I cared for that park, my park, the more desperately I wondered, "What can I tell them? . . . Look here, I want to say, for godsake folks, . . . look around; throw away those goddamned idiotic cameras! For chrissake folks what is this life if full of care we have no time to stand and stare? eh?"[63]

Time. Time to stand and stare. Sage advice, also from Abbey: "Better to idle through one park in two weeks, than to try to race through a dozen in the same amount of time."

There are nearly four hundred units in the National Park Service, including more than fifty full National Parks, several hundred National Monuments, dozens of preserves, historic sites and battlefields, seashores and lakeshores, rivers and recreation areas. The US Forest Service manages nineteen National Grasslands. The Fish and Wildlife Service has 556 National Wildlife Refuges and counting. The Bureau of Land Management oversees 253-million acres, including several Monuments and National Conservation Areas designated part of the National Landscape Conservation System. Beyond federal units, there are more than six thousand state parks and even more county and city parks. Then there are non-governmental organizations such as The Nature Conservancy, the Audubon Society, universities, and private museums that manage wild and semi-wild lands in America and around the world.

Around the world! Other countries have parks and preserves, reserves and conserves, World Heritage Sites and Wilderneses—so many places! So many beautiful, wild, wonder-full places!

It's impossible to experience and appreciate them all.

As much as I enjoyed wandering around the Painted Desert during my first internship, I didn't ever expect to go back to Petrified Forest. The world was wide; I was young. I had other plans. They fell through. I found myself returning to northern Arizona. Re-turn. Try again. This time, I told myself, I'll slow down. I'll bike. I'll camp. I'll find more petroglyph panels, learn all of the grass species, and see a mountain lion. I will hike to Pilot Rock.

I did indeed spend that autumn and early winter camping, biking, slowing down, and sitting. One day, while sitting at Pintado, I heard a man complaining to his wife about the speed limit—45 miles per hour—on the stretch of road between the Puerco River and Lacey Point. "I mean, 45?" he grumbled, "It should be at least 65. There's nothing to see."

Nothing to see. Nothing but the earth, the grass, the clouds, the sky. What was I supposed to do, quote Paul Gobster at him: "The dramatic, visual elements of the picturesque continue to give aesthetic pleasure, but so do the more subtle and ordinary landscapes"?[64] Or Larry McMurtry: "To those not attuned to their subtleties the plains are merely monotonous emptiness. But to those who love them, the plains are endlessly fascinating, a place where the constant interplay of land and sky is always dramatic; gloomy sometimes, but more often uplifting"?[65] Shout that I think the speed limit should be 25? Or 15? Better yet, no cars allowed, just bicyclists, equestrians, hopeless peripatetics? Shake him and say *LOOK*?

All the quotes and photographs, interpretive signs and inspirational movies, lists of animals and plants and fossils and artifacts in the world can't convince some people that prairies are anything except empty. Better to let them just speed on through, on by, the faster the better, go. Leave my places alone. I am happy to sit and stare in silence. *Zazen.*

1.5 Rhythms, Cycles, Spirals
Petrified Forest National Park, Arizona

Part I : Sun-sitting

I get that feeling [that I could stay outside and somehow become part of that world, grass, wind and trees, day and night itself] when I'm out in the open . . . The land, the 360 degrees of unobstructed horizon, invites you to keep on walking . . . A person could stand and watch this changing land and sky forever.

— **Kathleen Norris,** *Dakota: A Spiritual Geography*[66]

I spend a lot of time / outside / myself, / looking around

—**Byrd Baylor,** *I'm in Charge of Celebrations*[67]

After a brief attempt to live in a city and work a nine-to-five job in a windowless office, I again returned to Petrified Forest—my first summer there as well as my first chance to be a real, honest-to-goodness Park Ranger. (Visitors may not notice the difference between interns and employees, much less Park Ranger and Forest Ranger, but I was proud of my grey shirt, green pants, arrowhead badge, perpetually unpolishable boots, and, of course, the signature Smokey Bear-style hat, though I soon learned that it's hot and tight and rolls like a tumbleweed when caught by the breeze.)

For three months, I stood happily in the visitor center, welcoming road-weary travelers and answering their questions: *28 miles* (how long is the road?); *the Painted Desert Inn, Pintado Point, Puerco Pueblo, Blue Mesa, and Rainbow Forest Museum* (where should we stop?); *buried in mud, smothered by volcanic ash, and replaced with silica cell by cell* (how did the trees turn to stone?); *back outside, around to the left* (bathrooms?). I chatted about the weather, gave directions, sold postcards, started the interpretive film, and wished people a good day. As the schedule dictated, I went to the Painted Desert Inn and Puerco Pueblo or Giant Logs and Crystal Forest trails to facilitate emotional and intellectual connections to the park's natural and cultural resources (i.e., to give formal talks and "rove," making myself available for spontaneous, informal contacts: *Enjoying the park today?/ Yes, it's always this windy / That's a raven trying to con you out of your lunch.*) About once a week, I had "project time," during which I attended to my designated duty of preparing pen-and-ink illustrations of the park's most common and charismatic flora. (I drew flowers.)

To make accurate botanical drawings, I had to pay attention to the tiniest of details—how the tiny, slender leaves of blue flax alternate, for example, and how the fuzzy lobes of globemallow grow larger closer to the ground. That blazing red of Indian Paintbrush? Not actually the plant's flower; rather, the bracts. I shared these observations with visitors, too, when they saw me sitting near a trail, trying to look proper and scientific but more often sprawled akimbo, hat skewed to block the sun, identification guides and pads of paper flapping in the breeze. What are you doing?, they would ask. "Drawing flowers," I would look up and smile. Well, what kind of flower? Why? What's this one over here? Half an hour later, I would have explained not only the natural history of sacred datura but its relationship to deadly nightshade and the medicinal uses of sage.

I especially liked to draw flowers at Puerco Pueblo, where casual conversations about yellow buckwheat flowed seamlessly into animated discussions about agriculture and the Ancestral Puebloans who had cultivated their corn, beans, and squash nearby. "Yes, the climate may have been wetter in the twelfth century," I told twenty-first-century visitors who looked at the desiccated landscape and marveled at the idea that anyone could possibly choose to live there, "but the people were also smarter about their use of resources; they'd accumulated several generations' worth of knowledge about the place." They knew where to get raw materials—agate and chert, cottonwood, sandstone—for tools and shelter; they knew why to build on a slight rise and with a corner pointed at the predominant wind; they knew how to supplement their diet with wild herbs and game; they knew when to plant and when to reap, when to stay and when to go. With the river, the trees, the brush, the dirt, and the deposits of iron-red and manganese-purple stone all nearby, really, it's a great place to make a home.

"Let me show you," I would say, if the visitors seemed interested in not just the pretty flowers or the drawing ranger but in the wisdom and beauty of living in such a place. I would lead them through what's left of the prehistoric city—unassuming piles of rubble, partially reconstructed to suggest the size and shape of a central courtyard surrounded by a hundred-plus rooms—and point out features like a ceremonial kiva (square with round corners, evidence of a confluence of cultural influences), maybe find a pottery sherd or a lithic flake. Along the way, I would try to explain how archaeologists find and interpret clues to the past. When we came to the highest point on the trail, I would gesture to the sweeping landscape and describe the importance of viewsheds to inhabitants and travelers along prehistoric trade and migration corridors. Then we would follow the pavement down, away from the Pueblo—not far, just to the edge of the sandstone ridge, where a metal railing politely told us to stop.

"Stop," I would say, "what do you see?"

Most of the time, people looked up and out—affirming an instinctive tendency to scan the horizon. (Not much there. Another sandstone-capped ridge, a bit of a spring, some greenery; horsetails wisping through the upper atmosphere.) Then they would lower their gaze to focus on boulders nearby. Sooner or later, someone would gasp, *oh!* Rock art!

"Petroglyphs," I would corroborate, explaining that the stone symbols are, indeed, a form of creative expression, not a written language like hieroglyphics. Some people think they look rather crude or childish, but, judging from the amount of effort it takes to carve stone, the figures were likely imbued with much more importance than mere graffiti: "In order to chip carefully away at the dark 'desert varnish'—a manganese-rich compound that bacteria fix to exposed surfaces in arid places—to reveal light-colored stone underneath," I would explain the process, "their maker had had to exercise a fair amount of control and patience." Citing Ekkehart Malotki, an anthropologist who has worked extensively in and around Petrified Forest, I would tell visitors that "[m]ost Colorado Plateau rock art . . . constitutes attempts to propriate the gods and other supernatural forces to ensure individual or collective well-being. Intrinsically, therefore, rock art is a product of ceremonial and ritual activities."[68]

Anthropologists have tentatively identified some glyphs by consulting the legends and lore of modern Puebloan people, particularly the Hopi and Zuni. For example: a highly visible "stork carrying a baby" glyph at Puerco Pueblo might illustrate a story about a giant bird-man that carries off naughty children (or it could just be an ibis with a frog in its beak); female anthropomorphs surrounded by bighorn sheep and pawprints suggest "game mothers"; and the image of Kokopelli, found throughout the Southwest (and, thanks to the modern souvenir industry, on Southwestern-style pendants and bookmarks and lampstands around the world), is that of a seed-carrying, hunchbacked flute player. All of these symbols, notably, invoke ideas of fertility—appreciation and/or desire for food, water, and virility. Universal concepts.

Petroglyph panel on the bank of Lithodendron Wash

My personal favorites are the handprints and footprints, which evoke a visceral connection to humanness and humanity though no contemporary scientist can say exactly why they were made. So too, lonely cougars—are

they meant to express power, awe, danger that lurks with soft paws and
tawny eyes? Most enigmatic and elegant are the geometrics—abstract
symbols—dots and bursts, triangles and squares, spirals and mazes,
mazes and spirals, in and out, around, around, around.

> It was as if we were looking for the center of a whirling spiral. Every time
> we found the center, it slowly dissolved from under us, and we left to
> follow it elsewhere.
>
> —Craig Childs, *House of Rain*[69]

"Do you see the spiral?" I would point to a small glyph etched into a
boulder below the railing.

"Where? Oh yes, that. Hmm." Visitors tended to nod politely, perhaps wondering why I bothered with such an unassuming mark while
Kokopelli danced nearby.

"Any guesses what that means?"

"Um." The reply.

On "Newspaper Rock" a mile up the road, people can see spirals and
lines zigging and zagging in what anthropologists have interpreted as
ancient travelogues and/or travel guides. Out in the Wilderness Area,
hikers may encounter one of several different panels featuring spirals
with a dizzying number of precisely cut whorls—eight, nine, you lose
count after that. In June, a few other rangers and I woke at 3:30 A.M.
(cold and dark), piled into a truck (moon hovering low and orange on
the horizon), drove twenty-odd miles (stars beginning to fade), parked
where a minor fork of Dry Wash dips under the road (familiar landmarks
beginning to appear), hiked out along the slender strand of clay (pale
glow in the lightening sky), then stopped at the base of Martha's Butte
and waited for the sun to rise—all part of a pilgrimage to see a spiral
petroglyph.

A spiral. At dawn. On the summer solstice. "It had to be / sunrise," Byrd Baylor knows, "And it had to be / that / first / sudden moment. / That's / when all / the power of / life / is in the / sky."[70]

If you were to sit on the same rock day after day to watch the sun rise and set, rise and set, you would notice that it appears and disappears not just at different *times* each day, but so too in different *places*. Instead of popping up at exactly 90° east, tracing a perpendicular semicircle through the sky, and tucking obediently back in at 270° west, the sun rises and sets at points farther north in the summer and farther south in the winter, swinging at an angle relative to the latitude. (Though, to be fair, it's not the sun's whimsy, rather a matter of the earth's axial tilt and annual orbit.)

If you were to sit on the same rock day after day, year after year, you might notice that the location at which the sun crosses the horizon does not change at a regular intervals. Rather, like a pendulum, it starts at one end, gathers momentum and speed through the middle, begins to slow, eventually pauses and lingers before turning to begin the process again in the other direction. ("As breath turns from down to up, and again as breath curves up to down—through both these turns, *realize*," Paul Reps translates the Malini Vijaya Tantra, "Or, whenever in-breath and out-breath fuse, at this instant touch the energy-less, energy-filled center."[71])

If you were to sit on the same rock day after day, year after year, you might learn to pay special attention to these moments of pause—the solstices. It might become, as explained to Craig Childs by a park ranger at Chaco Canyon National Historical Park,

like morning prayer, to go to spots where, at certain times of the year, [you know] the sunrise [will] be dramatically framed by shapes on the horizon . . . this pursuit [feels] natural in this particular land, with the sky so huge overhead and the horizon picketed with cliffs and buttes. You can't help looking for the peculiar way the sun rises from one day to the next.[72]

You might even want to create some sort of marker for the moment. It wouldn't have to be something huge—no need for ziggurats or stone henges—just a row of doors or windows, neatly lined to channel the light on a solstice morning. Or a simple glyph, positioned so as to catch shadows or spaces between shadows cast by features nearby. That's all it takes to make a calendar—attention, time, and a few loops or whorls, spiraling in, out, both.

> The spiral becomes this expansion and contraction of energy . . . an outward motion in its evolutionary reach and an inward motion in its emotional drain. A spiral moves in both directions – clockwise and counterclockwise.
> —Terry Tempest Williams, *Red*[73]

The solstice marker at Puerco Pueblo amazes visitors. For good reason—it proves that Ancestral Puebloans achieved a level of natural acuity exceeding that of most modern people. In fact, westerners weren't even aware that ancient Southwestern societies had oriented elements of their lives—buildings, roads, rock art—to celestial features until the 1970s, when archaeologists and astronomers realized that structures at Chaco Canyon in New Mexico aligned to the solstice sun. Writing of "A Unique Solar Marking Construct" at Fajada Butte, first observed in June of 1977, Anna Sofaer and colleagues describe a "Sun Dagger" that tracks solar movement throughout the year. Creating such a glyph, they marvel, "required a sophisticated appreciation of astronomy and geometry for its realization."[74]

As in Chaco Canyon, there are several recorded archaeoastronomical sites in and near Petrified Forest—not just summer solstice spirals, but glyphs for winter, other important dates, possibly the movement of stars or planets or even elaborate lunar calendars. Almost all are in the

Self-portrait with sun

backcountry, some in sensitive locations that few people (myself not included) are allowed to know. The marker at Puerco Pueblo is readily accessible, however, and the Park Service is proud to point it out to visitors, especially in the weeks before and after June 21 or 22.

On those days, when I stood out at Puerco early in the morning, watching as the sun rose and shone through a crack in a nearby boulder, casting a "dagger of light" (why not a sabre or stylus?) toward the center of the spiral, I usually met a smattering of visitors and sometimes great hordes—too many to talk with all at once. But there were also stretches of solitude—long, beautiful hours, just me and the ravens; the rumble of trains, the rustle of wind; the spiral and a big cloudless sky.

Hundreds of years ago, I would think to myself, leaning into the hot metal railing and watching shadows part and light leak onto the glyph so slowly, so naturally, *somebody stood at the same exact spot.* And they watched. Watched the sun as it rose every morning, watched the light as it played on the stone; watched the skies storm and clear, watched the wildlife come and go.

That would have been me, I still like to think to myself, that would have been *my* job. I would have been what Least Heat-Moon calls a "site-watcher," or, to Childs, a "specialist in sunrises."[75]

I may be yet.

Part II : A Day

When not watching rocks, drawing flowers, giving talks, or selling post-cards, I was out walking. Every morning, every evening, and anytime I could in between, I headed off along the same route—the same old broken road through the same old dusty plains, new things to see every time. I didn't stop exploring the Wilderness and I biked often enough, but, for the most part, that summer was dedicated to discovering what Gary Snyder already knew: "Walking is the great adventure, the first medita-tion, a practice of heartiness and soul primary to humankind. Walking is the exact balance of spirit and humility."

Balance, meditation, adventure—it's as simple as this: left, right, left, right; breathe.

Everything begins as a promise.
—Charles Bowden, "The Emptied Prairie"[76]

A morning:

4:30 A.M. Wake. Strap on sandals, slip on a sweater, step out. Sky still deep and dark, maybe a sliver of moon, Venus ever bright. Lavender sky, scent of sage.

About a quarter mile from headquarters, turn onto the old dirt road, aiming east. This was once Route 66—America's beloved Mother Road, connecting Chicago to L.A. (Get your kicks!) It now leads to piles of gravel; beyond those, weeds. You would never notice it if you didn't know to look.

4:50. Sparrows begin to sing. Rabbits rustle and hop—excited, nervous, ears and noses twitching with anticipation. From a slight rise, you can see a line of white lights and another of red, together streaming all the way to the horizon. (Truckers zipping along I-40. If the wind's right, the traffic is audible too.)

Soon, you're beyond the large shrub that marks a mile. Beyond that, the old key embedded in the tar. Pass the spot where I once encountered a rattlesnake and another where I saw a mountain lion track. (That was it—a single print, the size of my hand. I wonder how much time had passed between the moment when the cat bounded across the dirt and the moment I stopped to look, bent over, touched the track, spread my fingers as wide as the pads of the lion's paw. Was it watching from the grass?)

5:10. Arrive at the fencepost where, by some act of Cartesian cartography and the politics of land ownership, the park's border jags in and out in a sharp, square corner. The actual end of the park—a gate, a fence across the road—is only another mile away, but this is far enough. Greet the post and turn around, head for home.

It's fairly light now, sky awash in pinks. Lingering clouds quickly dissipate. There's already a breeze, westerly—even the air rushes to greet the sun.

The sun! "Some people / say / there is / a new sun / every day," Byrd Baylor writes in *The Other Way to Listen*, "They say / you have to / welcome it."[77] Welcome it by walking, taking huge steps, feeling the earth rotate beneath your feet, as Annie Dillard suggests in *Pilgrim at Tinker Creek*.[78] Breathe deeply of the pre-dawn air, then stop. Stop! Here it comes! . . . Hold your breath! . . . 5:20 or 30, lighter, lighter, rays of light shoot up then out, skittering across the steppe, snagging on the sage, blinding, brilliant.

There it is! Good morning, sun.

5:45 A.M. Sunrise is a time of possibility, of promise, of hope. Aldo Leopold knew this, writing in *A Sand County Almanac* "at daybreak I am the sole owner of all the acres I can walk over. It is not only boundaries that disappear, but also the thought of being bounded. Expanses unknown to deed or map are known to every dawn, and solitude . . . extends on every hand."

This effect—let's call it the Dawn Effect—is even more pronounced in sweeping prairies and plains where, as N. Scott Momaday notes in *House Made of Dawn,* "you can see to the end of the world. To look upon that landscape in the early morning, with the sun at your back, is to lose

Tawa Point, dawn.

the sense of proportion. Your imagination comes to life, and this, you think, is where Creation was begun."[79] How can you *not* feel joy with a new sun, created every day, to illuminate the wild, wonderful expanse? Imagination and spirit soar. "It's an old emotion," writes Dan Flores, *"euphoria at spaciousness."*[80]

Summer days on the plains can quickly become hot and dull, however. Each morning, I made it back to the park's housing complex with just enough time to transition back to the real world. If I had to open the visitor center, I would take a quick shower, gulp down breakfast, and leave even before my roommates woke up. If I was scheduled to close, I had several hours—time to bike up to Pintado Point then return to make pancakes. On weekends, I tossed snacks and water bottles into my pack and tried to head out to the Wilderness before it became unbearably hot.

It was unbearably hot by 9 A.M.

By 10:00 A.M., the sky is stark, the air hazy; the ground shimmers with irradiated heat. Not a breath of air. Even the snakeweed looks dehydrated. Visitors are short-tempered: "It takes a whole *hour* just to *drive* through? *Ten dollars* a car? Why haven't we seen any *antelope*?"

Noon. Just as we consider telling people, "Sorry—you can't go in; the road melted," wisps of cloud tickle the horizon, so far away, so faint, that they're less substantial than mirages.

"The prairie landscape is so completely dominated by its skies that sometimes there seems to be no middle ground," Paul Gruchow's description of rural Minnesota fits Arizona as well:

There are summer days when the blue of the prairie sky permeates everything, when land and plants and air and water seem all to be molded from an identical blue material. The air on such days shimmers; it is difficult to say precisely where the horizon quits and the heavens begin.[81]

Clay, rock, and horizon baking in the midday sun

It's like that almost every day on the Southwestern sagebrush-steppe. May, June, and the beginning of July melt together into a hot blur of dry, empty blue. It would feel intolerable but for the knowledge that the hotter and drier these months are, the thirstier the ground gets; the thirstier the ground gets, the more likely it is to suck moist air masses up and over from the Sea of Cortez or Gulf of Mexico. These air masses, in turn, manifest themselves in the form of tremendous storms that sweep in like clockwork every afternoon for weeks at a time, August into September—monsoon season!

2:00 P.M. Slowly, almost imperceptibly, wisps build into puffs, then begin to multiply and cast speckles of shadow on distant mesas. Patches of cool shade sweep across the plains, then the clouds begin to develop

Sacred datura, opening for a storm

depth and drama. The land becomes a mere accomplice to the sky, there to "change and glow and darken under it," as Wallace Stegner observed in his plains memoir *Wolf Willow*.[82]

4:00. Although there might still be sunshine directly overhead, thunderheads swell to the east and north and west and south—black-bottomed, white-crowned billows that suck hot air from the ground and circulate it up to the stratosphere. Yes, Kathleen Norris, maybe it *is* our sky that makes us crazy: "[w]e can see the weather coming, and we like it that way."[83]

5:00. Energy builds, along with tension and anticipation; it's darker, darker, dark. Eerie, beautiful blue-black dark. Tendrils of virga sweep down, teasing the parched earth. Through the darkness, a flicker and a whoosh—lightning!

Lightning!

. . . Lightning!

It's rare to hear thunder—usually the storms are too far away for sound, but sometimes the clouds grumble and roar. Dust devils whirl furiously along dry washes. Clockwise?—all is well; stand and watch. Counterclockwise?—go inside, batten down. The air crackles in anticipation.

A whiff of ozone—fried air, mixed into the pungency of sage. And, if you're lucky—very, very lucky—you'll feel one cool drop, *sploosh*!, on your brow. Then another, *splash*! at your feet.

Plock, plock, big fat pockets of water, how could the sky have held anything that size?,

plock, plock,

plockplockplock,

patterpatterpatter,

pitterpatterpitterpatterpitterpatter,

and you're soaked, cold, drowned, happy.

5:20. The world is fresh and new. Frogs are singing. Clouds breaking. Sky lightening, light.

> (Ha!, one last kaboom.)

> "I come from brilliancy / And return to brilliancy. / What is this?"
> ...[Hoshin] shouted "Kaa!" and was gone.
> —Paul Reps and Nyogen Senzaki, *Zen Flesh, Zen Bones*[84]

I didn't know there were frogs in the desert. (Technically, spadefoot toads, which boast the remarkable ability to burrow deep into the mud and wait until they sense rain to emerge and breed.) I didn't know what "virga" was, or that, according to Navajo lore, one can identify a malevolent dust devil by its counterclockwise rotational pattern. I didn't know that rainbows could be full, that the sky can turn slate green, that lightning can fuse sand into twisted globules of glass.

I didn't know that you can live your whole day, every day, for just three moments: sunrise, sunset, and the raw scent of first rain—pure joy.

After a storm passes, the sky becomes blue again, but a quieter, more content blue than the parched exhaustion of noon or darkening shade of afternoon. Even if there hasn't been a storm—if the day has just stretched long and hot and flat—still, by late afternoon, there's a feeling of readiness, resignation, wu wei. Minutes linger, not because they're loathe to pass but because they're content to know the next will arrive soon enough. The sun will set, the earth will whirl. "In the reprieve at the end of a day, in the stillness of a summer evening," writes Barry Lopez, "the world sheds its categories, the insistence of its future, and is suspended solely in the lilt of its desire."[85]

To step out into this blueness—a blue tinged with pinks and purples and golds—is to experience a release. A rhythm. Exhalation, inhalation: continuity and change, if not infinity.

Perfect time for a walk.

6:20. Turn onto the same old path; pass the same little landmarks. But now, as William A. Quayle promises in *The Prairie and the Sea*, "[t] he prairie path leads to the sky path. The paths are one: the continents are two; and you must make your journey from the prairies to the sky."[86]

It wouldn't be hard to walk up instead of across. The air is buoyant; the earth exhaling. Grasses ripple in the breeze.

The grass! The slight rustle and soft touch of tall wheat lining the path is the only sensual tether to earth. As the sun dips lower, it caresses the vegetation with its long rays, making everything—alive or inanimate, rain-soaked or dry, real or imagined—glow like copper and gold. Cicadas start to sing.

Old Route 66, the morning after a monsoon

Fragrant grasses and white clouds / hold me here. / What holds you there,
/ world-dweller?

—Chiao Jan, 8th century Chinese poet[87]

6:40. If there are wildfires to the west, the particulates catch reds and oranges so bright that the color stings as much as the smoke. If thunderheads are still rumbling through, great shafts of light pierce through holes in the cloud layer and race in bright splotches across the plains. If the sky is empty—wonderfully empty, just ether and light—then your

Triticum—a wild wheat

attention is fixed on the great glowing sun—is it sinking or are the mesas stretching up to catch it? Beautiful, breathtaking, but so urgent that it makes you dizzy, or anxious, even—jealous, possessive. *Stop!* You want to shout at every fleeting moment, let me *look,* let me *see!*

I actually did shout "stop!" one evening, out loud, at the sun or the earth, desperate to make time stand still. Having just slipped away from a group at quarters (*Can't miss the sunset,* my excuse; *but the sun sets every night,* the response), I was determined to have the world be beautiful for me. I raced out old Route 66, seeking space, more space. When I stopped to catch my breath, I realized that the view was indeed extraordinary— deep purpley-blue mesas, deep blue-purple clouds, and, in between: a strip of light; Pilot Rock; wisps of virga dripped in gold. The prairie was newly washed, sage sparkling. Flowers were sprouting up from the soil and bursting into bloom; I could hear their petals open, no? Larks were larking, rabbits hopping, I should have broken out in song, gone skipping or dancing off into the prairie, mud soft and cool between my toes, but instead I shouted "stop!"

Stop! Hit pause, run back to quarters, drag everyone outside, out into that blazing evening, so alive, so alive, and say, *see?* Don't you *see?*

Stop! Let *me* see, let me stare, let me memorize every beautiful color and line. Let me sear the scene into my brain or seal it in a bottle or a box so that I can look at it whenever I want (or maybe just shake it sometimes; hear it rattle; remember it was real, had happened, was happening.)

Stop! It was the most beautiful thing I had ever seen, and soon it would be lost. I would never see anything that beautiful again. I would forget, forget, it would blur into the summer's worth of sunsets, sunrises, days and nights, moments, dreams, lost, forgotten.

I burst into tears.

What else can you do? There's a tinge of desperation in every sunset. Sunrise is for anticipation, then awe (*rise, sun, rise! . . .. Oh!*). Midday hours merge in a bright, brilliant glare. Come late afternoon, though, as the light begins to lengthen, you know the sun is going to slip away, slowly, surely, whether you want it to or not, whether you will it to or not, and then it will be dark. In the dark of night, you'll have to face a universe filled with far more empty space than solid matter.

"The Golden Hour," or even "Magic," photographers and cinematographers call it—those moments when the sun lingers near the horizon, embracing everything in its rich, warm glow. Who hasn't raced out to snap a shot of a brilliant dawn or fiery dusk? Though the images might look the same—you can't tell the difference between a rising sun and a setting sun unless you know whether landmarks face east or west—the experience is entirely different. The rise comes with a bit of a pop—an inhalation, a celebration, *oh!* Sunset: *a-u-m*, you exhale.

Though words can never convey the full meaning of such moments, if you delight in definitions: "awe," according to the *Oxford English Dictionary*, is "reverential or respectful fear; the attitude of a mind subdued to profound reverence in the presence of supreme authority, moral greatness or sublimity, or mysterious sacredness."[88] Awe can be what theorist Vladimir Konečni calls a "peak experience"—a state of being moved with fear and joy, boundlessness and humility[89]—or what others consider a mix of beauty, admiration, reverence, and respect. When filled with awe, people find their minds "expand to accommodate truths never before known," according to cognition researchers Dacher Keltner and Jonathan Haidt; we feel a part of larger phenomena—the great wide world, the infinite whirl of time, all that is sacred and divine.[90] (N. Scott Momaday: "The sun is at home on the plains. Precisely there does it have the certain character of a god."[91]) Truth, admiration, and reverence are for Aurora—the goddess of dawn; that bright beautiful sun peeking over the horizon once again. Awe-rora.

What of sunset, then? Sublime. Not "sublime" as in a change of phase from solid to gas (though that would seem to happen each night), nor "sub-liminal" as in below the threshold (though that would aptly describe the sun as it drops behind the horizon); rather, "sublime" as defined by eighteenth-century philosopher Edmund Burke—"the feeling of expanded thought and greatness of mind" provoked by an encounter with objects with great and ineffable power.[92] Power—a dimension of threat and terror—is what distinguishes that which is sublime from the merely beautiful, according to Allen Carlson[93]: Immanuel Kant cites an emotional reaction to a display of nature's power,[94] while Sigmund Freud describes an "'oceanic' feeling . . . a flowing out of the ego and into the totality of things."[95] Keltner and Haidt discuss a merging of *vastness*—"anything that is experienced as being much larger than the self"—and *accommodation*—the mind's struggle to comprehend challenging, confusing new experiences that leave an individual feeling small and powerless. What can one do when confronted, simultaneously, with one's own fragile mortality as well as one's presence in a vast, whole universe?

Well, you can burst into tears. Every night. Around 6:45 or 7 P.M. during the summer; more toward 5 during the winter.

Or you can just watch, with enchantment. "Enchantment" invites no dread, no terror, no thoughts of ego or Truth; no desire to pause or capture or cling. Nothing but beauty and peace. "To be enchanted," according to philosopher Jane Bennet, is to be "transfixed, spellbound . . . Thoughts . . . are brought to rest, even as the senses continue to operate, indeed, in high gear. You notice new colors, discern details previously ignored, hear extraordinary sounds, as familiar landscapes of sense sharpen and intensify."[96]

Let go of the mind, then, "the thousand blue / story fragments we tell ourselves / each day to keep the world underfoot," advise poets Jim Harrison and Ted Kooser.[97] Let your thoughts rest as blues change color. The sky grows vivid, glows, glows! as the breeze and the flowers and the sweet chirps of insects rise lightly from the land. The sun lingers on distant mesas, then is gone.

Enchantment

Some theorists say magic eventually gets dusty, dulls, thins: the sun sets each evening, day after day, year after year; after a point, who cares? "As experience increases, experience of the ordinary increases, and thus the odds of experiencing the exceptional decreases," Stan Godlovitch evaluates nature; "[m]any exceptional things have only one chance to be exceptional. Repeat them often and they become ordinary."[98] Ordinary. Boring. Plain.

And yet, in researching the "Aesthetic Experience"—moments when "we feel as though life had suddenly become arrested . . . We are wholly in the present with no thought of the past or future. There is no purpose or motivation behind our experience other than just having the experience for its own sake"— Richard Chenowith and Paul Gobster found that intense beauty can be and is often encountered in familiar places and ordinary landscapes.[99] Their research participants cited lakes, birds (especially ducks), sunsets, seasons, and storms as being particularly inspirational. Conclusion: there's no need for the stimulation of busy city streets or the splendor of forested mountains, just an ability to appreciate quiet natural beauty (and/or the presence of waterfowl.)

In fact, the better a person comes to know a place, the more attuned they may become to its subtle rhythms and rhymes. Even "less spectacular landscapes," geographer Karl Benediktsson concedes, afford a state of heighted emotional and aesthetic awareness "once one allows oneself to dwell therein."[100]

Dwell therein: "Abide in some place *endlessly spacious,* clear of trees, hills, habitations . . . Thence comes the end of mind pressures" the god Shiva shared one of 112 ways to open the invisible doors of consciousness (recorded in the Vigyana Bhairava Tantra[101]). Discover "that it is necessary, absolutely necessary, to believe in nothing. That is, we have to believe in something that has no form and no color—something which exists before all forms and colors appear," Zen monk Shunryu Suzuki Roshi urges.[102] Once one allows oneself to dwell therein—once one has emptied the mind of expectations, beliefs, easily acquired abstract knowledge—one is open to the feel of a place.

"The 'feel' of a place," according to Yi-Fu Tuan, is

made up of experiences, mostly fleeting and undramatic, repeated day after day and over the span of years. The "feel" of a place . . . is a unique blend of sights, sounds, and smells, a unique harmony of natural and artificial rhythms such as times of sunrise and sunset, of work and play.[103]

To experience the rhythm of space, stand out on the plains at dusk. After suffering long hours of harsh sunlight and/or the intense swirls of storms, the earth exhales with gentle relief. Release. Heat waves shimmer into the deepening air. Snakes and spiders crawl out to warm themselves on the pavement. Planets start to shine and stars begin to twinkle, one by one. Perhaps an owl, *whowho?*, or a meteorite, tracing a fleeting arc through the growing darkness.

Perhaps nothing.

Night sweeps over the Painted Desert Inn cabins

I know I was lucky to get to see each dawn and dusk and full night sky at Petrified Forest. The park is one of few that closes each evening—not just the visitor center, but the road. Law enforcement personnel gently encourage visitors out at a designated time, then close and lock gates behind them. Although this is done for resource protection (people continue to attempt to steal fairly significant amounts of petrified wood; they would take even more if they could come and go under the cover of darkness), I can see why the policy might be contentious. After all, the park is public land, ostensibly owned by all citizens; shouldn't every taxpayer have the right to see dusky light lingering on the Painted Desert?

"You can, in fact, see the sunset from any number of locations outside the park," I would tell visitors who were unable or unwilling to apply for a free backcountry permit and hike out a mile into the Wilderness Area (the only way, aside from working there, to legally be inside the boundary after hours); "there are Painted Desert overlooks north of Winslow and Flagstaff."

That's what I would *say*, nodding with polite understanding, but I'm secretly glad that I had sunrises and sunsets to myself—just me and the birds and the rabbits and the bobcats, letting the world lilt into sleep. Less secretly, I'm appreciative that I was able to experience not just one sunrise or storm or morning at the solstice marker, but a whole summer's worth, and autumns' and winters'. Months, years, of "clean air to breathe," as Edward Abbey extols the intangible benefits of working and living in a National Park:

> stillness, solitude, and space; an unobstructed view every day and every
> night of sun, sky, stars, clouds, mountains, moon, cliffrock and canyons;
> a sense of time enough to let thought and feeling range from here to the
> end of the world and back; the discovery of something intimate—though
> impossible to name—in the remote.[104]

Of course, you may be thinking, if *I* could live in a park for a summer, I too would learn the names of the flowers and cycles of the day. I too would walk out to where the path disappears into sky; I would visit the petroglyph panels, let the wheatgrass whisper between my fingers. I too would come to see the plains as beautiful.

To that, I wonder: would you?

I would like to say it's just a matter of time—time and an open mind—that's all it takes for a place to become your home, for a fit to be achieved, or peace, as Rick Bass writes[105]; if you let yourself dwell therein, any landscape can feel spectacular. Yes, I would like to say so, but I can't. How we perceive places says something about who we are; how we internalize them says something about how we want to live and who we want to be. Bass belongs in the Yaak. Ed Abbey in the desert. Annie Dillard at Tinker Creek, Aldo Leopold by his shack; the Muries in the Far North, John Muir in the Sierras, Henry David Thoreau on the shores of Walden Pond. Dan O'Brien is "cursed" to love South Dakota, Kathleen Norris finds North Dakota sacred, and in Minnesota, Paul Gruchow acknowledges that the "mystery has captivated me, and under the spell of it, I have meandered, like the drifts of snow, across the wide prairies." ("This sameness is the mystery, / Mystery within mystery; / The door to all marvels" observes Lao Tzu in the *Tao Te Ching*.[106])

We can't go looking for mystery, or peace, or place. We can't go drifting across fields, expecting if not demanding a landscape be always enchanting, awe-some, sublime. But if we find, as did Barry Lopez in the Arctic, that "[t]he land gets inside us," then "we must decide one way or another what this means, what we will do about it."[107]

What does this mean?

What will we do?

Interim : Sense of Place
Red Desert, Wyoming

In studying, each day something is gained. / In following the Tao, each day
something is lost. / Lost and again lost. / . . . / No matter how much you
manipulate / You can never possess the world

—Lao Tzu, *Tao Te Ching*[108]

Why do some people find seemingly dull, desolate plains landscapes beautiful? How do some people become attached to wild places and wide open space? And what do we do about it?

When I made my first conscious attempt to answer these questions, I let myself be muddled by preconceptions and misconceptions (conceptions in general). I gave myself a crash course in academic definitions of "place" and "space," starting with Yi-Fu Tuan's *Space and Place: The Perspective of Experience* ("What begins as undifferentiated space becomes place when we endow it with value"[109]), then progressing through *Topophilia* ("the affective bond between people and place"),[110] Paul Faulstich's "Geophilia" ("a human tendency to emotionally connect with landscape"),[111] and a spate of theories on place-attachment, place-identity, and place-dependence (terms that describe how people attach to, identify with, and depend on particular locations)[112] before finally settling on Antony Cheng, Linda Kruger, and Steven Daniels' review of "'Place' as an Integrating Concept in Natural Resource Politics."[113] Their research depicts a relationship between people's perceptions, management decisions, and the land itself, locating "place" at the nexus of Biophysical Attributes and Processes, Social and Cultural Meanings, and Social and Political Processes.

Hooray!, I thought, *a Venn diagram!*—Something into which I can neatly corral all of my wild, wide-ranging ideas!

Armed with a rudimentary understanding of "place," I blundered on in an attempt to distinguish phenomenological epistemology from that of social constructionism. From what I could tell (or at least quote), the former is "analysis and interpretation of consciousness, particularly the conscious cognition of direct experience" (Anne Buttimer, "Grasping the Dynamism of Lifeworld"),[114] while the latter pertains more to "shared meanings and expectations of appropriate behaviors to a place" (Cheng, Kruger, and Daniels). In other words, one explores an individual's encounters with the real world; the other, concepts created and maintained in the public sphere. Both perspectives seemed valuable to me, so I amended Cheng et al's Figure 1 to include a loop for personal experience—the sensations, perceptions, and ideas that form and inform an individual's relationships with a place.

Definitions and diagrams in hand, I was ready to deconstruct "place." Believing that I must maintain at least a veneer of objectivity, I decided

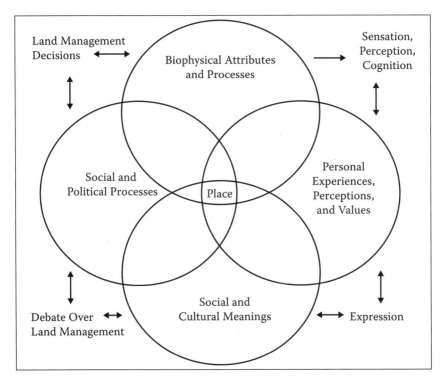

Dimensions of Place

not to delve into the natural and human history of the Painted Desert—
"my" desert; that patch of prairie I had come to love—but rather began
looking for a proper "study area"—some other stretch of semi-desert
sagebrush steppe that I knew and cared nothing about. A blank slate;
an empty space.

"Wyoming's Red Desert was chosen as a study area for two main reasons," I intentionally excluded myself from active-verb responsibility of
choosing: "recent debates over land management priorities in the region
and the natural landscape itself."[115]

The Red Desert is a windswept patch of clay soils and dusty shrubs,
ranchland and public lands, few roads and even fewer towns nested
between forks of the Continental Divide in south central Wyoming's
2.5-million acre endorheic Great Divide Basin. Or, as some locals put it,
the Red Desert is "miles and miles of nothing but miles." It does, in fact,
share many biophysical features with the Painted Desert: both are, for the
most part, low-relief plains, horizons punctuated by distant mountains
and buttes as well as distinct basaltic landmarks—the Neogene Leucite
Hills (including the photogenic "Boars Tusk") in the former and the
slightly older Bidahochi volcanic field (Pilot Rock!) in the latter. Aridisols
dominate both areas, overlain with quaternary alluvial and aeolian deposits and spectacular stretches of badlands. Both the Red Desert and
the Painted Desert receive about 7.5 to 10 inches of precipitation per year
(the former receives a fair balance of summer rains and winter snows,
while the latter has distinct seasonal variability) and are classified as
"semi-deserts," "shrub-steppes," and/or "shortgrass prairies" dominated
by widely spaced grasses, forbs, and xeric shrubs.[116]

Artemisia tridentata (big sagebrush)? Check. *Chrysothamnus viscidi-
florus* (rabbitbrush)? Check. *Atriplex confertifolia* (saltbush), *Opuntia
polyacantha* (prickly-pear cactus)? Check, check, along with exotics
Bromus tectorum (cheatgrass) and *Salsola tragus* (Russian thistle, better

known as tumbleweed). The main difference, vegetation-wise, is that the Red Desert has a significant amount of *Sarcobatus vermiculatus* (greasewood) while the Painted Desert boasts more grasses, such as *Bouteloua gracilis* (blue grama) and *Bouteloua curtipendula* (sideoats grama) as well as the succulent *Ephedra viridis* (mormon tea).[117]

Turning to animals, the Greater Green River Basin is home to several large vertebrates, mainly *Antilocapra americana* (pronghorn) and *Odocoileus hemionus* (mule deer)—of which there are an estimated 50,000 each (Biodiversity Conservation Alliance 2009). More charismatic species include the occasional *Cervus elaphus* (elk); carnivores such as *Taxidea taxus* (badger), *Lynx rufus* (bobcat), *Puma concolor* (mountain lion), and the ubiquitous *Canis latrans* (coyote); and the exotic but well-loved *Equus caballus* (wild horse), sheep, goats, and cattle. Notable smaller mammals include *Peromuscus maniculatus* (deer mouse) and *Lepus townsendii* (jacktail rabbit) as well as the endemic *Cynomys leucurus* (white-tailed prairie dog), *Thomomys clusius* (Wyoming pocket gopher), *Spermophilus elegans* (Wyoming ground squirrel). Avian species such as *Atheme cunicularia* (burrowing owl), *Aquiila chrysaetos* (Golden eagle), *Buteo regalis* (ferruginous hawk), and of course *Corvus corax* (raven) are present year-round, while several migrating waterfowl, including *Anus platyrhynchos* (mallard), *Anas crecca* (green-winged teal), and *Branta canadensis* (Canada goose), use wetter pockets for breeding grounds; *Centrocercus urophasianus* (Greater sage grouse) are important game birds. Typical reptilian species include *Pituophis melanoleucus* (gopher snake), *Crotalis viridis* (prairie rattlesnake), *Sceloporus graciosus* (sagebrush lizard), and *Phrynosoma hernandesi* (horned lizard). Although the region is estimated to host several thousand insect species, including multiple types of endemic grasshoppers, entomologists have not yet catalogued many of them. (Indeed, writer and grasshopper expert Jeffrey Lockwood calls the Red Desert "an exercise in scientific humility.")[118]

While the Painted Desert does not host the same number of larger animals, members of the same families are present, with *Sylvilagus audubonii* (desert cottontail), *Lepus californicus* (black-tailed jackrabbit), *Ammospermophilus leucurus* (antelope ground-squirrels), and *Cynomys gunnisoni* (Gunnison's prairie dog) replacing their counterparts to the north. Adding to the list of birds, reptiles, and insects: that southwestern icon *Geococcyx californianus* (roadrunner), showy *Crotaphytus collaris* (collared lizard), *Cnemidophorus* (whiptail), *Lampropeltis getula* (kingsnake), and the storm-serenader *Spea bombifrons* (spadefoot toad). *Theraphosidae* (tarantula) are also present, though not quite as prominent in Park Service publications.

You get the idea. Formal descriptions of biophysical attributes; checklists of animals, plants, climate, relief—what makes a place a place?

Susan Dakin, a researcher with expertise in landscape aesthetics and environmental management, writes that "[p]eople are not mere viewers of landscape: they participate in a way that influences their understanding."[119] Among many other scholars, Emily Brady agrees: "there is no meaning internal to landscapes. We bring meaning to them."[120]

People—is it *people*—history, culture, society that make a place a place? As with the Painted Desert, people have been living in the Red Desert for millennia. Plains tribes followed herds of animals from place to place (the northern landscape was more amenable to a nomadic lifestyle than to agriculture), embedding their geographic knowledge and beliefs as deeply in the landscape as did Puebloan farmers; Ute and Shoshone people still consider the region sacred. In historic times, Euro-American mountain men, explorers, and settlers preferred to pass on through, following branches of the Oregon Trail, Cherokee Trail, and Overland Trail to more hospitable lands. Railroads brought more people and, with them, a need for supply stations at particular distances along the easiest route—now cities such as Rock Springs and Rawlins. Aside from the occasional attempt to mine gold, silver, or uranium, grazing seemed to be the only suitable use for the land; the Red Desert boasts a ranching heritage stretching back several generations.[121] That also sounds like the Painted Desert, crossed by the Santa Fe Trail and the Camel Corps and the railroad, punctuated by railroad towns such as Holbrook and Mormon-camp-turned-railroad-towns such as Joseph City, and still surrounded by ranchland.

The "desert values" published by the conservation group Friends of the Red Desert read just like my pleas for the Painted Desert (replace "scope" with "sketchbook"):

The Red Desert is a land of contrasts. Its emptiness and incessant wind can overwhelm visitors at first, but as you explore and look more closely, the desert has a way of drawing you in. It may be the unexpected flash of pink bitterroot poking up through barren sand, or the sight of a herd of wild horses racing across the sagebrush. It may be sighting a pronghorn buck in your scope after hours of crawling stealthily on your belly through the sage. Whatever it is, the Red Desert has captivated hundreds of thousands of people over the years. . .

". . .But now"—here's an important distinction—"this area faces threats—in the form of oil and gas development—that may change it forever."[122]

Due to accidents of geology and not-unrelated issues of land ownership, a significant portion of the Painted Desert, with its petrified wood and phytosaur fossils, has been preserved by the National Park Service for more than a century; the Red Desert, meanwhile, long seen as nothing but scrubby ranchland and habitat for some birds and antelope, became a checkerboard mix of private, state, and public lands left to the care of the Rawlins and Rock Springs Offices of the Bureau of Land Management (BLM)—a federal agency tasked with balancing uses from grazing to mining to recreation to wilderness preservation. Though local citizens have made sporadic efforts to designate the Red Desert a game preserve or wildlife refuge, few people outside of Wyoming knew, much less cared, about the region until extensive deposits of oil and gas were deemed recoverable. Then it became a battleground—ground of and for "an ideological battle . . . among those who value what is here. Some value what lies on the surface; some value what lies beneath," in the words of journalist Hal Clifford.[123]

When the BLM expressed interest in expanding oil and gas leasing in the Red Desert, local conservation groups campaigned for a Citizens' Red Desert Protection Alternative that would prohibit any further energy development in sensitive areas. In September 2000, the BLM received more than 12,000 public comments on their draft Environmental Impact Statement for the Jack Morrow Hills Coordinated Activity Plan (JMHCAP), many of which supported the Protection Alternative. The following summer, national organizations such as the Sierra Club and The Wilderness Society joined the push for designation of Jack Morrow Hills—a 620,000-acre stretch of wildlife habitat and active sand dunes—as a Natural Conservation Area.[124] By the time the comment period on the JMHCAP closed, the BLM had received a record number of statements, many of which expressed the fear that oil and gas development would bring fencing and roads, directly altering habitat, disrupting migratory patterns, and introducing several pollutants to a larger "road-effect zone."[125] Friends of the Red Desert interprets the Final Environmental Impact Statement (FEIS) for the Jack Morrow Hills, released in July 2004:

> The [allowed] 255 wells is the minimum number to be drilled and therefore it is not a cap, which leaves the area vulnerable to even greater industrialization. Friends of the Red Desert is highly disappointed with the BLM's decision that discounted over 80,000 comments calling for no mineral

extraction in the Jack Morrow Hills and the lack of acknowledgement that Wyoming's citizens want some unique and special lands left for themselves, for wildlife, for wildlife habitat, and for open space.[126]

Open space. When I moved to Wyoming to begin graduate school, I had never heard of the Red Desert. It was in central Wyoming; I was in eastern. It offered no notable attraction; I was happy hiking the Medicine Bows and climbing Vedauwoo. But as controversy over management principles and practices in some place called the "Red Desert" infiltrated local and national media, I began to pay attention. Radio segments. Newspaper articles. Travel guides, letters-to-the-editor, and, especially, websites—the more I learned, the more intrigued I became. The descriptions, the photographs—the place looked just like my Painted Desert![127] Open space, wild beauty—people were expressing and uniting behind their love of sagebrush steppe! Why and how had they come to care for a forgotten patch of windswept plains? How did they assert the value of emptiness and desolation, that feeling of grandeur that plains afford? I wanted to learn more.

It seemed simple enough. Step 1: Read available documents—everything from biological reports to land management records, op-ed articles to environmentalist brochures. Step 2: Talk with stakeholders and decision-makers in an attempt to ferret out personal opinions from professional positions. Step 3: Find and focus on common themes, recalibrate readings and transcripts. Step 4: Synthesize results.

Of course it's more complicated. To begin with, the Red Desert has a variable and ill-defined location and extent. There is a town called "Red Desert," located in south-central Wyoming, just off Interstate 80. There is also a "Red Desert Basin" topographic quadrangle and the toponym sprawls in large letters across state highway maps. The "Red Desert" is touted in tourism brochures, cited in scientific studies, dissected in energy development projects, defended in environmentalist brochures, and debated in newspaper columns, magazine articles, radio programs, and short films.[128] Two recently published books have "Red Desert" in the title—one a comprehensive if somewhat resigned overview of the region's natural and cultural history, edited by the Pulitzer Prize-winning author Annie Proulx; the other an unabashedly loving (and stunning) photographic journey compiled by the Executive Director of Biodiversity Conservation Alliance, Erik Molvar.[129] The BLM's Draft Environmental Impact Statement pointedly covered leasing in the "Green River Resource Area," but the barrage of comments referred to the fate of the "Red Desert."[130] No one seems to know exactly where such a place is. Or rather, everyone thinks they know where it is, but the borders, whether mapped or not, rarely coincide. ("Researcher: 'Well, to start, where is the Red Desert?' Rancher: [laughs] 'That's a good one!. . .'"[131])

You'd think that if you can't say exactly *where* a place is, it would be hard to discuss *what* it is, much less what it should be. In fact, it's quite the opposite. Toponyms are place-holders, used to contain and convey conceptions of a geographic feature. To those who are campaigning for environmental protection, "Red Desert" stands for pronghorn and mule deer and sage grouse; wild horses; volcanic necks, sand dunes, and fossils; petroglyphs, trails; public lands! In an attempt to "educat[e] the public and show them what's out there, so that we can burst this myth that it's just this empty void that's just waiting for drilling rigs and bulldozers to make dollars out of it," conservation groups such as Biodiversity Conservation Alliance flooded the media with species lists and economic statistics and political histories as well as glossy photographs depicting gorgeous sunsets and thunderstorms.[132] Articles and brochures juxtapose images of wide open plains with grim shots of development pads and power-lines, with the intent to, as Cheng *et al.* theorize, "generate a response from people, even among people who have never even been to the place in dispute." (Their Proposition 3 is that "Social Groups That Seemingly Emerge Around Using, Protecting, or Altering the Physical Attributes of a Location May Be Engaging in More Fundamental Processes of Defining Significant Social and Cultural Meanings to That Place"; according to Proposition 5, "Groups Intentionally Manipulate the Meanings of Places Hoping to Influence the Outcome of Natural Resource Controversies.")

To people who see or read the materials, "Red Desert" becomes a symbol—a symbol for the rugged, spectacular "Wild Heart of the West" brochures promise. It's a rallying cry for those who strive to "balance industrial uses of my public lands with the needs of public recreation, clean air and water, and desert wildlife," as Friends of the Red Desert proffer in a letter template. But to individuals with firsthand experience, reference to the "Red Desert" evokes memories of particular locations— The Haystacks! Honeycomb Buttes! Most often and most passionately, Adobe Town! (A Wilderness Study Area of spectacular clay canyons and hoodoos, abutting the "Desolation Flats" Project Area—how's that for a symbolic name?) When asked to describe the place, people happily shared stories about hiking or camping or driving "out in the Red"—stories about encounters with golden eagles or moose or wayward tourists; stories of first impressions and mornings in camp. (Cheng *et al.* Proposition 2: "People Perceive and Evaluate the Environment as Different Places Rather Than an Assemblage of Individual Biophysical Attributes.") Trusting in the power of stories, Friends of the Red Desert urges citizens to write to their governmental representatives "about personal experiences and what you enjoy doing in the Red Desert."[133] In case people hadn't yet had "the thrill and enchantment of hiking through the maze of Honeycomb Buttes without another person or sound but that of the wind," the Wyoming Wilderness Association insists "[e]very Wyoming outdoors person must take a trip soon to the Red Desert" and the Biodiversity Conservation Alliance offers guided field trips.

That's all it takes!, one activist explained to me:

The best way for people to feel investment in these landscapes and to understand the need to protect them is not to send them a ten-page diatribe
or talk on the radio or be in the newspaper —that doesn't convey it. All
you have to do is set people in front of this landscape, and without saying
anything to them at all, they get it.[134]

They get it! I nodded eagerly, all you have to do!—just let the earth, the
grass, the sky work their magic; who wouldn't be amazed by the wonders
described by another interviewee: "wide open spaces . . . spectacular
geological landforms . . . an abundance of wildlife . . . [and] endless views
to the horizon?" The Red Desert!

Confession: I didn't interview anyone who'd written to the BLM to
voice approval for the energy development. I didn't try to understand
those who might have told me that it was just space—nothing there
to worry about. I didn't lurk along I-70 to flag down travelers and ask
them what or, worse yet, *if* they thought of the landscape—the monotonous, barren non-landscape. My intent evolved into an investigation
of Cheng *et al.*'s Proposition 1: "People's Perceptions and Evaluations
of the Environment Are Expressions of Place-Based Self-Identity." I
wanted to analyze individuals who identified with the Red Desert, or
at least those who defended it most vociferously in the public sphere.
I tried to sort out personal perceptions from political positions and
assert the importance of personal experience and emotional attachment. I rallied against theorist Thomas Brown's dismissal of "value in
the relational realm" as mere interaction between a person and place
rather than some intrinsic quality; to his claim that relational value is
unobservable and "only at the feeling level,"[135] I wanted to shout: *only* at
the feeling level? What is there *but* the feeling level? Granted, humans
are rational, social animals, but we are also individuals with individual

emotions. The whole point of researching the fight for the Red Desert was to understand how and why people could feel such love for a seemingly empty, dusty space.

In his presidential address to the American Sociological Association, Douglas Massey chided:

> Sociologists have unwisely elevated the rational over the emotional in attempting to understand and explain human behavior. It's not that human beings are not rational—we are. The point is that we are not *only* rational. What makes us human is the *addition* of a rational mind to a preexisting emotional base. Sociology's focus should be on the *interplay* between rationality and emotionality, not on theorizing the former while ignoring the latter or posing one as the opposite of the other. Attempting to understand human behavior as the outcome of rational cognition alone is not only incorrect—it leads to fundamental misunderstandings of the human condition.[136]

He may well have been speaking to land managers (Brian Eisenhauer et al.: "Emotional attachments to place are a type of sense of place that is based on an appreciation for the land that goes beyond its use value"[137]), landscape architects (Appleton: "we do not have the same understanding of those emotional reactions which arise from our experience of our inanimate environment as we have of grief, anger, joy, etc., resulting from our relations with other people"[138]), and, especially, geographers. J. K. Wright's words, spoken more than 60 years ago, still ring true: "Budding geographers have been cautioned . . . against employing such adjectives [that carry emotional connotations] on the ground that they reflect the personal emotions of the writer and are not universal common denominators in the symbolism of science."[139] Though some have continued in the humanist vein pioneered by Anne

Buttimer, Edward Relph, and Yi-Fu Tuan, many scholars squirm at the seemingly unprofessional "I." It feels like an act of not just release but outright defiance to "turn to the individual being," as does Edmunds Bunkše, "first discovering new emotional and intellectual territories for myself before . . . attempt[ing] to add something to the wider discourse on landscapes."[140]

Thinking it might be interesting to compare the current campaign for a Conservation Area in Wyoming to the historic fight for a Wilderness Area in the Painted Desert, I read the "official report of the proceedings of the Wilderness hearing in the matter of Petrified Forest National Park, 23 May 1967."[141] It seemed promising, even inspirational at first: citizens testified that "[t]he Painted Desert country has a character of . . . openness and the hint of loneliness . . ." *Yes! Openness! That wistful hint of loneliness! Character!* But then, to my horror, emotionally resonant statements dissolved into bland facts: "due to lack of vegetation and strong topographic relief." The Wilderness Society (the Society, note—a national organization, not a living, breathing person) provided a checklist of attributes and recited statistics. (Oh, Aldo Leopold, Howard Zahniser, Mardy Murie, what has happened?) A representative for the Sierra Club, meanwhile, made a plea for "a place, where, once you get close to the land . . . you can truly learn what it is to walk through color, learn how full of interest and beauty a 'barren waste' can be."

To walk through color (*Hal chiitah*), how beautiful! How true! Such interests and beauties lay like hidden jewels in a "barren waste"—the representative for the Sierra Club *said* all the right things, and said them terribly eloquently, but did they *care*? Had they *walked*, had they *crawled*, for years, was red dirt caked in their knuckles and knees? I'm sure they believed deeply in abstract ideals of wildness and open space, but did they care for *the Painted Desert*? For *my* Painted Desert?

Daniel Williams and colleagues warn of the importance of distinguishing between two types of place attachment: "attachment to the specific area itself and attachment to the type of area it represents."[142] Writer and activist Dave Foreman slightly more crankily insists that "wildness" is an idea; "wilderness" is a place.[143] A real-world, hard-rock, bright-sky, lived-in, breathed-in tangible spot on earth. Gary Snyder: "Our relation to the natural world takes place in a *place*, and it must be grounded in information and experience."[144]

Information *and* experience. After several months of research, I could draw an outline of particular features and map the location of important points in the Red Desert; I could rattle off names of charismatic species, list pertinent federal regulations, even classify different statements into sociocultural and sociopolitical theories. But I didn't know the texture of Boars Tusk, the aura of Adobe Town at dawn. I didn't know the cry of a hawk or the dust of an access road. I had come to care about the imminent loss of abstract wildness, but found it hard to care for the Red Desert as a place. I had never experienced it firsthand.

Finally, mid-May, I equipped myself with directions, maps, extra water, a spare tire, and a whole host of expectations along with preconceptions. I planned to start in Rock Springs, spend a few days (a few days, as if I could learn all I needed to know in just a few days!) exploring some of the more notable sites north of the interstate, then wander south from Rawlins. I would see those petroglyphs! The wild horses! Killpecker dunes, the Haystacks, even Adobe Town and "Desolation Flats"! The Red Desert!

Instead, I got a lesson on Wyoming weather. Sometime during the night, while I was huddling sleeplessly in my cold little car (all the hotel rooms in Rock Springs were sold out, thanks to the oil and gas boom), the wind started howling and a front swept in. As I later noted, day dawned to a landscape of featureless whiteness buried under a shadowless grey sky. I stubbornly tried maneuvering the "Wild Horse Loop," but when my car rebelled against the mix of clay and ice I returned to the main road and headed northeast away from Rock Springs. At some point, I passed the most photogenic features—Killpecker Dunes and Boars Tusk—but I don't know when or where; I couldn't see through the storm. Turning vaguely eastward, I stopped to read a historic marker, but the winds were so fierce that I didn't get out of the car. A Visitor Center in Lander was closed, so on southeast to Rawlins, where I merged back on to Interstate 80 and found myself again [whipping across] the heart of the Red Desert.[145]

So much for experience. Friends of the Red Desert insist that their place "invite[es] you to explore its mysteries," but it was telling me to go away.

I went away. Fled south. Cold, tired, hungry, I didn't care any more about theories of social constructionism and phenomenology, lists of environmental attributes and iterations of management plans. I didn't care about people's attachment to some place called the Red Desert. None of that mattered.

I was on my way back to the Painted Desert—*my* swath of semi-desert sagebrush-steppe.

A couple of years ago I spent a day with a sheep rancher from Rock Springs, Wyoming. . .

Many people from the coasts don't like this part of Wyoming, or what they see of it from Interstate 80. It is dry, and a lot of it is flat. Late in the day, however, we came up over the top of one of the great ridges that surround Rock Springs, and when I mentioned the coastal opinion of sagebrush, he flared up and said, "Christ, I love this country."

— Bret Wallach, "The return of the prairie"[146]

1.6 The Quest
Pilot Rock, Painted Desert Wilderness Area, Arizona

Maybe we have lived only to be here now.

—Shipwrecked companion of Rockwell Kent[147]

In the larger scheme of life, a few months—a winter here, an autumn there, one all-too-short but oh-so-beautiful summer followed by another—is not much time. In 12–14 weeks, you can memorize and forget mathematical formulas and scientific nomenclature, float into and out of friendships, move to and away from a place you may call home; time passes with barely a trace.

Then again, a lot can happen in a few months. Or a few weeks, days, hours; minutes for that matter. It may take but a second for a fleeting sensation to etch itself on your memory—to experience true peace, to fall fully in love, or to root yourself so deeply into a landscape that you will always, always, even years later, hundreds of miles away, feel like you've left a part of yourself behind—some skin, a few bones, still out there, bleaching into the godforsaken plains.

It was only my fourth season at Petrified Forest. Other rangers had been there for twenty seasons or forty years—*they* had rightly earned the reputation of "desert rats"; *they* had rightly earned the respect of peers; *they* had earned the right to call the Painted Desert *their* place, *their* park, *their* home. Maybe. (Probably not, Ed Abbey would say.)

In a transcript made available to all Park Service employees in 2012, a high-ranking official mentioned to the Director that his biggest pet peeve is when rangers call a unit "my park" or "my monument." The sites belong to all Americans, he insists, not just the select few that work or live there. I understand where he's coming from, but, dear former deputy director, it really *is* my Painted Desert. I am happy to share it with others, but it is mine. I cannot own it much less control it, but I can claim it as a part of me. I could say that cells in my brain have been permanently configured in the shape of a dry wash; dust from the prairie is glommed deep in my pores; I sweat sage. Or I could just explain: Pilot Rock, you see, Pilot Rock.

I should have known that something would be different—that I was clinging too desperately to delight or that infatuation was tipping toward obsession. There were hints during training week, starting when a supervisor told our gaggle of eager seasonal rangers that we must remain

Pilot Rock, summer noon

considerate of the visitor and leave our personal opinions unexpressed. Surely, she meant something like "don't get embroiled in political debates," "listen to all religious views," or "be polite, even when you feel tired and cranky"—basics of front-line interpretation—but I immediately stiffened. Why should I have to compromise my love for the place? How was I supposed to curtail my passion? If a visitor made a deprecatory remark about the "boring" landscape or "empty" plains, I tended to either issue ardent injunctions (*Look! Pilot* Rock!) or bristle and fall silent (*Fine then, get out of my park, go on your way, shoo.*)

And what was I supposed to do when my new roommate hated the place? "I knew it was a desert," she spent the first week in a mild state of despair, "but I didn't think it would be like this! A *desert*! How can I live here for a whole summer? There are no *trees*!" (My initial attempt to comfort her—"Well, actually, it's not a desert. It's a semi-desert sagebrush steppe"—didn't seem to help.)

By the second week, though, she had begun to appreciate the nuances of the landscape. I'd like to take credit for that (here, use my bike; go watch the sun set. *Granted, it may not look like the places you're used to*, I offered unsolicited counsel in aesthetic appreciation, *but it's even more beautiful once you get know it)*, but it was actually a matter of her own willingness to stay and explore with open hands.

Meanwhile, I made every possible effort to get out of the visitor center, off the paved trails, and into the backcountry. I volunteered to go out with the paleontology crew to search for bone scatters and lug plaster casts. (I became an aficionado of teeth, unable to find the grander skull cases of giant crocodilian phytosaurs and instead attuned to the enameled surface of centimeter long serrated *Desmatosuchus* dentae). I joined the wildlife biologist on night drives along the park road (*Lampropeltis!* she would find, or *Theraphosida!*, while I only managed to identify a herd of cattle that had broken through the fence.) Most memorably, I helped the archaeologist relocate and assess hard-to-access sites. The fourth week of the season—June, pre-monsoon, hot—I offered to accompany him on a multi-day trek through the Wilderness Area, beginning in the far northeast corner, heading around, up, and along Chinde Mesa, following the northern fence line, and cutting diagonally back to the Painted Desert Inn after looping behind Pilot Rock.

Ah, Pilot Rock.

I'm a walker, a wanderer, not a peak-bagger. I don't care much for "conquering" high points and would be just as happy to circumambulate significant landmarks, round and round, with or without prayer beads. You see more that way—get a feel for the country, not just a view from the top.

Or so I tell people. In truth, I hate being goaded by peaks. They're domineering, relentless. If they're there, well, then, you have to climb them, right? Maybe that's why I like plains—knobs and knolls don't taunt, just expand gently then roll back down.

Pilot Rock, though, is different. How so? It's the highest point in the park, and the farthest too, but that isn't it. As a volcanic neck composed of six-million-year old basalt, it's also one of the youngest features and certainly the darkest. I don't think that's it either. Perhaps it's the name: despite the superlatives, it's not Pilot Mountain, nor Distant Big Dark Rock—just Pilot Rock, evoking flight as well as the feel of solid stone; a navigational beacon as well as unassuming rock-ness. Pilot Rock. I can't really tell you what "it" is, or what "that," exactly, makes it different. It just is. Pilot Rock.

I don't think I was quite as obsessed with Pilot Rock the first time I was at Petrified Forest. Of course, I had tried to hike out to it—one of many adventures in those breathless months of first acquaintance. One particularly benign winter day, I woke early, packed my water bottles and bags of granola, laced up my boots, stepped out into the wilderness, aimed my internal compass at the peak, and walked until, five or six miles out, I ran into an insurmountable cliff—a wall in the badlands, a barrier, high and steep, too high and steep to scramble up, too crumbly to even get partway. I tried to climb it, then conceded defeat—a mix of inability and naïveté—and found other wonders to keep me entertained. ("Don't start/with a mountain /. . ./Start with/one seed pod/or/one dry weed" advises Byrd Baylor.)

When I returned for a second season, I was slightly more determined to reach the top of Pilot Rock. Or at least its base. I had spent so many months drawing its profile, dreaming its view, staring at its scrunch of lines on the topographic map that I just wanted to touch it—to know it was real. Solid. Rock.

I strapped a sleeping bag and pad to my pack and carried extra water and apples and cookies, planning to be out overnight. I also took a notebook, a sketchbook, and, of all things, a copy of Annie Dillard's *Pilgrim at Tinker Creek* ("This is our life, these are our lighted seasons, and then we die."[148]) I regretted the extra weight as I trudged down the social trail, along the Lithodendron and its tributaries, past the lumpen sandstone hoodoos of Angels Garden, past the giant fossilized logs of the Black Forest, past the petroglyph panels and the lone juniper gnarling its way out of rock and clay, past everything. Everything except that cliff. It was still there—even higher, steeper, more crumbly than I remembered. I tried scrambling up, then paced back and forth in search of any slight gap, any drainage, any series of footholds, handholds, other people had hiked out there, there *had* to be a way. A Way? Away. I couldn't find it. Retreated in sweaty shame, nothing to show for the trip but bloody knees and elbows.

Rinse, repeat.

Three times—three times, I tried, I tried, I tried, Pilot Rock! That only increased the allure. I had to earn its respect. (It's a rock. It doesn't respect me. I respect it. Re-spect.)

The third time I was at Petrified Forest, I learned how to get to Pilot Rock. Early in the summer, a couple of gung-ho young rangers asked if I wanted to join them on their excursion to the high point. (They wanted to check it off their to-do lists before moving on to bigger, higher peaks). They'd asked a veteran employee for directions; ever-willing to share, he'd happily informed them of a gap in the badlands cliff and mapped a clear route to the summit. (He trusted everyone with the place and its secrets; why do I guard them so jealously?)

We dashed out and back in just two days. It was a test of endurance, no lingering to look for fossils or stopping to smell the yucca along the way. Instead, we practically slid off Chinde Point, ran across Lithodendron Wash, skipped Angels Garden and the Black Forest, paused only to consult the map before racing into a slim canyon that wound up through that formidable wall in the badlands. We didn't even bother to rest when we reached the upper expanse, just moved on along Digger Wash, flung our overnight packs down at a lonely cottonwood oasis, and, freed of the weight of sleeping bags and water bottles, flew up the pillar of Pilot Rock. No stopping until we reached the wooden cairn and USGS marker at the summit, where we reveled breathlessly in our sense of accomplishment.

Pause. Anticlimactic, almost profane.

[S]ince wilderness is a place, and wildness is a quality, we can always ask, "How wild is our wilderness?" and "How wild is our experience there?" My answer? Not very, particularly in the wilderness most people are familiar with, the areas protected by the Wilderness Act of 1964.

—Jack Turner, *The Abstract Wild*[149]

A few years ago, I was asked to try writing a short piece on a good weekend hike for an outdoor adventure magazine—perhaps the directions to Pilot Rock? I couldn't bear the idea of people tackling the landmark with that peak-bagging, high-pointing mindset, oh no, not my Pilot Rock. (Pilot Rock will never be mine). Yes, I will provide directions, I decided—instructions on how to explore Wilderness seeking wildness.

"Step to the edge of the Painted Desert," I wrote carefully, almost painfully, "You'll see a dark shape looming on the horizon, towering over the polychromatic expanse of dry washes and sagebrush flats. That's Pilot Rock." *Am I demeaning the landmark? I wondered, I hope not. Listen here, all you outdoor adventurers, let me tell you how this works.*

"Many people snap photos of the basaltic neck, located in the far northeastern corner of Petrified Forest National Park, Arizona, but few dare to traverse the miles of crumbling clay, scrubby prairie, and sandstone ledges that separate it from paved overlooks.

"Go. Dare." *Will you really go? Will you really dare? That first day— that first cold, grey, windy day when I stepped to the edge of the Painted Desert—I was awed, but afraid. Afraid of wandering out on my own, unprepared, no maps, no trails. Afraid of the big grey sky, the desolate red earth, that dark formation that separated the two, wonder-full, awe-full. Afraid, you; be afraid too.*

"The experience of watching the sun set across that landscape, with only a touch of wind and cry of a nighthawk for company is well worth the effort." *It is. Well worth it. But let me tell you just how much effort is involved.* "As the farthest landmark in a designated Wilderness Area, Pilot Rock doesn't have any trails leading to its summit. Instead, you have to find your own way, negotiating eight to ten miles worth of labyrinthine washes and cliffs with a topographic map, an eye to the horizon, reliable directions, and lots of water." *No trails. Do you hear me?—no trails. Find your own darn way. You can always see Pilot Rock; it's the highest point on the horizon. Figure out how to get there.*

No, sigh, *I understand.*

"Maps, with contour intervals useless to the casual day-hiker but handy for longer treks, are available at the park's visitor centers, as are free overnight permits." *I hope you come to me to ask for a permit! I'll size you up, warn you well.*

"As for directions:" *Here we go, breathe,* "start at the west side of the Painted Desert Inn, where a wilderness access trail switchbacks down into a gully, then flings you out into the unmarked desert. An unmaintained social trail will lead you one mile west before it's cut off by the Lithodendron Wash. Follow the wash southwest (if it's not too muddy, you can walk right in the channel) until you've skirted the hills of the Black Forest region (named for its unusually dark petrified wood). Turn into the easternmost tributary, heading northeast toward Chinde Mesa (a high feature that demarcates the northern boundary of the park) for about four miles. After winding your way up a gap in the steep badlands cliff and emerging in Digger Wash, follow the streambed west two miles until you reach a small grove of cottonwood trees. This oasis, situated another two miles from Pilot Rock, makes a nice place to camp. Drop your pack and pick a route to the summit, where you'll find a wooden cairn, a USGS marker, and a wild sense of peace."

All true, but good luck making any sense of it without knowing the desert, or having time to learn. It took me years. Years! That cliff is steep and covered in desert pavement—little pebbles of rock and clay that are like marbles. You can't just scramble up. Believe me; I have the bloody knees and bloody elbows to prove it. Then again, I get scraped up every time I'm out in the desert. Expect to. It's part of the experience—trade a little skin for rock.

"A warning: water is an absolute necessity in this arid environment. It's advisable, even in cooler temperatures of autumn or spring, to start out early in the morning, find a juniper (or tamarisk) to relax under at mid-day, then continue hiking as afternoon shadows lengthen. It's even more advisable to bring lots of extra water—far more than you think you could ever need or even drink."

Bring. Lots. Of. Water.

"I know how to get there!" I told park personnel, "I'm familiar with the Wilderness Area; I can get back from Pilot Rock! [And I want to go to Chinde Mesa.] I'll go!"

Thus I became a volunteer field assistant. The archaeologist would determine what sites to visit, plan the route, carry the relevant files and safety devices; I would be there as an extra set of eyes and, more so, as a safety precaution. Because it was June—hot, premonsoon, as in 100-degree-plus temperatures and relentlessly clear skies—and we were planning on being out there for several days, he arranged for two water drops: one set of bright plastic containers were placed by horseback "in the shade of a tree at the foot of Chinde Mesa"; another were left "by the gate in the fence at the far northwestern corner of the Wilderness Area." That settled, the archaeologist and I set off late one Sunday afternoon, bumping an old Dodge truck as far down the park's western border as possible before continuing on foot. When dusk began to descend, we settled in to camp on the open plains.

It was a beautiful evening—slight breeze, soft sky, the epitome of serenity. No need for a tent, just stars (*so many stars!*) and birds (*so many birds!*), singing happy praises into the night. Later, in the wee dark hours, lonely howls floated into the air. ("Together," Kathleen Norris promises, "monks and coyotes will sing the world to sleep."[150])

I should have known, though: there are some places that people are only meant to see, to dream—not actually visit. I was hiking through and sleeping in the big sweep of prairie that I'd spent several seasons contemplating every morning and every evening on my walks down old Route 66. The landscape ought to have been left to the horizon, never solidified into actual grasses and dirt.

The next morning, then, we woke before dawn and aimed for the first site—a blown-out dune filled with pottery sherds and lithics. Right away—an intact arrowhead! Then another! Both were knapped out of the finest of chert, one smokey, the other rich reds and purples. (Why so unused, perfectly preserved, presented?) I could have spent all day there, crawling around on hands and knees, calling out "pottery!" "base!" "shells!" while the archaeologist tried to sketch everything into his records, but there were many miles to go, other sites to see, and the day was beginning to bake under that blazing sun.

Not long after we'd begun hiking in earnest, hoping to reach the first water drop by early afternoon, we encountered a skull. Mule deer, judging from the antlers. Various other parts, too—vertebrae here, jawbone there, all bleached a smooth white but not yet splintering with seasons of exposure. With no time to take a photo much less make a sketch, I just imprinted it on the amygdala.

Aside from that discovery, mid-day hours and miles melted into a blur of sandy slopes and slight ridges, dusty washes and tangles of brush, a detour to a rather unimpressive couple of sherds then a long, open flat overgrown with dead plants. Dead sage, dead yucca, dead cacti, brown and crumbling, broken and bent—it looked like they'd decided en masse that the desert's no place to grow. By the time we reached the foot of Chinde Mesa, I was taking slow steps, looking for hoofprints, anxious to find the shade of a tree. Shuffling up a wash, around blind curves, until . . . a cairn? Big white jugs? Water! Blessed water! We happily collapsed, stared up at the eternally blue sky through the boughs of a lonely piñon.

Thirst quenched, spirit refreshed, we refilled our bottles and continued up to the top of the mesa, where I was surprised to discover that the landform is broad and flat. Yes, I know "Mesa" means "table" and, as such, the term is applied to table-like features with steep sides and a broad, flat top, but I had spent so long looking at Chinde from afar, knowing it as the defining border of the northern horizon, that part of me expected it to drop off on the other side as if it were stage scenery or a movie set—a cardboard cutout, a wooden façade, two dimensions, not three. The horizon is supposed to be a distant border, the attractive edge of a landscape, which can, to paraphrase Barry Lopez, quicken expectation and shape human curiosity.[151] The horizon is what Ralph Waldo Emerson called a "point of astonishment" where land meets sky, visible drops off into invisible, and known is clearly, sharply distinguished from invisible, unknowable.[152] "The essential feature of the prairie is its horizon," Paul Gruchow avers, adding the seemingly obvious stipulation, "which you can neither walk to nor touch."[153] You are *not* supposed to be able to stand on the horizon.

Yet there I was.

While I was grappling with that idea, the archaeologist realized he'd left something at the water drop and went to retrieve it. I nestled into the base of a juniper, ate a few cookies, made a few sketches, watched clouds divide then recombine. In the cool shade of a hot summer day, I possessed and maintained what Rick Bass describes as "a strange and unreplicable mixture of happiness and despair and dreaminess and urgency."[154] I was seeing new places and learning new things about a place I thought I'd known and even thought I owned. *Ah Painted Desert*, I exhaled, *how much you have to teach me!*

But soon I began to feel a touch of unease. The earth was shimmering, the juniper clawing. Somewhere overhead then all around, a raven craw-craaawed. I remembered, then, while sprawled in the shade of that gnarled tree: "Chinde" is the term for a ghost or spirit exhaled by Diné with their dying breath. According to the legend behind the toponym, there had once been a hogan (Navajo dwelling) on this mesa, abandoned and shunned after its owner passed away inside. One day, so it goes, a geologist was out making field maps and somehow got soaking wet. (Were there storms? Was it monsoon season? The story begs for embellishment, but it's not mine with which to tinker.) He went to the hogan to dry off. Some Navajo sheepherders happened to ride by, saw a pale figure lurking in this place of death, and raced off to warn others of the chinde that had taken up residence in the cursed place.

Simply a matter of mistaken identity mixed with superstition, no?

I had also heard a co-worker—a perfectly logical, rational, experienced hiker—tell me to never, ever go near the accursed Chinde Mesa.

Onward. The archaeologist came back. We checked off two more sites then opted for a short rather than smart route, dropping off the steep, unconsolidated side of the mesa. Having safely descended and breathed sighs of relief, we tromped through a Georgia-O'Keeffe-esque scene— huge creamy-pink hills with black and white and red striations; over them, a half-moon floating in a turquoise sky. (This is the moment—the exact, identifiable moment—I fell in love with turquoise. Yes, Ellen Meloy, "It is the stone of the desert. It is the color of yearning."[155])

There was, according to the charts, an archaeological site located a few hundred meters south of the Wilderness Boundary, centered between Chinde Mesa and Pilot Rock. We tried to stick to the fenceline, figuring that it would be easier to follow it than the squiggly topography. *Ha!*, we soon learned, as we dipped into another ravine then dragged ourselves back up the other side. This was the craziest fence I'd ever encountered: it plunged down cliffs, perched on boulders, and pranced across fields, never wavering from its destination. Pilot Rock.

Just as I was going to propose that we take a flatter detour, the archaeologist told me to keep my eye out for the site. It's somewhere nearby, he said, looking back and forth between the GPS and a paper form. The former told us where we were, the latter where wanted to be. Roughly. The original surveyor wasn't exactly sure of the site's coordinates, nor did the notes mention what, exactly, we were supposed to be looking for. Petroglyphs? Pottery sherds? A pueblo?

People have been scouring the Painted Desert in search of artifacts for more than a century. Most early twentieth century visitors merely stopped to see "Indian Art" or collect an arrowhead en route to the petrified forests; John Muir was one of the first people to conduct a more systematic survey of cultural resources. Herbert Lore, an early homesteader and original proprietor of the "Stone Tree House" on the site of today's Painted Desert Inn (still there, way on the horizon), took people on tours in the 1920s, likely leaving more material behind than he took (old tin cans, broken glass; there's even a full, rusted-out Model T Ford at the base of Chinde Mesa, though no one's quite sure how it got there). As the Park Service acquired land and developed resources in the early- to mid-twentieth century, Civilian Conservation Corps crews partially and semi-accurately reconstructed Puerco Pueblo and Agate House (an eight-room dwelling at the south end of the park, built entirely out of petrified wood), paved trails to petroglyphs at Newspaper Rock and the Picnic Gallery (the latter now inaccessible due to rockfalls), and, mostly, left the Wilderness Area alone. (Too much space; too desolate to bother.) Nonetheless, a few intrepid teams of archaeologists ventured out and found an astounding abundance of resources—not just petroglyphs and flakes, but evidence of long-term settlement in the form of manos and metates, building blocks, grand kivas and pueblos. Standard protocol entailed giving each find a number, writing out a detailed description, and marking the location with a stake—wooden, at first; later, metal.

That's what we were looking for—the archaeologist and I—some sort of stake, with some sort of resource nearby. We had passed several lithic scatters and pottery sherds throughout the course of the day, few of which warranted paperwork. Even I was becoming inured after my initial delight at the intact arrowheads (just that morning?). By late afternoon, having covered more than 20 kilometers, we were hot, tired, and couldn't find the site—the darn mid-north site. We were surrounded by mud-cracked clay and cobbles, not even a bush nearby. What could be here; why couldn't we see it? There's a lot of land "about 500 m south of the boundary, centered between Chinde Mesa and Pilot Rock." (Pilot Rock.)

We were about to concede defeat, give up and move on, when, almost simultaneously, we spotted a strange little vertical (straight lines still odd in a land of undulation)—the stake! We rushed over, only to find . . . a rock. A volcanic bomb, a chunk of basalt, perhaps used to pound some sort of tool? Oh.

Onward, Pilot Rock.

From this vantage, we could only see and aim for the false summit—a slightly lower knob to the east of the actual top. Though I'd always known it was there, or at least that Pilot Rock was more oblate than pyramidal, I had never really considered that side in its own right. Why bother? From afar, it's but a little dip, a little lilt, a diminutive cousin of the sinistral summit. By this point in our hike, though, even second-best seemed daunting enough, rising as it did some several hundred feet from the plains below. We kept hiking toward it, but it didn't seem to be getting any closer. We were walking on pure bentonite—a cracked skin of red clay. The sky was assertively blue. It was difficult to gauge progress much less distance between the two flat planes, so I was relatively startled when the archaeologist broke into my mindless trudge, "Should we stop for water first?"

Water? Stop? Before what? Oh, we were at the base of Pilot Rock. And I was thirsty. We paused to get bottles out of our packs and plan a route up. After an hour's worth of across, a bit of up required recalibration. Should we aim straight for the peak?—aside from a bit of a cliff toward the top, the series of brush-filled gullies looked challenging but do-able. The fence had made us leery of straight lines and "shortcuts," though; we decided to climb up about halfway then traverse a contour around to the north, where the terrain smoothed out a little. There was no longer any sense of urgency—the afternoon was lingering into early evening; still plenty of light, so near the solstice, along with the promise of cooler temperatures. We dawdled up, pausing frequently to catch our breath (a luxury I'd not been afforded on my first whirlwind of a trek.)

As we were half hiking, half looking for artifacts somewhere partway around the northern slope, a rock caught my eye. Just a rock. A smooth, round, dull tannish chunk of sandstone about the size of my palm. I leaned over and picked it up—no small investment of energy by this point. I just wanted to hold it in my hand—to hold its solid, sun-warmed weight. (By now, I know, you're wondering why I'm telling you all of this; I'm wondering why I'm writing it. Why so much detail, why care about a rock, much less the dalliance of fencelines or the legend of Chinde Mesa? Lessons of the prairie: be patient; pay attention to detail; nothing is as it seems; nothing is nothing. Abbey: "Yes . . . Touch stone. Good luck to all."[156])

Then, who knows why, I shifted the rock to my other hand. I'd picked it up in my right and transferred it to my left—a simple move, but it transformed the rock from a rock into something else: a tool—a mano; a magic talisman. It fit perfectly in my palm, like it had been made not just for me but *by* me—that I had been holding it, using it for years and years, grinding my corn against my metate and thinking: this is my rock, this is my food, this is where I live; I am home. I wrapped my fingers—long, skinny fingers that never fit into premade gloves but that fit the rock perfectly—around the mano. In so doing, I realized that my odd long hands are the same exact size and shape as those of someone who had held the tool centuries before. And, I knew, that person—whoever they were, wherever they were going, whatever they ate or felt or believed—that person was here; they were at Pilot Rock (what did they call it?) They were sinistral.

When we reached the lower summit of Pilot Rock, I gazed out across the expansive landscape with contentment, looking back to where we'd come from (east) and west to where we were going; north to the Navajo Reservation, then south to the entirety of wilderness. The archaeologist, meanwhile, poked and puzzled about the place where we were standing. "Hmmpf," he said eventually, hinting that he had something important to say. "These rocks," he contemplated a pile of black boulders, then "hmmpf"-ed again. He looked up, scanned the horizon, and, upon finding what he was searching for, a third "hmmpf," a nod, and a smile, "I'll bet it was a shrine."

A shrine? He may not have used the actual word "shrine" and "hmmpf" is not an exact transcription, but I remember realizing that the place held something sacred—something between a cairn and a cross, meant to mark the sightline from Black Knoll (far to the south, visible from the Puerco River corridor) to Pilot Rock to its Bidahochi volcanic field contemporaries (far to the north, on what's now Navajo land, part of newer lore).

But why, I never asked him, would the shrine be on the false summit, the lower side? As I looked across to the actual high point—tall, dark, desolate—I thought I understood. I didn't want to go there. There was something about it, too forbidding, too foreboding, too awesome.

I didn't understand at all. Pilot Rock.

We dropped our packs in the saddle then clambered up a basalt cliff to the twentieth-century cairn and USGS marker. Yet again, we couldn't locate the archaeological site we'd set out to survey—perhaps it was that pile of boulders back east?—but it didn't matter by that point. We were done for the day, ready to return to our packs and collapse in exhausted appreciation for the view and for twilight and for sleep. Deep sleep, blessed sleep. Light breeze, a billion stars. Badger, we thought, listening from a ledge nearby.

Upon waking in the quiet, pale pre-dawn, we packed up, ate a quick breakfast, and finished most of our water. Oh, innocent indulgence—I even splashed some on my face. It felt good to get rid of a couple days' grime; besides, there was no reason to carry the extra weight around.

We began threading our way down the northern slope of Pilot Rock, planning to survey the last few sites, refill our bottles, and start the long trek back, entertaining the vague hope of making it to the edge of Black Forest before night. My thoughts were already in that part of the wilderness, with the Old Dead Juniper (which had, by now, become capitalized in my mind).

I'd never seen it at night, wouldn't it be wonderful to sleep right there? To see its silvery branches shadowed against the dark sky, to see its stolid roots shimmer and dance in the starlight? Before I knew it, it was 8 A.M., two of the sites were surveyed, my legs were tired, and it was hot. Baking. I was thirsty.

Water, soon, "by the gate in the fence at the far northwestern corner of the Wilderness Area," right? We began looking. Fence? Check. Northwestern corner? Check. Gate? Uh oh.

We walked back and forth, north-south, then east-west, where the fence turned a sharp corner, back and forth, forth and back, where was this gate? No gate, no water. Water. Why hadn't we insisted on GPS coordinates, or a good old-fashioned mark on a map? Why hadn't we brought more water?

The sun rose higher in the sky, 8:30, 9. Brighter, hotter, no longer a benevolent god. I began to feel slightly nauseous. We needed shade, needed to get away from the unforgivingly barren flats.

The radio didn't work; the thick shadow of Pilot Rock separated us from any signal. No radio, no gate, no water. "Worst case scenario," the archaeologist finally said, voicing what I hadn't dared to think, "one of us hikes back to the Painted Desert Inn, then sends the LEs [Law Enforcement] out to get the other. We can't both go and we can't just sit here until they send out a search party."

Can't go. Can't wait. Between the two of us, we had half a liter of water. Summer, June, 100-degree-plus temperatures and we had half a liter of water. Half a liter of water, two apples, a topographic map, and eight to ten miles worth of labyrinthine clay hills and sandstone ledges separating us from civilization. Can't call. Can't wait. Can't go. Farthest corner of the wilderness, beyond Pilot Rock.

Pilot Rock.

We reconvened at the fence, rigged up a tarp for shade, and sat in the dust. What to do? Draw straws. Just a formality, in my mind—of course I would go. I was lighter, smaller, knew the terrain. I had been to Pilot Rock and back, I knew the cottonwoods, knew the gap. [This was *my* desert.]

He drew the short straw, but I protested, reasoned—lighter, smaller, know the terrain. *Can't just sit here and wait for someone else to retrieve me from my desert. I am ready.* I shed my overnight gear—sleeping bag, pad, extra socks, even my sketchbook—strapped on a little daypack containing the apples and the GPS, and headed off, aiming for—what else?— Pilot Rock. It was the easiest way to go, up and over again, rather than around and into a series of deep gullies and crumbling slopes. Pilot Rock.

I don't know how I got there, but I remember pausing at the summit, looking back in the direction of the fence then forward toward the Painted Desert Inn—both too small to see. North, then south. West, east, I inhaled deeply—air thick with challenge, adventure; had I finally found it? Pure wilderness, true wildness!

Then I exhaled. Oh.

Whether we live or die is a matter of absolutely no concern whatsoever to the desert

—Edward Abbey, *Desert Solitaire*[157]

As I climbed gingerly down from the summit—a malevolent pillar of hot black basalt—I was already worrying about the cliff in the badlands. For that matter, I was acutely aware of every little ridge and ravine, rock and root—what if I turned an ankle? How would anyone find me, or even know where to look? 43,020 acres. Forty-three thousand twenty acres. That's a lot of space.

Space.

If I can just get to Old Dead Juniper, I thought to myself as I approached the cottonwood oasis, I can make it. I can crawl back, need be; I can drag myself through the Black Forest and Angels Garden, across the Litho, up the trail. I paused in the shady sanctuary of the cottonwoods to eat an apple and try to swallow heavy thoughts. "The terror of the country you thought you knew bears gifts of humility," Terry Tempest Williams promises, "[t]he landscape that makes you vulnerable makes you strong."[158]

Leaves rustled. I had to go. I stepped out into Digger Wash, aiming for the drainage that cuts through the wall and closing my mind to another possibility: a landscape that makes you vulnerable can also make you weak; tired; a little crazy. ·

> I have feared that if I go too far I will myself erode into nothing . . . And I have also feared that I will live, but will be left unable to speak, my mind handed over to this ineffable vastness.
>
> —Craig Childs, *Soul of Nowhere*[159]

Although prairies and plains are rarely thought to confront travelers with the same sort of challenges that, say, a mountain range or a raging river pose, they are, in fact, full of dangers, perhaps all that more perilous because of their hiddenness, their diffidence, their quietude.

To be sure, there are large, unmistakably dangerous phenomena—tornadoes and brushfires, blizzards, dust storms, swarms of grasshoppers. There are also smaller but much more animate threats—everything from rattlesnakes and scorpions to ticks and hanta virus. The howling of wolves filled many a homesteader's heart with fear.

But then there are the hazards that lurk unseen. You begin to cross what looks like a perfectly flat field only to realize that it's incised with a dozen steep-sided ravines. Or you eagerly approach a spring or watering hole only to learn that it's brackish. Drought—how can you anticipate or quantify that, but in desiccated plants and dead cattle? Distance—without a sense of scale, how can you tell how far away a storm is, or how fast it's moving? Lightning bolts strike out of the blue.

The most ineffable and thus terrifying peril of the plains, though, is the sheer exposure—the nakedness, the relentless emptiness. Paul Gruchow knew well: "[t]here is no place to hide."[160] No place. No thing. It's not a simple matter of lack—no trees, no water, no landmarks (no gate in the fence at the northwest corner). Nor is it a matter of elements from which one would hope to hide—sun, rain, snow, wind, always wind. It's not even a combination of these factors. No—"it," in this case, is the feeling of a rapacious presence, an emptiness so vast so as to have acquired gravitational force. Exposed to the weight of the prairie sky and the sprawl of the prairie earth, a person cannot help but feel naked, lost somewhere between two infinite entities, belonging to neither, excoriated by both.

If I have to, I told myself, perhaps even said aloud once no one was there to hear or say it for me, *I'll just slide down.*

I was skirting the top of the badlands cliff, back and forth, searching for the right route, not finding it, not knowing whether to keep looking—just keep looking, while the sun rose higher, hotter, hothothot—or to give up and try to slide down. *A controlled slide,* I mumbled to myself, unconvinced, *a calm, smooth slide.* No straws to pick, no coin to flip, I finally decided to go for it and tumbled gracelessly down, fingers and toes grasping for clay cobbles.

When I came to rest at the bottom, I paused, exhaled, and assessed. Intact, unscathed? No broken bones! No gushing wounds! I had made it down past the wall! I was practically home free!

But, you see, I was already free. I was already home.

This is what I don't understand, don't know how to explain: Midday, out past Black Forest still, sun high hot blazing blinding overhead, I was lost in the tortuous meanders of some anonymous little wash, following my feet down the dry channel rather than attempting to pick my own way through the prairie's sand and brush. I vaguely thought that I was on the right track—that this little wash might lead to a slightly larger one, and that, in turn, to a tributary of the Lithodendron—but I couldn't be certain. There were no dramatic features nearby, no beautiful flowers in bloom, nothing by which I could mark my passage, nothing, nothing, that's what I don't understand, there were things all around me—dirt, brush, sky—but all incomprehensible, insensible. My mind had dissociated from my muscles and bones. I could, for all I knew or cared, have been going around in circles or simply standing still.

I stood still. I came to a curve in the bank that boasted a deep undercut. In the undercut bank in the curve was a pocket of shade. In the pocket of shade, I stood. Stopped walking; stood still; how cool the shade felt, how pungent the clay. I leaned into the cool clay bank, pressing my forearm and forehead into the earth while my legs folded beneath me. I sat. Ate the other apple. Curled my knees in to meet my chest; curled my back into the ground. Let my spine conform to the shape of the bank, vertebrae filling gaps in the clay. Let my attention turn to the swath of blue sky; let sweat evaporate off my skin and my flesh sink into the prairyerth. Bones bleach out in the sun wind snow.

Exhale.

What do we know? What do we really know? He licks his dry cracked lips. We know this apodictic rock beneath our feet. That dogmatic sun above our heads. The world of dreams, the agony of love and the foreknowledge of death. That is all we know. And all we need to know? Challenge that statement. I challenge that statement. With what? I don't know.

—Edward Abbey, *The Monkey Wrench Gang*[161]

"Bring lots of water," I wrote for my guide to a good weekend hike, but couldn't let that be the final word. "If you'd prefer not to have to worry about trails or travails," I tacked on an extra paragraph, "50,000+ acres of designated Wilderness (total between the Painted Desert and Southern sections) are open for exploration—spend as long as you like scrambling around the prairie looking for fossils, listening for birds, or smelling the sage. You don't have to stand on the summit of Pilot Rock to breathe a touch of wildness." *Don't ever go to Pilot Rock.*

I got a note back from the magazine's editors saying they liked my submission, sounds like a great place, but we wouldn't want people getting lost in the wilderness—could I please provide better directions; where exactly is the trail?

I must have picked myself up and continued on. ("On," not "back." "Back" lost all meaning; "forward" too. To where do I long to return?) I don't remember or care to remember how. All I remember, all I know, is the smell of clay, its cool embrace, and, overhead, an empty blue sky.

when you see the entire sky endlessly clear, *enter such clarity*
                              —Centering, from Vigyan Bhairava, Sochanda Tantra,
                                        and Malini Vijaya Tantra[162]

If I had to name favorite places in Petrified Forest, Pintado Point would be there, of course, along with the old dead juniper, the petroglyph at Puerco Pueblo, the key embedded in the pavement a mile out old Route 66, and the porch of the Painted Desert Inn.

Now a museum and a registered National Historic Landmark, the Painted Desert Inn hasn't been available for public lodging for decades. Its rooms echo with years' of use and abandon, bustle and silence, and even, according to local lore, a ghost. (Every proper historic structure is haunted.) The first building on the site was constructed by a private entrepreneur, Mr. Herbert Lore, in the early 1920s. Recognizing an opportunity to capitalize on the emerging tourist industry, Lore built a hotel out of petrified wood he'd lugged up from the Black Forest. Despite the spectacular scenery and the uniqueness of a "Stone Tree House," as he advertised it, it wasn't necessarily the best place to build a business: not only did Lore have to drive a long, bumpy 10 miles south to retrieve visitors (and water) from the railroad, but the constant shrinking and swelling of the clay foundation threatened to topple the unstable structure. When the Park Service expressed an interest in expanding Petrified Forest National Monument, Lore happily sold both the land and the crumbling building to the government in 1935.

Because it was easier, policy-wise, to "renovate" an existing structure than to erect an entirely new one, the Park Service asked Lyle Bennett—a little-known yet extremely gifted artist who also designed elegant "Pueblo Revival"-style visitor centers and ranger cabins at White Sands and Bandelier national monuments—to reenvision the building. Bennett poured his talent and appreciation for southwestern cultures into every facet of construction: the exterior looks like an extension of the surrounding landscape, crouching low and pink with thick walls and a jumble of rooflines that mimic the clay hills of the badlands, while the interior is filled with details such as glass ceiling panels hand-painted with designs found on Ancestral Puebloan pottery, hand-carved corbels and hand-adzed vigas and savinos (pillars and roofbeams, made of ponderosa pine and aspen from the nearby White Mountains), Spanish-mission style tin chandeliers, and geometric designs in the cement floors, meant to mimic Navajo rugs. As supervisory architect Lorimer Skidmore attested in 1936, "The building . . . blends harmoniously with the surroundings. It is entirely in character being located in the heart of Hopi, Navajo, and Zuni country."[163]

Not long after construction was completed in 1940 and the Painted Desert Inn (as it came to be known) opened for business, America became embroiled in World War II and people stopped traveling to parks. The Inn closed, and Lyle Bennett disappeared into dusty corners of the federal bureaucracy. Today many visitors assume that the building was designed by an equally talented and far more famous early twentieth-century architect—Mary Jane Colter, known for buildings such as La Posada in Winslow and the Watchtower, Hermits Rest, Hopi House, and Phantom Ranch at Grand Canyon. Indeed, Colter had a hand in the interior decoration of the Inn: after the war ended, the Fred Harvey Company, which was expanding away from luxury railroad resorts to operate facilities in national parks, hired her to update the building to make it a vibrant rest stop along Route 66. (Rather than open the six tiny guest rooms to overnight travelers or expand lodgings to an economically feasible scale, the company planned to open a curio shop, soda fountain, and dining room catering to the daily tourist.) Legend goes, when Colter came to see Bennett's structure for the first time in 1947, she exclaimed that it was beautiful just the way it was.

She did make a few cosmetic changes, though—enlarging the windows in the curio room (thus affording a much wider view of the wilderness), choosing a paint scheme that brought the vibrant colors of the desert inside (summer-sky blues, creamy pinks, the palest of sage green trim), and hiring Hopi artist Fred Kabotie to paint murals on the walls, as he had done with great success at Grand Canyon. Kabotie, in turn, chose themes to fit the location and the facility's intended uses: in the room with the lunch counter—a spot for travelers to catch a quick bite—he painted images of the Tawa sun symbol and of four buffalo dancers in his usual, realistic style; in the sit-down dining room, however, he chose to tell a story, using the clean lines and characters of legend.

"I had been thinking over what subject I should do," Kabotie said at the mural's unveiling, as transcribed by historian Laura Harrison, "when it occurred to me that the Hopi people . . . used to travel right through this country to go after their salt."[164] He went on to explain the traditional journey: two youths leave their home and family at the Hopi mesas (center), pass several wild creatures such as ants, prairie dogs, coyote, pronghorn, and bear, retrieve salt from the Salt Lake near the Zuni pueblo in New Mexico (overseen by a Goddess figure, top), and finally return home. The mural depicts several rituals specific to the coming-of-age tale: the boys must run, brandishing sticks, as they approach the lake (upper right);

Mural by Fred Kabotie, dining room, Painted Desert Inn Museum

they are expected to visit Puebloan cousins at Zuni (upper left); and they know to light a fire upon their return so that their cousins and aunts can prepare to welcome them home (bottom right).

Departure, initiation, return: it's an old story, the monomythic Quest. As described by Joseph Campbell in *The Hero with a Thousand Face*: the hero bravely severs himself from home and family, undergoes several tests or trials of character, culminating in "a supreme ordeal," achieves some sort of triumph—intrinsically an "expansion of consciousness and therewith of being (illumination, transfiguration, freedom),"—then integrates back into society with newfound wisdom.[165] The heroes with a thousand faces: Hopi youth venture forth (answering the "call to adventure"),

traverse a path lined with supernatural beings (a "road of trials," filled
with dangers as well as protectors or guides, such as the Goddess of the
lake), successfully gather salt (finding the "ultimate boon" or "magic
elixir"), visit their Zuni brothers (proving their comfort and mastery of
"Two Worlds"), then cross the final threshold back into Hopi life—the
triumphant return!

When I first worked at Petrified Forest, the Painted Desert Inn was falling
apart. It had been abandoned in 1963 after a new visitor center / admin-
istrative offices / housing complex was built two miles away, courtesy of
the Park Service's "Mission '66" construction craze. (Architect Richard
Neutra's modernist brick walls are now full of bentonite-induced bulges
and cracks as well.) After several years of unuse, the Inn was so filled with
mice and cobwebs and water stains that it was scheduled for demolition.
Local citizens rallied on its behalf, however, and had it declared a National
Historic Landmark in 1987. Still unfunded and still unused, it remained
closed until just a few years before I arrived for my internship. At that
time, park management decided to open it for visitors to see—creaks,
cracks, hanta virus and all.

The building was dark and lonely. At some point someone had plas-
tered the exterior a dull grey, painted the interior a dull tan, and slathered
the corbels and vigas with coats of dull, dark brown. It was cold, too—an
old boiler system sometimes clanked and clattered to life, but when I was
working there, I spent most of my time huddled by a space heater or out
on the porch, trying to catch the pale warmth of the winter sun. I don't
know that I saw ghosts (either the Harvey Company employee who had
died in a fire there or the cigarette-smoking phantom who paces the roof
at dusk—Herbert Lore, some say, but I like to think Lyle Bennett), but I
certainly heard squeaks and felt shadows. (Once, years later, I witnessed a
locked and bolted door fly open of its own accord.) I loved that building.

When I returned in 2006, the Inn was closed for extensive renovations. The park historian had tracked down old blueprints, photographs, and original furniture as well as the funds necessary to return the place to its Route 66-era glory. Workers stabilized the foundation, fixed the leaky roof, stripped ugly paint, replaced rotted beams, cleaned the skylights and chandeliers, restored the Kabotie murals, and, in the most startling and revitalizing step, replicated Mary Jane Colter's paint scheme—blues! Pinks! Greens! Creams! I loved the building even more.

Then, one day—one hot day in June, my fourth season—I found myself tucked into a corner of the porch, pressing into the cool, rough stuccoed walls and cool, smooth cement floor. I vaguely knew that someone was getting me water and someone else was arguing that I shouldn't drink water, that I needed electrolytes. (Magic elixir!) I vaguely knew that someone was getting permission from the neighboring landowner to drive a truck out to the boundary fence for the archaeologist. I vaguely knew I was at the Inn, but had no idea how I'd gotten there. I looked at the walls of the porch: a deep, smooth, salmony pink—the same pink as the clay wash; I looked at the sky beyond: a deep, rich, summery blue—the same blue as the wilderness sky. The air smelled of baking juniper.

That is all I knew. All I needed to know.

Yes, an old story, taking place not just in Hopi lore, but in deserts and forests, on mountains and seas around the world: go to the wilderness to find oneself; to touch holiness. From John Muir to Jon Krakauer, Jesus to the Buddha, adventurers and saints, sinners and heroes have ventured into the wild to strip themselves of outer veneers and bare their souls and/or spines.[166] Religious historian Mircea Eliade theorizes about the "eternal return," in which man "detaches himself from profane time and magically re-enters the Great Time, the sacred time" by performing rituals and enacting myths.[167] According to Carl Jung's psychoanalysis, the hero (or just the average person) disorients and dislocates him- or

Pilot Rock, evening storm

herself from society in order to confront suppressed elements of the undesirable-unconscious *shadow* and integrate them with a conscious *ego* and desirable-unconscious *anima* in order to arrive at an integrated "self."[168] Set forth; overcome trials; learn to be self-reliant and self-assured in any situation, when facing any danger. The shadows, the tests, the crossing of the very first threshold—those are typically considered the biggest obstacles to integrated "self-" hood. The biggest danger on Kabotie's mural, for example, is the enigmatic mountain lion-like figure with a spirit line, spear tongue, and sharp whirling claws, encountered at the very outset of the journey. Compared to that that, even the bear looks goofily benign.

But of what, dear Mr. Kabotie, do the boys dream during their last night under the stars? As our heroes light their signal fire, do they think happily of their aunts and piki bread, or does something in them resent a return to the literal daily grind? Having tasted freedom and adventure, sipped water from clear, tadpole-packed pools, will they now be content to tend their corn, beans, and squash?

What, Mr. Campbell, Dr. Jung, Dr. Eliade, do you have to say about the integration, the return? How and why do heroes want to cross the final threshold, to go back to town? What happens if they can't fully return to society, having left something of themselves in the wilderness?

The shadows, out there over the plains—are those clouds? ravens? or chinde, ghosts.

I spent the rest of the summer trying to regain a semblance of balance and wonder, if not a sense of curiosity and delight. (Light, light—how hard I tried not to be dark, dull, heavy.) I went out again with the archaeologist the very next week, ostensibly to locate the sites we'd missed but really to show Pilot Rock it had not won—I was neither lost nor alone, much less afraid. (It didn't seem to care.) I continued to walk sunrise and sunset; saw several new petroglyph panels and found more *Aetosaur* teeth. Bought a turquoise ring and a copy of Terry Tempest Williams' *Red*; biked to Puerco Pueblo, sat out at Pintado Point, camped by the Lithodendron Wash, talked with my roommate, dined with other seasonals, welcomed the monsoons, danced in puddles, and then

Night. August. It was raining. An unusual rain—neither thunderous downpour nor a teasing sprinkle; a soft, steady summer rain. The air reeked of life.

Normally, the sky is full of stars. Stars and planets, planets and satellites, satellites and a sliver of moon, a moon so bright you have to squint—that's the prairie at night. But this night, it was dark. Dark with rain, drizzling dark. So dark that I couldn't sleep.

I drifted out of bed; out of my room; out of the apartment. I was barefoot, clad in soft black pants and a black top. Dark. My feet found their way along the cold, wet sidewalk, then onto the black pavement. Dark. Past the sleeping cars, onto the road, closed for the night. Along the road, past old 66, all the way to Tiponi Point. I couldn't see a thing.

I felt the wall—the low stone wall that separates the parking lot from the wilderness, the overlook from the overlooked—and felt, mmm, the rock warm with residual daylight. That's one of my favorite things about the semi-desert steppe—while the temperature of the air swings madly from extreme to extreme, the ground is slower to react. I had often nestled into warm thrones of sandstone at sunset or spread out on the sidewalk to keep my back warm while cold droplets fell from the sky. On this evening, in this moment, the warmth of the stone wall offered more than physical comfort; it was a psychological tie. The rain, the darkness, the night—the wildness loomed all around me, the wilderness near me, drawing me out into its empty heart. All I would have to do, something tugged at my soul, would be to step up and over the wall; from there slide down the nearest ravine, slip through the brush, splash across the wash, and there I would be, mud soft and smooth between my toes, rain erasing any trace of my passage—oh, the possibility!

Up and over the wall I went. Then paused. I was shivering and the stone was warm. So warm. It was so dark. What would happen when it was no longer so dark, so empty, so abstract? What would I do the next morning, when the sun would rise and the darkness would dissipate and there, there would be rocks and dirt and plants and animals and maybe even some clouds skittering lightly through an open sky? Did I belong in that world?

In rain during a black night, enter that *blackness* as the form of forms.

When a moonless raining night is not present, close eyes and find blackness before you. / Opening eyes, see *blackness*. So faults disappear forever.

—the 62nd and 63rd of Shivas's 112 ways to open

the invisible door of consciousness[169]

The 64th of Shivas's 112 ways to open the invisible door of consciousness:

Just as you have the impulse to do something, *stop*.

Stop.

Eventually, I fell asleep, clinging to a rock somewhere between the parking lot and the Painted Desert. Woke woozy and goosebumped in the dark, drizzly pre-dawn and stumbled back to bed, dreamless.

Yes, Kathleen Norris, it *is* "a dangerous place, this vast ocean of prairie . . . Something happens to us here."[170]

Interim: Dream of Place
Laramie, Wyoming; and the Painted Desert, Arizona

There are more things in the mind, in the imagination, than "you" can keep track of—thoughts, memories, images, angers, delights, rise unbidden. The depths of mind, the unconscious, are our inner wilderness areas, and that is where a bobcat is right now . . . I do not mean personal bobcats in personal psyches, but the bobcat that roams from dream to dream.

—Gary Snyder, *Practice of the Wild*[171]

In making a case for the necessity of wild spaces, Stephen Trimble testifies: "People smile when they remember such particular places on the earth where the seasons and textures and colors belong to them, where they know, with assurance and precision, the place and their relationship to it."[172] Smile! You own seasons, you know your place! Right?

After the summer of Pilot Rock, I began to rethink and rescind my claims to textures and colors, much less seasons. It's the other way around, I came to realize—rather than knowing and owning the Painted Desert, I was possessed by it.

Early one morning, deep in December, I was trudging down the sidewalks of Laramie, Wyoming, boots gripping the icy cement, head bent to the howling wind. Most of my attention was focused on staying upright and moving forward, but then I blinked or breathed and oh! Red dirt! Blue sky! Silver sage, sunshine? I stopped, gasped and gaped at the gritty sandstone ledge in front of me. The Litho? I was standing in a dry wash . . . in Arizona . . . on a dusty summer day? Before I could believe what was happening, I blinked or breathed and was back on the wintery sidewalk in Wyoming. My nose was cold, but warm desert air swirled in my lungs.

That's how they began—my dreams of the wilderness. Not just any old wilderness—the Painted Desert Unit of Wilderness, all 43,020 acres of open-skied, coyote-tracked, sagebrush-scented semi-desert shrub-steppe. And not just any dreams—dreams so real and unexpected that I'd call them hallucinations if not actual time-space wormholes. I'd be working in my stuffy white office, poring over papers scattered across a big wooden desk, when I'd hear a rustle and look up to glimpse a jackrabbit hopping out from behind a shock of Indian Paintbrush. I'd be standing in my little white room, stirring a pot of hot chocolate, then sneeze to find myself stirring up clouds of dust, face open to the bright warm sun. One moment here, the next there; a whiff of sage, a raven's garble, and I'd find myself in my beautiful desolate wild open park. Not thinking about it, merely indulging in nostalgia, but actually *there*, under the brilliant blue sky, a bit disoriented, a bit dizzy, but happy, home.

My imagination has always been vivid. I see a photograph of the Red Desert's Killpecker Dunes and feel sand between my toes; someone says "grassland," I hear meadowlarks sing. I've walked the prairie with Laura Ingalls and Wallace Stegner; seen the plains through the eyes of George Catlin and Michael Forsberg. Like Paul Gruchow, when reading O. E. Rolvaag's *Giants in the Earth*,

> I could see a moonlit winter night. I could see the whole landscape covered with sparkling snow until it revealed not a single distinguishing feature. I could hear the emptiness and the wolves howling. I could see the tiny hut and Per and Beret sitting in the dim light of the fire . . . I could see them sitting empty-handed and silent, nothing to say, nothing to do, no place to turn around in, nowhere to rest their eyes, even. I could feel time dragging endlessly on.[173]

But this wasn't a matter of imagination, much less daydreaming. I had no control over these moments, much less any warning. They came in flashes, bolts, hypersensual bursts. Some were memories of specific experiences—I'd touch the old dead juniper again, or trip over Onyx Bridge for the first time repeatedly. Others were more general feelings— I'd find myself rolling my sleeping bag out onto the pale, gritty sandstone of Angels Garden or trudging a Seussical stretch of dead yucca at the foot of Chinde Mesa. Most unnervingly, some were fleeting impressions of places to which I'd never been or things that I had never experienced, but *knew*—knew, somehow, just knew, still know—exist, are out there, either in this world or some parallel universe?

Rather than try to figure out M-Theory, I raided the psychology section of the local library and came to the conclusion that it was some sort of neural misfiring. My brain meant to process a regular sensation—walking, say, down the sidewalk; cooking dinner; climbing—but electrons were sucked into a stronger, already-made, deeply embedded path, like a flood continuously drawn back into an older, well-incised channel. It was what Terry Tempest Williams describes as "a matter of rootedness, of living inside a place for so long that the mind and imagination fuse."[174]

Mind and imagination, okay. Rootedness, though, that's a different matter. If you allow yourself to become deeply rooted, to fuse with a landscape, well, then, when you leave, you feel loss. At a loss. Lost. You wither. Pulled out of place, a person, as does a plant, wilts.

Like most parks, Petrified Forest has a decent reference library. Mixed in with the bureaucratic files, anthropological studies, plant and animal identification guides, and tomes on Triassic paleontology are a number of seminal works on conservation philosophy. *Quiet Crisis. Silent Spring. Desert Solitaire. A Sand County Almanac*, next to a biography of its author written by Curt Meine. In reading about Aldo Leopold's life, I learned, during my very first internship, that he felt that there are six "necessaries of life": Adventure, Work, Love; Food, Air, Sunshine.[175] (I always think of them in that order, with that rhythm: Adventure, Work, Love. [*Pause.*] Food, Air, Sunshine.) I found these precepts so compelling that I made them into signs to hang on my wall—purple letters and mountains for Adventure, blue and clouds for Air, et cetera. I carried them around with me for years, tacking them up everywhere I went. They brought me cheer, or at least a reminder of what's truly important. It was like Leopold was there, whispering: *remember, the important things: Adventure, Work, Love; Food, Air, Sunshine.*

At some point during that winter in Wyoming, the signs began falling off my wall. I would come home to find Sunshine or Love, always Food, on the floor, face down, as though they'd quit and were no longer a part of my life. Deciding that it probably had something to do with tape drying out or drafts slipping through cracks, I tried hanging them back up—bought new tape, then tacks. It didn't work. Eventually, I stopped trying—let the walls reclaim their whiteness. "Adventure" remained hanging for the longest, clinging by a corner until it too was gone.

I had returned to Wyoming intending to continue researching perceptions of the Red Desert (from a safe distance, of course) and in so doing create a wall of objectivity between the plains and my own psyche. It is, however, unwise to immerse oneself in theories of the construction of meaningful place when one is still reeling from lonely exposure to desolate space. And it is, perhaps, even more unwise to run away from a land of whirling dust and wind-rent skies to a town where icicles grow sideways from the eaves. I was cold, tired, and, worst of all, lost—lost in a city, a cold rectilinear shell of civilization. There were plenty of places to go, things to do, but no tumbleweeds swirling down the road at noon, no rabbits quivering by the courtyard at dusk; even the beautiful snow-capped peaks of the Medicine Bows just to the west couldn't rival the mesas and buttes of the semi-desert steppe. Where's the adventure in neatly gridded city streets? Where's the meaning in "hellohowareyouim-fineseeyoulater"? Where's the hope in the small, blank walls of office and apartment? I missed wild tangles of washes and brush; I missed coyote howling for the moon to rise. I missed the plants and animals and rocks and sky, oh that prairie sky. I was lonely.

So I dreamed myself back into place.

William Least Heat-Moon suggests that we must dream our way into landscapes, particularly prairies. About a fifth of the way into his epic *PrairyErth: A Deep Map*, he realizes:

> I'd come to the prairie out of some dim urge to encounter the alien—it's easier to comprehend where someplace else is than where you are. . .. I was coming to see that facts carry a traveler only so far: at last he must penetrate the land by a different means, for to know a place in any real and lasting way is sooner or later to dream it. That's how we come to belong to it in the deepest sense.[176]

In time, he invites the reader to join him: "Now: you are dreaming, walking in your dream, here in the hills, alone. If you continue you will find what I have hidden for you, if you want it."

I wanted it, whatever it was that was hidden. As long, cold, empty nights dragged endlessly on, I found myself walking in the hills more and more, eating less and less, never quite sure where I was or where I ought to be. I vaguely began to wonder if I should worry about my dreams, my dizzy spells. In tackling the "open question" posed by geographer Pete Shortridge—to what extent have "aridity, space, highly variable weather [and other physical realities] . . . modified the psyches of plains people?"[177]—I realized I had pursued only the exhilarating, uplifting elements: wildness! Space! Room to think, to breathe, to walk and walk. All of my interviews, all of my readings, and all of my research were biased to corroborate the fullness and worth of open places. I had thought "emptiness" and "desolation" pejoratives to counter and obstinately ignored warnings posed by David Pichaske and Scott Russell Sanders, namely: "[e]mpty space may be an opponent against which humans struggle for survival, identity, or sanity";[178] "the expanse and indifference of the grasslands could drive its inhabitants to 'prairie madness.'"[179]

Prairie creatures are hunted by loneliness, Sanders cites Gruchow, making it sound as though loneliness is a beast that lurks in the grass unseen. Maybe it is. This belief—that there is "something inexpressibly lonely in the solitude of a prairie: the loneliness of a forest seems nothing to it"[180]—has been voiced by everyone from Washington Irving in 1832 to William A. Quayle in 1905 ("Loneliness, thy other name, thy one true synonym, is prairie"[181]); Thomas Scanlan ("The land is linked to suicides and madness, to defeat and conformity and spiritual deadness"[182]) to Tom Rafferty, a third-generation resident of Havelock, North Dakota, who was quoted in *National Geographic Magazine* in 2008:"'There were a lot of suicides,' he says [of the town in the first half of the twentieth century]. 'I think in many cases it was financial—they were down and out—and in other cases, it was the loneliness.'" (When Rafferty looked through his granddad's diary from 1908, he reflected, "'a lot of the entries are about wind.'"[183])

It's important to distinguish loneliness (*sabishisa,* in Zen tradition) from aloneness (*sabi*) and, especially, solitude. "Solitude" connotes desirable space and time—a person seeks solitude so that they can think and breathe in peace. (Is it accident that the term contains the Latin word for sun?) Alone-ness meanwhile, is simply a matter-of-fact state of being. A person may find they are a lone, one—no others around and no thought of whether that's good or bad; it just is.

Aah, but loneliness. Loneliness is alone-ness with the ache of desire for un-alone-ness, for companionship, for society. It's the acute awareness

of unbidden solitude, solitary confinement, or, in the case of the plains—
solitary exposure. Loneliness is looking out at the world, asking for beauty,
for wonder, for comfort, for anything—*please!*—and seeing nothing nothing nothing; how the wind does howl.

That ultimate world, he thinks, or rather dreams, the final world of meat,
blood, fire, water, rock, wood, sun, wind, sky, night, cold, dawn, warmth,
life. Those short, blunt, and irreducible words which stand for almost
everything else he thinks he has lost. Or never really had.

And loneliness? Loneliness?

Is that all he has to fear?

—Edward Abbey, *The Monkey Wrench Gang*[184]

1.7 Beauty and Desire, Beauty and Despair
Petrified Forest National Park, Arizona

*People's desires and aspirations [a]re as much a part of the land as the
wind, solitary animals, and the bright fields of stone . . . And, too . . . the
land itself exist[s] quite apart from these.*

—Barry Lopez, *Arctic Dreams*[185]

By now, it's a familiar refrain: bid farewell to a place, make other plans;
those plans fall through, you're back. Leave and return. Return and leave.
Again and again. "The landscapes we know and return to become places
of solace," writes Terry Tempest Williams in *Refuge*, "We are drawn to
them because of the stories they tell, because of the memories they hold,
or simply because of the sheer beauty that calls us back again and again."[186]
Beauty. Solace. Return.

After a full year of feeling uprooted, placeless, lost and tired, I again returned to Petrified Forest, this time carrying with me a copy of a blessing published in Momaday's *House Made of Dawn*[187]:

"Happily I go forth.

My interior feeling cool, may I walk. / No longer sore, may I walk.

Impervious to pain, may I walk. / With lively feelings, may I walk.

As it used to be long ago, may I walk.

Happily may I walk. . ..

May it be beautiful before me, / May it be beautiful behind me,

May it be beautiful below me, / May it be beautiful above me,

May it be beautiful all around me.

In beauty it is finished"

I thought that if I sang this often enough—if I looked hard enough and wished deeply enough—I would find beauty in the wild, windswept plains. The landscape would, as Stephen Trimble promises, "nourish and teach and heal." It would keep me sane, give me strength. It would afford "restoration, protection, release from dark anxieties and complexities, the chance for a fresh start," according to David Pichaske.[188] Oh, Barry Lopez, why did you write it would teach me to "imagine beauty and conjure intimacy . . . [to] find solace where literal analysis finds only trees and rocks and grass"?[189] *Please be beautiful; in beauty may I walk.*

The Painted Desert was, of course, beautiful. It was late August: the harsh glare of summer was beginning to lengthen and tilt toward autumn. Monsoon storms swept through in bursts of power and light. Everything was still there—all of the colors, all of the shapes, the Litho! Chinde! Angels Garden, Black Forest! And, of course, Pilot Rock.

I wasn't strong enough to make it all the way out to Pilot Rock. I had returned to the wilderness as bare bones as the semi-desert, all sinew and dreams. My first weekend back, I loaded up my pack and set off, eager to visit Old Dead Juniper. Happy possibilities rose in my mind: perhaps I'll swing by Onyx Bridge along the way, I thought, or look for that silly BLM benchmark. Old friends.

Down the wilderness access trail I went (quadriceps quaking slightly), then out to the very muddy Litho (legs like lead); mucked along meanders east, west, (trudge, trudge); east (breathe), west (pause), onto the sandy flats (gasp) then into one of those drainages (the farthest left or the farthest right? It didn't really matter.) I collapsed, exhausted. Beauty? Too tired to look. I didn't really care by that point whether I saw the Bridge; I just wanted to sit. Rest. Barely even two miles out and I couldn't go any farther.

No longer sore, may I walk./ Impervious to pain, may I walk.

There was no way I could make it to the juniper. I'd be lucky if I could make it to my favorite camping spot—a little sandstone saddle in Angels Garden with high views of every horizon. There, I thought, I can sit and think. Really think. *Where am I? Who?* Had I, like Annie Dillard, "walked too much, aged beyond my years?" Had I too "been there, seen it, done it"; did I believe "the world is old, a hungry old man, fatigued and broken past mending"?[190]

If, as Anne Whiston Spirn avers, "dialogues with ourselves and with the landscape . . . help us know ourselves and our place in the world,"[191] then plains are the perfect landscape for contemplation. Forests are full of distractions and seashores lull you to sleep (*crash*, the waves break, *crash,* two three, *crash,* two three, *crash*). Cities are disorienting, suburbs even more so; wood-lined fields too bucolic and mountains too forbidding. Yes, prairies and plains afford just the right balance of clean horizons and intricate details: good, solid earth and wide, open sky; movement and pause; expectation and surprise; space, space—ever more space than the mind can possibly fill or fathom. Deep thoughts rise, expand, iridesce, then turn to dust; the wind sweeps them away and you are light and free.

At least, that's the desire.

Mary Oliver: "Whoever you are, no matter how lonely, / the world offers itself to your imagination, / calls to you like the wild geese, harsh and exciting — / over and over announcing your place / in the family of things."[192]

Scott Russell Sanders, introducing Gruchow's *Journal of a Prairie Year*: "never despair of nature"; life will keep "breaking through."[193]

Possibilities. Never despair. I made it to Angels Garden, then rolled out my sleeping bag and settled in to wait. Wait for the sun to set, for stars to appear, for coyote to sing. Wait for the sun to rise, datura to bloom, raven to trace grand spirals on the upwelling wind, *craw! Craw!* Oh, wild geese, where are you?

Establishing legislation for the National Wilderness Preservation System (Public Law 88-577) mandates that designated lands provide "opportunities for solitude or a primitive and unconfined type of recreation" "for the permanent good of the whole people." Wholeness. Goodness. Recreation. Re-creation. (*Being as it used to be long ago, may I walk. / May it be beautiful before me.*) Again, that myth, that mantra: go to the wilderness to heal thyself, to confront thy true nature and return Whole. Doubly so for plains places: "disorienting and dislocating us from familiar references," prairies, in the words of Jodi Kinsey, "offer us a prospect from which to confront our own true nature." It's so easy to fall under the expansive spell, to believe under that grand and open sky that one has found some greater meaning, deeper Truth. ("The SKY!," remember Georgia O'Keefe? "the sky, the sky!" And Willa Cather: "[T]he thing all about one, the world one actually lived in . . . the sky, the sky!"[194] Even Prince Andrei in Leo Tolstoy's *War and Peace*, "All is vanity, all falsehood, except that infinite sky. There is nothing, nothing, but that."[195]) Since the pioneer era, such openness has made people ponder life "on a grand and utopian scale," according to Shortridge: "Where land holdings and sky both are large, it seems logical for human aspirations to expand as well."

Euphoria! Utopia! U-topia. No place. "But even it does not exist," was Tolstoy writing of the sky or of the truth?

There I was, sitting out in Angels Garden, waiting. Just me and the stars. Star light, star bright. With nothing to block the edges of the universe, I found myself wishing to see a shooting star, *please*, (to whom was I pleading?, with whom did I speak?), I *need* to see a shooting star.

Nothing. The sky was silent, the night still.

Pernicious!, the promise that Old Spider Woman will come, that Tawa will rise, that there will be wild geese; "[w]ith every dawn"—I believed you, Paul Gruchow!—"[w]ith every dawn, every place on earth is a new place." I lay awake, waiting, wanting a new place. The sky grew darker, the stone colder. Stars. Moon. Breeze and tiny little gnats. My fingers and toes tingled as my heart alternately skipped and raced. I didn't belong there. Where did I belong?

When the sun finally rose—a pale blush into the sky, a quiet lightening across the land, good morning, sun, good bye—I packed my bag and slowly, softly, left the Painted Desert.

Headquarters area, Badlands National Park

CHAPTER 2

Mixedgrass

2.1 Wonderlands
Badlands National Park, South Dakota

*I felt motion in the landscape; in the fresh, easy-blowing morning wind,
and in the earth itself, as if the shaggy grass were a sort of loose hide, and
underneath it herds of wild buffalo were galloping . . .*

—Willa Cather, *My Ántonia*[1]

Green! Lush, luxurious green!

So *this* was the legendary sea of grass; *here* was the soft growth of
Poaceae; *now* was Willa Cather's "spring itself; the throb of it, the light
restlessness, the vital essence of it everywhere: in the sky, in the swift
clouds, in the pale sunshine, and in the warm, high wind—rising suddenly, sinking suddenly."[2]

I thought I needed to try something more spectacular—less desolate
and more inhabitable—so headed northeast, destination South Dakota. I
arrived at Badlands National Park on a glorious day, mid-May—a sunny,

blue-sky-with-puffy-white-clouds, air-throbbing-with-spring sort of day. I should describe the drive: how I was so eager to get to there from Denver that I woke pre-dawn and zipped all the way along the Interstate instead of lingering on scenic back roads; how I hadn't even turned off I-80 at Wall to drive through the bulk of the park, but rather stayed on the highway until I reached the exit nearer the Ben Reifel Visitor Center; how I had slowed slightly and opened my windows to let the fresh morning air and the liquid songs of meadowlarks permeate my car; how I caught my first glimpse of the jagged, pink-cream-red-striped mountains of clay, passed the parking area for the Notch Trail and Castle Trail, then rolled down the steep hill after Cliff Shelf and finally stopped at the visitor center; how I had introduced myself to a half-dozen new faces, then gotten directions to my new quarters; how I had begun to unpack my car, but, halfway through, finally looked up and around and realized, I'm *here!* I dashed out the back door, scrambled over a hill, flung myself down into a soft carpet of spring grass, and let my mind explode with, *Green!* "Bad" lands?

(That night, a front moved through. The rest of the week was cold, grey, and drizzly. Hills turned to muck; wildflowers exploded.)

The mixedgrass prairie of western South Dakota receives an average of eighteen inches of precipitation a year, most of which comes in the form of late spring-early summer rainstorms. Compared to the shortgrass and semi-desert farther west, where a good year might bring half that, this abundance of moisture nurtures riotous growth. The high plains are susceptible to climatic extremes, though—harsh blizzards and withering droughts; raging lightning-lit grassfires and periodic floods. Grasslands here teeter on the brink of barrenness.

The term "bad lands" doesn't refer to weather conditions, however—rather, the earth itself. Whereas some stretches of the unglaciated Northwestern Great Plains ecoregion are underlain by rich, dark soils, the Badlands are made up of siltstones and clays (the Chadron Formation),

Foxtail barley, *Hordeum jubatum*

capped by layers of gravelly sandstones and siltstones (the Brule) and ash-laced fluvial and aeolian sediments (the Sharps). Like Arizona's Painted Desert / Chinle Formation, Montana's Hell Creek Formation, and the Little Missouri River badlands in North Dakota, the capital-B Badlands can't support much vegetation: highly absorbent clay swells when wet, then shrinks when dry, leaving large cracks and curls in the surface and making it difficult for plants to take root; moreover, steep and siliceous hills erode at a rate of up to an inch a year, sloughing seedlings.[3]

Slick surfaces and rugged topography also make travel difficult. Indeed, the Badlands were named not for their inhospitableness or uninhabitability, but because French trappers and fur traders found them *les mauvaises terres a traverser*—"the bad lands to cross." For the most part, early nineteenth century explorers, travelers, and even native plains people tried to avoid the heart of the rugged region, particularly the sheer "wall" of clay that extends about 100 miles from the park to what is now an eponymous town. (The feature gained renown in 1890 when Lakota leader Spotted Elk escaped the United States cavalry by leading his Lakota Sioux people down a seemingly impassable cliff, through the *mako sica* "land bad," and, ultimately, to Wounded Knee.) In the 1840s, though, the geologic formations became a destination: after a few curious discoveries—bones of creatures unknown to contemporary naturalists—were brought to the attention of Easterners, scientists working in the budding field of paleontology rushed to find their own fossils in the southwestern section of the Dakota Territories.[4]

In 1846, Dr. Hiram A. Prout of St. Louis published the first paper (under the heading "Miscellaneous Intelligence" in the *American Journal of Science*) describing a fossil from "the 'Mauvais Terre' on the White River." He identified it as the maxillary bone of a "Gigantic *Palaeotherium*"—an Oligocene-age rhinoceros-like creature, later renamed *Titanotherium prouti*. The next year, Joseph Leidy of the Academy of Natural Sciences of Philadelphia described "a remarkable genus of *Ruminantia*, very different from any that has been heretofore described"—a sort of ancestral camel. By 1852, Leidy had filled the Academy's proceedings volumes with descriptions of ancient "Ruminantoid Pachyderma," "Two New Genera of Mammalian Fossils," and even "A New Rhinoceros."[5] Rhinoceroses! Camels! And, soon enough, land turtles, pig- and sheep-like mammals, carnivorous creodonts, sabretooth cats, and even three-toed horses—the race to find and name new fossils was on in what the Park Service now calls the "birthplace of American vertebrate paleontology."

Even the land surveyor Ferdinand V. Hayden got into the paleontology craze, describing dozens of new species and genera in his 1857 reports of explorations in the Mauvaises Terres. But apparently Hayden wasn't as awe-struck by the abundance of fossils, the rugged badlands, and the lush, open swaths of prairie as he was by a wild land of fire and brimstone he was sent to survey fourteen years later—the great basin of the Yellow Stone Lake. According to popular lore (and park historian James Kieley), members of an earlier to the Yellowstone region (the Washarn-Langford-Doane Expedition of 1870) had been so amazed by the "fairyland of un-ending wonders" they encountered there—geysers! Mud pools! Waterfalls and canyons, forests and wildlife—that

> [a]s they sat around their campfire the night of September 19, 1870 . . ., [they] quite naturally fell to discussing the commercial value of such won-ders, and laying plans for dividing personal claims to the land among the personnel of the expedition. It was into this eager conversation that [Montana lawyer Cornelius] Hedges introduced his revolutionary idea. He suggested that rather than capitalize on their discoveries, the members of the expedition waive personal claims to the area and seek to have it set aside for all time as a reserve for the use and enjoyment of all the people[6]

—a National Park.

Although this "campfire myth" proved romanticized if not outright untrue, the idea of creating a national park or preserve was circulating by the end of 1870. According to research by historian Aubrey Haines, when the Smithsonian Institution and US Congress gave Hayden the duty of "secur[ing] as much information as possible, both scientific and practical" about "the geological, mineralogical, zoological, botanical, and agricultural resources of the country," he assembled a team of not just scientists but artists, including the well-known painter Thomas Moran and pioneering photographer William Henry Jackson.[7] The group re-turned from their travels in October of 1871 armed with maps, descrip-tions of ecological attributes and curiosities, specimens, sketches, and Jackson's folio of negatives, some of which still rank as some of the most iconic landscape photographs ever taken. These materials—particularly the images—helped convince Eastern legislators and citizens that the region was, indeed, a land full of wonders meriting protection. Nathaniel Langford (from the 1870 expedition) introduced a Yellowstone bill into the US House of Representatives on 18 December 1871 and Public Lands Committee Chairman Samuel C. Pomeroy followed with a version in the Senate soon thereafter. President Ulysses S. Grant signed it into law on 1 March 1872, establishing the world's first National Park.

In designating "a public park or pleasuring-ground for the benefit and enjoyment of the people," legislators set several precedents. The first, according to environmental historian Jerry Sheppard, was that the scenery destined for preservation as a national park had to be spectacular and unique. Second, "the area under consideration for national park status had to be commercially worthless to logging, mining, grazing, and agricultural interests." Third, "the land had to lie within the public domain."[8]

Spectacular! The rugged Mauvaises Terres of South Dakota certainly are breathtaking and awe-inspiring, especially at dawn or dusk when the long, oblique rays of the sun deepen the hills' warm hues and sharpen the relief with dark shadows. Artist Frederick Remington wrote in an article for *Harper's Weekly* in 1891: "[n]o words of mine can describe these Bad Lands. . . . One set of buttes, with cones and minarets, gives place in the next mile to natural freaks of a different variety, never dreamed of by mortal man . . . The painter's whole palette is in one bluff."[9]

Unique! Writing to ask the federal government to designate a section of country near "the headwaters of the White River" a national park in 1909, the South Dakota Legislature asserted that "nature has carved the surface of the earth into most unique and interesting forms, and has exposed to an extent perhaps not elsewhere found . . . this formation is so unique, picturesque, and valuable for the purpose of study that a portion of it should be retained in its native state."

But agriculturally worthless? Public domain? The badlands bluffs are but islands of wonder in a sea of mixedgrass prairie. As soon as the region was opened to homesteading, the grasslands began filling with intrepid settlers; by late 1906, second-generation resident Leonel Jensen attests, there was "a homestead shack on practically every quarter section of land."[10] Because the siliceous soils and climatic extremes proved harsh for farming, the federal government decided to expand allotted acreage from 160 acres to 320 (via the Enlarged Homestead Act of 1909, implemented in South Dakota in 1915) and then to 640 (via the Stock-Raising Homestead Act of 1916), quadrupling the rate at which lands could be claimed. "Between 1910 and 1920," note Badlands historians Ray Mattison and colleagues, "increasing amounts of land in western South Dakota passed out of the public domain and into private ownership." Thus when US Senator and former governor Peter Norbeck began campaigning for a National Park in 1922, he faced a great deal of opposition "on account of the land having gone into Private ownership. The Federal Government will not purchase land for park purposes."[11]

Moreover, several legislators and federal officials simply didn't believe that the place was worthy of park status. Maybe a monument, they replied, exemplifying what Sheppard calls the fourth precedent—one on par with if not subsuming the first. National parks, a la Yellowstone, are established not just for their geological, ecological, and/or archaeological importance, but for their potential to provide for the enjoyment of the American public. (Pleasuring grounds.)

As of the early twentieth century, the Mauvaises Terres were still bad lands to cross. Because travelers couldn't easily access and thereby enjoy the wonders, there was little motivation for Congress to declare them recreation areas. Senator Norbeck introduced bill after bill, attempting to establish first the "Wonderland National Park in the State of South Dakota" in 1922 (Wonderland!), then reintroducing a renamed "Bill to establish Teton National Park in the State of South Dakota" in 1928 (the first Tetons! As Grand as, though, admittedly, very different from, the currently named Teton range), but he received little support. It wasn't

Sunset in the Wonderlands

until after the Great Depression and Dust Bowl blew away the prospects if not the dreams of local homesteaders and, simultaneously, led to the creation of the Works Progress Administration and Civilian Conservation Corps that the idea of a National Park unit seemed more feasible. In the mid-1930s, federally funded crews finished building roads into the heart of the Badlands and the Emergency Relief Administration began considering purchasing land from failed homesteaders. The National Park Service issued a report proposing a Badlands Recreational Demonstration Project in 1935. Four years later—on 25 January 1939—President Franklin Delano Roosevelt signed Badlands National Monument into existence. Nearly forty years later, it was redesignated Badlands National Park.

("Badlands"? What happened to "Wonderlands"?)

"Dear Granny," I addressed a letter not long after I'd begun to settle in; rains had stopped and the prairie felt even greener, wilder than it had when I first arrived,

I'm writing from atop a little clay island in a big sea of grasses. As the breeze picks up, rustles ripple by and even the crickets stop to listen. Earlier, the sky was blue—a far deeper, more purely blue blue than what Crayola packages and sells as that of "sky"—but big white and grey clouds just swept in. Looking up and south, all I see is grass and a puny little fence struggling to define the boundary between the park and Buffalo Gap National Grassland; north, a rugged ridge of mudstone and sandstone, horizontally striped in layers of tan and beige and vertically striated by steep erosional channels. Other people have likened this landscape to European cathedrals and monstrous teeth, but I just think of it as a huge tangle of dirt / a graveyard for ancient grassland species. (Camelids!) It's so full of fossils that it's hard to walk anywhere without stepping on a 35-million-year old turtle shell or teeth of an ancestral horse. I could spend all summer exploring the area within a mile of my apartment and still not see what's hidden in every nook and cranny (or rather "knoll and crag.")

I would try to make sketches for you, but I don't know of what—huge swaths of green, beige, blue? Thin stalks of grama, curling out of mud cracks? Better yet, the chorus of birdsongs! The smell of dirt! The warmth of the sun, oh, I know, those don't fit in an envelope.

Instead of drawing, instead of writing, I feel like all I should do is spin around in circles or try floating up into the clouds. Or I could burrow into the dirt, around the mat of roots, join the ladybugs. Does this make sense? : imagine what it would be like to walk out to the middle of Lake Erie, or the ocean for that matter. On a calm day, you'd be surrounded by an abundance of fish and seaweed and birds—that's what it's like to stand on the grasslands, teeming with life. But on a stormy day, you'd be engulfed by towering whitecaps, both beautiful and terrifying. That's what it's like to stand in the badlands. I'm drowning.

It's wonderful.

2.2 National Grasslands
Buffalo Gap and Comanche National Grasslands, South Dakota and Colorado

You must not be in the prairie, but the prairie must be in you . . . That alone will do as qualification for biographer of the prairie . . . He who tells the prairie mystery must wear the prairie in his heart.

— **William A. Quayle,** *The Prairie and the Sea*[12]

Two years after Badlands was set aside as a national monument, Victor E. Shelford, a former chair of the Ecological Society of America's Committee for the Study of Plant and Animal Communities reflected on the fact that "Great Plains national parks and monuments were established to preserve features—'badlands, outlying mountains, etc.'—other than grasslands" and were "not typical of the great grassland community."[13] As cited by Jerry Sheppard, Policy Guidelines for the National Park Service issued by the Department of the Interior in 1969 went so far as to declare

> [t]he National Park System should protect and exhibit the best examples of our great national landscapes . . . There are serious gaps and inadequacies which must be remedied while opportunities still exist if the System is to fulfill the people's need always to see and understand their heritage of history and the natural world.[14]

Grasslands were (and still are) one of the most egregious gaps, not considered wonderlands meriting preservation. Until 1991, when Tallgrass Prairie National Preserve—"a new kind of national park," the National Park Service congratulates itself[15]—was carved out of former ranchland in the Flint Hills of Kansas, only accidents of geology (the Badlands, along with Wind Cave, Petrified Forest, and Fossil Butte) and/or history (Theodore Roosevelt, Lewis and Clark, and assorted former forts and battlefields) resulted in prairies' inclusion in the National Park Service system. Even then, proposed establishment of units such as Theodore Roosevelt and Tallgrass Prairie met with vociferous protest—the former was considered too "stark," writes Sheppard, and the legislative history of the latter admits that opponents expressed a "deep-seated philosophy . . . that the government should not own land."[16]

Ah, but Park Service "Crown Jewels" are not the only—nor necessarily the most important, much less the most beautiful—public lands in America. In addition to the 270 million acres of leftover land—mostly shortgrass prairie and full-fledged desert—now overseen by the Bureau of Land Management, the US Forest Service (USFS) manages twenty units containing 3.8 million acres of rolling ridges, woody draws, and an astounding variety of plants and animals—America's National Grasslands.

Badlands shares borders with Buffalo Gap National Grassland—nearly 600,000 acres of mixedgrass prairie and rugged clay hills, including more than 48,000 acres of proposed Wilderness. Aside from a few scraggly signs and a spindly fence upon which red-wing blackbirds like to perch, there's little to separate the two on the ground; they share the same geological, ecological, historical, and scenic characteristics. In fact, visitors to the National Park can't help but experience the Grassland too: the sweeping view from Notch Trail? Mostly Buffalo Gap. Conata Basin Overlook, White River Valley Overlook? Buffalo Gap. The Pinnacles Entrance, the Northeast Entrance, the Interior Entrance, even the lesser-known gravel road leading from Scenic to Sage Creek? You can't get into or out of the North Unit of Badlands without crossing Buffalo Gap. (Once, when I recommended to a visitor that he return to Rapid City via Highway 44 and thus see the beautiful expanses of Buffalo Gap, he replied that he didn't want to see any old prairie; he'd come for the *Park*. I didn't warn him that the majority of his scenic photographs are likely contaminated with Grassland.)

Although not as well-known as national parks, grasslands boast an impressive array of significant landscapes, lifeforms, and resources— colorful badlands and deep canyons, carpets of wildflowers and lonely cottonwoods, keystone prairie dogs and endangered black footed ferrets, dinosaur tracks and historic structures. Rather than being established out of public appreciation for their ecological and aesthetic integrity, though, they are tattered remnants of a failed "Great American Garden"—products of boom, bust, dust, and (mis)management pervasive on the Plains.

After intrepid homesteaders persevered through decades' worth of droughts and wildfires, tornadoes and blizzards, loneliness and labor, the one-two punch of the Great Depression and Dust Bowl forced nearly two and a half million people to abandon their seemingly worthless small

Boundary between Badlands and Buffalo Gap

farms throughout the Great Plains. Striving to curtail socioeconomic and environmental catastrophe, federal legislators passed the Emergency Relief Appropriations Act of 1935 and Bankhead Jones Farm Tenant Act of 1937, giving the government the power to provide loans to "encourage and facilitate farm ownership" and also to purchase land in order to directly "control erosion, produce more forage, and ensure economic stability for remaining rural residents," according to environmental historians Eric Olson and Terry West.[17] From 1938 to 1954, the Soil Conservation Service oversaw the Land Utilization Program, which broadened its objective from simple range improvement to becoming models for wise land use. Tracing the National Grasslands' origin and development, historian Douglas Hurt explains:

The land-use projects were not the panacea capable of solving all the regional, economic, social, and erosion problems that many New Deal social
scientists had hoped . . . [but did halt] wind erosion, . . . [restore] a sound
agricultural base . . . [and ensure] best conservation and land-use . . . As a
result, the National Grasslands [today] serve as wildlife refuges, sources of
mineral wealth, and public recreation areas in addition to grazing lands.[18]

The acquisition history and management paradigm may help explain
why 5.5 million acres of livestock-supporting LUP grasslands were transferred not to the BLM (previously the US Grazing Agency) but to the
Department of Agriculture's Forest Service in 1954. Employing its prin-
ciple of "wise-use," the USFS was quick to "continue and expand upon . . .
improvement activities" through implementation of resource surveys and
development of recreational sites, Olson notes. After quietly designating
3.8 million acres as National Grasslands on June 20, 1960, land management officials continued "to correct maladjustments in land use, and
thus assist in controlling soil erosion, reforestation, preserving natural
resources, mitigating floods, . . . and protect . . . the public lands, health,
safety, and welfare," as mandated by the Bankhead Jones Farm Tenant
Act of 1937, only amending the legislation to add "protecting fish and
wildlife" and "not to build industrial parks or establish private industrial
or commercial enterprises" in 1962, "protecting recreational facilities" in
1966, and "developing energy resources" in 1981.[19]

Foresters trained to measure timber harvests and suppress woodland
wildfires were a bit unsure about what to do with arid, open grasslands,
however; personnel have sometimes struggled to define management
objectives and negotiate evolving usage of the ecosystem. USFS officials
admitted to researcher Francis Moul that they sometimes "kind of look
down on [grasslands]" as a "desert"; the absence of trees makes the units "a
step-child" within the agency.[20] In the mid-1990s, a Management Review
Team found that "direction, standards, and guidelines are lacking for

many significant resources, values, and issues outside of commodity issues"— officials were able to plan for uses such as livestock grazing, mineral development, and hunting, but unprepared for hiking, biking, and photography.[21]

The Review Team's solution called for "[c]reation of a commonly understood vision for the national grasslands" as well as a communication plan meant to "articulate and implement" that vision. From a broader perspective, the Forest Service is transitioning away from their traditional mantra of "multiple-use, sustained yield" and attempting to integrate "human needs and requirements, the ecological potential of a landscape, and economic and technical considerations" into management protocol, USFS researchers Sally Collins and Elizabeth Larry assert.[22] Agency policies and outreach materials are beginning to articulate the importance of "ecosystem services"—an array of attributes that the United Nations' Millennium Ecosystem Assessment report defines as:

> benefits people obtain from ecosystems . . . includ[ing] *provisional* services such as food, water, timber, and fiber; regulating services that affect climate, floods, disease, wastes, and water quality; *cultural services* that provide recreational, aesthetic, and spiritual benefits; and *supporting services* such as soil formation, photosynthesis, and nutrient cycling.[23]

In order to articulate the shift toward more holistic management, the Forest Service hopes to embrace what Collins and Larry deem "a new language"—one that resonates more deeply with residents of local communities as well as travelers. Official documents used to be filled with detailed technical information that informed specialists but hardly inspired citizens to understand or take pride in their public lands. (A Scenery Management Handbook uses flow charts and classifications of "landscape elements of landform, vegetation, rocks, cultural features, and water features" based on "their line, form, color, texture, and composition,"[24] for example, and thus compares "which *sites* are beautiful, [but] not which *ways* each site may be beautiful or interesting," landscape management specialist Neil Evernden realizes[25]; meanwhile, vague references to "an open, scenic landscape," as is written in the Buffalo Gap National Grassland Management Plan Review, neglect the fact that, Evernden also points out, "[t]he prairie is an experience, not an object—a sensation, not a view.") The USFS has issued newer documents that take multiple approaches—from economic efforts to "capture the true value of nature's capital" to ecological intent to "car[e] for our natural assets" and from "[c]ontrol [of] agricultural pests" to "[p]rovid[ing] research opportunities."[26] In so doing, they hope to connect with people's myriad interests.

Although it can be difficult to translate bureaucratese into clear, meaningful language, some officials, scholars, and local citizens have demonstrated an ability to provide lyric interpretations of ecosystem services. Dakota Prairie Grasslands, for example, welcomes visitors to a place "where pristine vistas inspire the imagination; where the rugged unspoiled beauty of the land invites exploration; and where the sights and sounds of the wide, rolling prairie stimulate the senses"; Francis Moul's *Guide to America's Undiscovered Treasures* introduces readers to a "seemingly infinite expanse of grass and sky where the solitude and beauty take time to assimilate"; and Thomas Henry's *Great Plains Adventure Guide* entices travelers to experience "the few wildernesses left where you can actually sleep under the stars . . . just you and the coyotes and the grasses and the wind and the sky—oh, that sky!"[27]

Perhaps most importantly, "sense of place" is, according to social scientists such as Dan Williams and Susan Stewart, "finding a home in ecosystem management."[28] Each of the national grasslands has site-specific concerns to acknowledge and address: mining and drilling on some units; overcrowding on others; checkerboard ownership involving different local players at several. Each also has unique natural and cultural assets to celebrate. As officials seek to to identify the meanings and uses assigned to specific Grasslands and articulate "appreciation for the land that goes beyond [commodity] value," to cite Cheng *et al.*[29], they reap what Gary Snyder calls "the ecological benefits . . . of cultivating a sense of place . . . [namely] that then there will be a *people* to be the People in the place"[30]— a people to continue living in rural communities and a people to serve as prairie stewards. When local residents and land managers together recognize and cultivate the ecological, socioeconomic, and aesthetic values of the national grasslands, World Wildlife Fund researchers Steve Forrest and colleagues aver, they are actively "restor[ing] the biodiversity of the plains . . . restor[ing] the spirit and livelihoods of those who live and work here, . . . [and] recaptur[ing] the imagination and interest of people throughout the world."[31]

Imagination! Interest! Sense of place? Where, buried in this management history of Grasslands, Badlands, wonderlands, is the sense of place?

While in South Dakota, I visited the National Grasslands Visitor Center in Wall, taking the opportunity to learn about American prairies' natural and cultural history, marvel at an exhibit of photographs from each of the units, and speak with a USFS employee who radiated enthusiasm for the plains. "Here!," she gave me a stack of reading materials and a topographic map of Comanche, "You have to go to Comanche! You'll love it! There are ridges and canyons and petroglyphs and dinosaur tracks, you have to go to Comanche!" (Some people speak in exclamation points; some people's eyes shine when they think of places they love. She is one of them.)

I saw her again, along with dozens of other people who have dedicated their lives to caring for public lands, a year later at the annual meeting of National Grasslands managers. There, officials brainstormed ways to "tell the grasslands story" and better communicate the principles of conservation and multiple use to local community members as well as visitors. (USFS personnel insisted on calling visitors "visitors," shuddering at the idea of hordes of national park-type tourists). Managers expressed appreciation for the landscapes' natural beauty, respect for the human histories, a duty for responsible stewardship, and, mostly, a fierce pride in the land and people. Nametags and water bottles were emblazoned with the quotation: *Anyone can love the forest. It takes soul to love the prairie.*

Soul. What do I know of soul? I've barely dipped my toes into a handful of grassland units, much less spent weeks, seasons, years, prowling them in search of their secrets. If you want to know of soul, look at Don Kirby's images in *Grasslands*, which evoke the feel of all of the units in all different seasons, at all different scales.[32] (His technique: "Photograph something for what it is. And what else it is.") If you want soul, read Dan

Ah, Matsuo Basho, how much I too desire!: "Inside my little satchel, / the moon, and flowers"[34]

O'Brien's *Buffalo for the Broken Heart*, which describes how he formed a lasting, symbiotic relationship with the land bordering Buffalo Gap. (His inspiration, shared with writer John Price: "I feel deeply about cows and grass and falcons, so I gotta stick with that . . . It's not a matter of choice."[33]) If you want soul, go to the National Grasslands Visitor Center in Wall and listen to the people who live near and with the prairie on a daily basis; listen to the people who have it in their soul.

If you want soul, go to Comanche National Grassland, perhaps late one afternoon, mid-August, when you're the only person present for miles and miles. Go when you have enough time to wander off and become deliciously lost—disoriented even—in the knee-high grasses that carpet Vogel Canyon's draws and flats. Go just before the sun gently sets and the sky fades away. Follow the historic stagecoach trail back through the chorus of crickets toward the spot where the bright, fat full moon rises while a small herd of pronghorn leaps lightly alongside.

There you may feel the stirrings of soul.

2.3 Animal Encounters
Badlands National Park, South Dakota

Part I : The Theory of Birds

I was lucky / on Coyote Day, / because / out of all time / it had to be / one moment / only /
that / a certain coyote / and I / could meet — / and we did

—**Byrd Baylor,** *I'm in Charge of Celebrations*[35]

Within a week or two of arriving at Badlands, I had made friends with the local deer as well as the rabbits, to whom I'd politely nod and greet "Good Morning" each dawn. I began to notice subtler changes in the vegetation—phlox spreading out one moment, primrose popping up the next. There was so much I wanted to remember, so much I was afraid to forget, that I began keeping a record of daily weather patterns, wildflowers, and animal sightings—a feeble attempt at a naturalist's diary, since I couldn't identify half of what I encountered. "Salsify!," I might learn and label excitedly, or "Switchgrass!" If I identify just one plant and one animal per day, I thought to myself, I'll know nearly a hundred of each within three months!

Badlands National Park boasts more than 460 plant species (including 60 grasses alone), at least 37 mammals, 15 reptiles and amphibians, 69 butterflies, and 206 different birds.[36] Oh.

I am not a birder. People assume that I am because I lead a birder lifestyle: I enjoy getting up before dawn, learning species' names, and, above all, sitting and studying the world around me. The problem is that I can't claim a crucial fourth characteristic—love of birds.

In my youth, instead of waking before dawn and settling in somewhere with a set of binoculars, I wanted to throw pillows at ducks paddling quackily past my window. Unlike true naturalists such as Aldo Leopold, who could appreciate great honky vees of geese as "a wild poem dropped from the murky skies upon the muds of March,"[37] or Terry Tempest Williams, who finds symbols and solace in everything from burrowing owls to avocets and stilts,[38] I couldn't get past the fact that pigeons are mean and seagulls belligerent. While watching cardinals and bluebirds squabble over birdseed in the backyard, I always, secretly, rooted for the squirrels to get to the feeder first. Birds just couldn't hold my imagination—I could never look into their beady little eyes and see a fierce green fire, feel a connection with something greater, wilder.

At Petrified Forest, I became acutely aware of hawks sweeping wide circles over the steppe, roadrunners peeking into doorways, hundreds of little brown sparrowy somethings singing from the brush, and ravens—ravens everywhere. But visitors kept asking me to identify distant specks, forcing me to shake my head and admit I couldn't identify flight patterns, silhouettes, or songs; couldn't recite families, genuses, species; didn't much care to learn. Too much to learn. How was I supposed to hold the binoculars steady enough to see the darn things before they flew away? How was I supposed to remember plumage male vs. female, juvenile vs. adult, summer vs. winter? Above all, how was I supposed to distinguish all of those cheeps and chirps, trills tweets warbles? That, in turn, made me feel like I was a bad ranger, a poor excuse for a naturalist; how could I not know my birds? Finally, one day, after listening to obnoxious squawks emanating from a tree just outside the visitor center for what seemed like an entire morning, I went outside armed with loads of books, determined to identify the medium-sized black bird whose only distinguishing feature was its yellow head. On this—my first serious attempt at birding—it took me a full hour to determine that the creature was, indeed, a yellow-headed blackbird.

I tried, but simply didn't have a passion for birding. I tried going to see cranes in Kearney, but couldn't concentrate on anything but the cold air, the bind's scratchy hay bales, and the long wispy cirrus that swept across dawn's pale pink-blue sky. I tried going to see swans in the Laramie basin, but tuned out the lessons on migratory patterns and instead filled a sketchbook with doodles of prairie dogs and mountain-scapes. Eventually, I decided, there was no point in trying anymore—I am just a flower-gatherer, a rock-collector, a hopeless topophile; I watch clouds, not birds.

Then on one of my first evenings at Badlands, I was sitting on my front step, watching a storm tie the sky in knots, waiting for grumbles of thunder and hoping for cool patters of rain, when I heard a strange snort fall from the air. Maybe it was more like a huff? A humph? An angry bison standing on my roof? I called for my roommate to come listen. A grunt? Was there a badger around? What does a badger sound like? We had no idea.

"A nighthawk!" laughed one of the rangers when we told him the next day. He was an expert on astronomy with a passion for birds, happy to share what he knew. His infectious enthusiasm acted as a catalyst; I couldn't help but take a bit more interest in those nighthawks. When I heard them dive and whoosh again the following evening, I smiled and thought to myself, "aha! Nighthawk!"

A few days later, I timidly asked Ranger L about the aggressive birds who didn't like me walking one particular patch of road—top-heavy things with long skinny legs and squat grey-brown speckled bodies? "Sandpipers!," he told me. The pairs that populate the visitor center parking lot, showing off their long, iridescent-black tails and flashing white wing stripes? "Black-billed magpies!" The flocks that flit into and out of nests in the badlands wall? "Cliff swallows!" And, of course, the first species I learned to identify by their song, which is as cheery yellow as their breast: Meadowlarks!

I still didn't like birds, but upon beginning to learn their names, I grew curious about their habits. I asked my mother to send me her father's *Golden Field Guide to Birds*, dusted off the bookshelves at home. After reading about the common species and spending a considerable amount of time trying to decipher the sonograms, I decided to purchase my very own bird book—not a Sibley's, nor an Audubon, but the Cornell Lab of Ornithology's *Bird Songs*, complete with audio recordings of 250 species.[39]

Bird Songs! I played the Common Loon (*Gavia immer,* number 002) incessantly, until my roommate threatened to remove the batteries. Then I moved on to the mourning dove (*Zenaida macroura,* number 186), Say's phoebe (*Sayornis saya,* number 194), and, of course, the western meadowlark (*Sturnella neglecta,* number 244). Despite the book's awkward size, I began lugging it along on my daily walks, letting my feet find the path while I concentrated on training my ears to recognize rhythms and melodies. One evening, one regular old evening—as hot and humid as any that had come before or would come later; sky its usual blue-fading-into-pink; nothing remarkable, nothing memorable—my bird book and I went up to Cliff Shelf Nature Trail. It was the perfect time to be there: campers were settling in for dinner, travelers were on their way to Wall or Murdo, so it was just me and the path and, of course, birds twittering happily from the treetops. After listening for a while, I began to press buttons. I didn't know what I was playing (hadn't yet learned to identify more than a few)—six, seven, twenty different calls, chosen at random—before, pause, something sang back from the real world. The same melody I'd just heard in the book.

I hit "play" again. First the book, then the same half-dozen notes echoed from the air. Again? Again! What was it, number 214? Two-fourteen, two-fourteen . . .. Mountain bluebird! I was hearing a mountain bluebird! Not just hearing it; it was hearing me, and singing back! Just like that, I "[caught] the animal excitement," to borrow a phrase from environmental ethicist Holmes Rolston III; "I rejoice[d] in the stimulus of spontaneous life."[40]

Wildlife-watching adds an important dimension to people's perceptions of natural landscapes, according to researchers Roy Ballantyne, Jan Packer, and Lucy Sutherland,[41] whose quantitative surveys and qualitative analyses confirm that encounters with wild animals can "produce strong and vivid memories" and help visitors develop emotional connections that "[lead] them to care about the animal's well-being." Writing of the Aesthetic Experience of Wildlife, Rolston muses:

> The mountains and rivers are *objects*, even the pines and oaks live without sentience; but the squirrels and antelope are *subjects*. When perceiving an item in the geomorphology or the flora I see an "it." But with the fauna, especially the vertebrate, brained fauna, I meet a "thou" . . . I see them; they also see me . . . The aesthetic experience differs because of reciprocity.[42]

Reciprocity. I was singing with number 214—a mountain bluebird, *Sialia currucoides.*

Visitors to Badlands often asked where they could see animals, especially the bison, the bighorn sheep, and the cute squat little prairie dogs. (Although the latter may be rodents, they're a captivating keystone species; the park road clogs with slow-traveling wildlife-gawkers alongside colonies.) "Sage Creek," we would tell people who wanted to see bison, which roam freely through a designated Wilderness Area in the park's North Unit, as well as prairie dogs, who pop anxiously up from and back into their burrows in Robert's Prairie Dog Town. Pinnacles Overlook for sheep, especially when researchers are tracking radio-collared individuals in the area. Birds? Cliff Shelf, as well as Prairie Wind Overlook for meadowlarks, the Visitor Center for magpies, and anywhere along the wall for turkey vultures, which lurk on thermals that rise up the cliffs. We kept wildlife updates (magnets that we could shuffle around whenever sightings were reported) on a large map of the park in the visitor center, but could not, of course, guarantee that the animals would stay there, posing for people's photographs. As Rolston continues:

> a principal difference between scenery and wildlife is that the observer knows that the mountain or the cascades will be there, but what about the redtail hawk perched in the cottonwood . . .? The latter involve probability, improbability, contingency, which add adventurous openness to the scene . . .. [T]ime brings to the animal freedom in space, and aesthetic experience of that freedom must delight in the spontaneity.[43]

Wild + life = Freedom! Delight! Surprise! You never know what will pop out of the brush or swoop down from a cloud, never know what will happen when you step out of your door. The prairie is *alive.* You have to be there to experience it.

Part II : Rewilding

Today, Badlands' mixedgrass prairie teems with wildlife—with wonders—but when the original Monument was established, it lacked several
of its most charismatic and ecologically important species. By 1939, the
fences, plows, and guns of industrious homesteaders and hunters had put
a severe dent in the pronghorn and mule deer populations and caused
the demise of great herds of bison, elk, and bands of sheep. "Problem
animals" such as coyotes, swift fox, and wolves had fallen victim to the US
Biological Survey's "predatory animal extermination program," according
to Mattison et al., and prairie dogs were considered "so deleterious to
agriculture and stock raising that their presence in some localities c[ould]
not be tolerated," according to the official policy of the US Biological
Survey.[44]

As the "problem animals" disappeared, people began to notice what
modern ecologists such as Robert Askins and colleagues confirm:
"[k]eystone mammal species—grazers such as prairie dogs and bison. . .
— played a crucial, and frequently unappreciated, role in maintaining
many grassland systems."[45] Along with drought and fire, grazing is one of a
trifecta of large disturbances that maintain balance in prairie ecosystems.
The mixedgrass of western South Dakota needs large herds of bison (and,
to a lesser degree, elk and pronghorn) to graze, wallow, and stampede
their way through the taller grasses, creating a "shifting mosaic" that
periodically allows shorter grasses such as blue grama and buffalo grass
space to grow. Black-tailed prairie dogs, meanwhile, not only impact the
vegetation with their nibbling and burrowing, but create habitat and/or
act as a food source for species such as the burrowing owl, the prairie
rattlesnake, the coyote, and the black-footed ferret.

More than 460 plant species! Thirty-seven mammals! Fifteen reptiles
and amphibians, 69 butterflies, 206 different birds! Remove a few mammals, let a few exotics grow wild, change the habitat for the birds and

the butterflies and the toads, and what happens to the mixedgrass sea of green?[46]

In 1987, Deborah and Frank Popper expressed their scholarly interpretation of the Great Plains as "the largest, longest-running agricultural and environmental miscalculation in American history," predicting that "over the next generation the Plains will . . . become almost totally depopulated," leaving the federal government free to "take the newly emptied Plains and tear down the fences, replant the shortgrass, and restock the animals, including the buffalo."[47] This idea was not without historical precedent, but the East Coast academics were surprised to find that their "musings . . . set off a torrent of discussion about the region's future."[48] Kansan Pete Shortridge explains: "plains people came to view the study as an attack on their way of life" by geographic and philosophical outsiders.[49] Locals accused the Poppers of painting an exceedingly negative picture of the Plains and journalists of milking the sensation[50]; meanwhile, the Poppers and colleagues accused locals of "exploit[ing] . . . nature for profit" and assuming "that the value of land lies in the intensity of its use—that it is more valuable when it is plowed, sold, or developed."[51] Several years later, the Poppers' reinterpretations of the so-called Buffalo Commons as "a literary device, a metaphor that would resolve the narrative conflicts—past, present, and, most important, future – of the Great Plains"[52] asserted not controversy but success: "There have been several initiatives to increase bison and to preserve grasslands across the Great Plains," they noted in 1993, explaining, "[t]he groups most involved are ranchers, Native American tribes, land preservation organizations, and public land managers."

Indeed, ranchers such as the owners of Wild Idea Buffalo Company ("a vision of environmental health, animal health and human health," located on a "certain little patch of prairie" just west of Badlands[53]) have realized both the ecologic and the economic benefits of raising bison, while non-governmental organizations such as The Nature Conservancy have brought back thousands of animals in an effort to "restor[e] the ecological and cultural values" of regions from Canada to Mexico.[54] Meanwhile, Custer State Park (carved out of the Black Hills region in 1912 by the same Peter Norbeck, then governor of South Dakota, as later campaigned for Wonderland National Park) started with 36 bison in 1914, was overgrazed by nearly 2500 head in the 1940s, and now balances around 1300[55]; neighboring Wind Cave National Park protects one of only a handful of genetically pure, free-ranging *Bison bison bison* (Plains subspecies) herds.[56] (Yellowstone boasts another.) From Ted Turner's 50,000 head of bison to Kevin Costner's giant bronze Tatanka statue (and interpretive center and gift shop and snack bar) outside Deadwood, Buffalo-Commons-esque examples abound.

And yet, as a team of scientists, government officials, NGOs, and tribal members throughout the international Great Plains write in the essay "The Ecological Future of the North American Bison: Conceiving Long-Term, Large-Scale Conservation of Wildlife," those who are interested in reintroducing bison must ask themselves: "What is our vision for bison restoration? Is it the animal itself . . . or is it also the interactions between bison and their environment that need to be conserved? . . . What aspects of the human relationship to bison—economic, cultural, aesthetic, spiritual—should be restored?"[57] How do you restore a spiritual relationship with a species, much less an ecosystem?

After witnessing the abundance of wild life roaming freely about in the Dakotas in 1832, the artist George Catlin wrote: "Nature has no where presented more beautiful and lovely scenes than those of the vast prairies of the West. . ."

It is a melancholy contemplation for one who has travelled as I have, through these realms . . . to contemplate [the buffalo] so rapidly wasting from the world . . .

And what a splendid contemplation too, when one (who has travelled in
these realms, and can duly appreciate them) imagines them as they *might* in
the future be seen . . . preserved in their pristine beauty and wilderness, in
a *magnificent park* . . . What a beautiful and thrilling specimen for America
to preserve . . .! A *nation's Park*, containing man and beast, in all the wild
and freshness of their nature's beauty![58]

It would be 131 years before bison would return to the mixedgrass
wilderness of Badlands.

From its inception in 1916, the Park Service has been tasked with what
some scholars refer to as a dual mandate: "to conserve the scenery and
the natural and historic objects and the wild life therein and to provide
for the enjoyment of the same in such manner and by such means as will
leave them unimpaired for the enjoyment of future generations." In an
effort to restore the tattered remnants of prairie to their natural glory,
managers of Badlands have researched the feasibility of reintroducing
native species. After evaluating "the ability of [a] species to prosper under
the park's current conditions; [t]he public opinion of the local community
and the nation; [e]conomic impacts to the park and its neighbors; and
[e]nvironmental impacts to the local ecosystem"—note that only two of
the criteria are ecologically based; the others are sociocultural—park
managers have condoned the return of bison, bighorn sheep, ferret, and,
most recently, swift fox.[59]

Bison were the first to be brought back, in 1963. They proved so successful in their home range that wildlife biologists have had to execute
annual round-ups to cull the herd back to 600–800 members (and gather
important data on the population's genetic makeup and overall health),
transferring extra animals to the Oglala Sioux Tribe and other Native
American Tribes through the Intertribal Bison Cooperative (a group based
out of Rapid City that includes 51 member tribes and more than 10,000

animals). Bighorn sheep came a year later, and now more than 100 clamber around the clay hills. Ferrets fill more of a surprising and precarious position: the prairie-dog dependent predators were so greatly impacted by the widespread extermination of their prey that by 1987, they teetered on the brink of extinction, with only 18 individuals known to science. A successful captive breeding program allowed scientists to reintroduce ferrets to wild prairies such as Badlands and Buffalo Gap; since 1994, they've expanded to reach a population size of nearly 300 (though wildlife biologists currently fear that bubonic plague may sweep through prairie dog communities in the area, again decimating the ferrets). Finally, swift fox! The cat-sized, grey-tan canid with big ears and a bushy black-tipped tail has been back at Badlands for less than a decade, sleeping in its dens during the day and prowling the prairie in search of rabbits, grasshoppers, and berries by night.

Early one morning, while a sliver of moon still hovered languidly in the pre-dawn sky, I joined a team of wildlife biologists as they set off to monitor the swift fox population; we found three or four individuals—all healthy, happy to be free to wander off to their daily routines—waiting patiently in cage-traps set the night before. But when I joined the same biologists in their quest for black-footed ferrets late one night, all of their tricks—radio telemetry gear, a great big spotlight, several pairs of human eyes straining to see the tell-tale green glow of Mustelid eye-shine from the fields—failed. We encountered only cattle, mooing dully from the darkness. After hours of driving and sitting, watching and listening, waiting, we finally had to call it a night, turn on the engine, and head back to headquarters. I'd barely figured out where we were—around the corner from the Fossil Exhibit Trail, where the road slips between ghostly pink hills—when something small and grey slipped into the sweep of the truck's headlights.

Swift fox? My heart leaped.

Ha! Coyote pup, glancing back over its tail with its trickster's grin. Not a scientific success story, but a creature thriving, laughing even, on its own terms. Wild life enough for me.

There's no wilderness left here . . . so don't fool yourself . . . [but] There's
still something wild and powerful in the land here, more than some other
places, and that's what sustains me.
  — Dan O' Brien, quoted in John Price's *Not Just Any Land*[60]

Interim: Medora to Marmarth (with some dinosaur statues in between)
South Dakota, North Dakota, Montana, and Wyoming

On the highways that dissect North Dakota, horizon always beckons.

—Eugene Richards. Photograph caption for "The Emptied Prairie"[61]

"Oh, it'll be fun!" I tried to convince my parents that they should get up
at 5 A.M. and hike a mile and a half to watch the sun rise over the open
grasslands; "It's a great view." They had just arrived at Badlands after a
long day of traveling and likely wanted nothing more than to sleep in the
next morning, but I was eager to show off the place. The prairie would
be at its freshest and most beautiful at dawn, I felt, and the notch high in
the badlands wall would afford the most expansive, awe-inspiring view.

Sigh. They agreed, trusting my insight or enthusiasm or simply because
I was their daughter and this would be neither the first nor last time I
would drag them off on some adventure or another. (I may already have
asked if they'd be interested in driving up to North Dakota and Theodore
Roosevelt National Park, perhaps swinging through the tiny town of
Faith, South Dakota—home of Sue the T-Rex!—along the way?) I didn't
plan this hike well, though, forgetting:

(a.) it's generally dark before dawn;

(b.) cold too;

(c.) Mom's not a big fan of heights;

and (d.) as soon as I promise we're perfectly safe, of course that's when we'll encounter a rattlesnake. Welcome to Badlands!

Granted, it was a baby rattler, trying to drag off a dead, fly-ridden mouse. (Just what everyone wants to see before breakfast.) And, granted, Dad and I were willing to slow down and navigate the trail carefully, especially the sections that skirt a shallow but steep wash (not much we could do about the part where Mom had to climb up the ladder; sorry). Most importantly, though, the sun cooperated and put on a good show, first painting the sky with a soft blush, then quietly slipping up over the horizon, spilling light across the grass and onto the hills. "Beautiful!" Mom exclaimed; beautiful!, I agreed. Dad, meanwhile, narrated for his new video camera: "Now, that's the sun coming up . . ."

Thus we began our Great Northern Plains vacation.

The Plains are not everyone's first choice for a destination. Though there are a number of attractions—everything from parks to petting zoos and pow-wows! Scenic Byways! Heritage festivals! The geographic center of the United States!—few people plan specifically to see sites in the Dakotas. Rather, they have to be enticed off the highway by oddities or curiosities—albino prairie dogs or Wall Drug (World Famous!, ubiquitous signs proclaim). Tourists may spend a few hours looking around, then continue on their way to the Black Hills or Yellowstone or home to Ohio, whizzing past mile after mile of flat, windswept prairie.

Even those who do take the time to wander the backroads may witness thousands of acres of ranchland laced with sun-bleached fences, dotted with haybales, and punctuated only by lonely siloes or the occasional weatherbeaten barn. There's a poignant sense "of things ebbing," wrote Charles Bowden for an article published in *National Geographic Magazine* in 2008—"of churches being abandoned, schools shutting down, towns becoming ruins."[62] His words, accompanied by Eugene Richards' haunting photographs, paint a stark picture of rural North

Dakota as not just "The Emptied Prairie," but "a giant skeleton of abandoned human desire." (A "giant skeleton of abandoned human desire"!
How do you counter that?) The portrait of a dying heartland surprised
and touched readers worldwide, but local residents and scholars were
already concerned that, as Bowden writes, "out on the land, the population has relentlessly bled away." Sociologists and rural geographers have
been discussing the implications of persistent population decline in North
Dakota and throughout the Great Plains for decades, noting that waning
birth rates, an advancing age structure, and out-migration of youth are
symptoms as well as catalysts for further socioeconomic and even cultural
decline.[63] As rural communities court everything from businesses and
baby boomers to garbage dumps and prisons in an attempt to diversify
their economies away from agriculture, some scholars and residents
question whether there's any way to save rural communities from what
Bowden deems "irreversible decline" and Frank and Deborah Popper
see as "near-total desertion." Just as philosopher Edmunds Bunkše found
of desolate flats farther west, "[d]riving through this landscape alone
[can bring] forth an interminable sense of longing and loneliness, and a
constant wish to escape from it as quickly as possible"; it represents, he
continues, a "'landscape of broken dreams.'"[64]

What journalist Richard Wood calls unique "purple cow" attractions can
spell the difference between life and all-out death.[65] When my parents
and I detoured to see Sue and other paleontological specimens tempo-
rarily on exhibit in Faith, South Dakota, for example, we supported the
local economy by eating at a local restaurant, peeking in a local jewelry
shop, and, of course, purchasing a dinosaur T-shirt that changes color
when exposed to sunlight. Not every town has a remarkably complete
and famous *Tyrannosaurus rex* skeleton on hand, however; nor do many
people go see one. Instead, other communities try to capitalize on their
cultural history (Medora, North Dakota, boasts the former ranch of

Theodore Roosevelt, for example), their geographic location (if not at the center of the nation outside Belle Fourche, at least along the interstate corridor), their natural beauty (found in hundreds of public and private parks and preserves), and/or the quirky humor of local artists (including everything from Carhenge outside Alliance, Nebraska, to the biggest ball of twine in Darwin, Minnesota, not to mention the astonishing plethora of dinosaur statues standing in random fields. South Dakota has to be the world capital of giant homemade metal dinosaurs.)

While some towns have struggled to remain socioeconomically and demographically relevant, others have "succeeded," only at the expense of their local identity. For example, Medora—a town of 100 permanent residents—now makes way for 300 seasonal workers and more than 250,000 tourists each summer. The tourism bureau claims that they come to "one of the premier family entertainment destinations in the country" seeking "a modern 'Old West' experience that [they] will never forget."[66] Unforgettable, indeed. My parents and I went to Medora eager to see the land that had inspired our twenty-sixth president to become a pioneering conservationist. Theodore Roosevelt National Park itself, with its rolling grasslands and thundering herds of bison, did not disappoint us. The town, however, had been planned and polished with such deliberate "Old West" kitsch—strategically spaced restaurants, shops, lodging, and attractions including an Ice Cream Parlor, Fudge and Ice Cream Depot, Corner Corral Gift Shop, Sacajawea Trading Post, Chuckwagon dinner, and, above all, the "Medora Musical" that nightly sings and dances its way through a romanticized history of the region—that it felt more like a movie set than an authentically thriving community. (Nonetheless, we experienced the "Old West" in the form of delicious steak dinners and my new cowboy hat.)

One place inspired me more than Medora, more than Faith, more than any of the other towns or landscapes we saw as my parents and I circled

west (so Mom could see Montana. She slept through County Road 7 while
Dad refused to stop to let me take pictures of fence posts), then south
(to Devil's Tower National Monument, where we again woke bleary-
eyed before dawn and were rewarded with the hollow echoes of bugling
elk), and finally back east toward Badlands. The place that kindled my
imagination, that glows in my memory was Marmarth, North Dakota.

I have no idea why.

When we drove past the town's isolated, weatherbeaten railroad station and newly restored Mystic Theatre, I didn't know that a hundred
years earlier, Marmarth had been a booming stop on the railroad, with
two banks, two hotels, a large elementary and high school, and even a
theatre and Opera House serving a population of 1000 people, according to Katharine Garstka's *Welcome to Historic Marmarth.*[67] When we
drove past—what else?—the dinosaur statue standing on a hill next to
Highway 12, I didn't know that every summer, teams of paleontologists
and interested volunteers prowl the famous Hell Creek Formation in
search of more late Cretaceous specimens like "Dakota"—a hadrosaur
complete with skin impressions—while the town celebrates "Dino Daze."
I didn't know that "[t]his small town of 140 people invites you to come
and enjoy its beautiful scenery, wildlife, history, dinosaur and fossil digs,
and relaxing lifestyle"; I didn't know that it urges travelers to "stop and
see us; you'll be a stranger only once." I only knew that the afternoon
sunlight was shining through the leaves of the cottonwoods, a couple
of dogs were lolling happily along one of the dusty side streets, and as
we rolled past the modest grocery mart and toward the open plains, I
thought, oh, this town has everything I could ever want, I would like
living here, Marmarth!

Residents of rural communities on the Great Plains cherish and champion their desirable "quality of life" —a healthy natural environment,
quiet pace, friendly neighbors, and good schools. Twenty years after the

Poppers learned that "[m]any people felt a possessiveness about their Plains—positively, exuding pride and love, and negatively, resenting outsiders,"[68] North Dakota governor John Hoeven bridled at "The Emptied Prairie," firing off a letter to the editor of *National Geographic Magazine* to tout the state's growing economy (including "the nation's 3rd largest pasta manufacturer") and insist that "small town, rural enterprises reflect [North Dakota's] spirit and ingenuity."[69] Readers wrote into an online forum to celebrate other attributes— "a view of a cornfield, a community where everyone nods hello when I pass, air that doesn't make me wince and water I can drink out of the tap . . . All the stars I could ever care to look at." "Let it be what it is!," one exclaimed, as much to his governor as to the author, "a big flat nothing with the most beautiful skies . . ."[70]

"Debate about the Great Plains has now spilled beyond economic issues," Pete Shortridge observes:

> People have noticed, for example, the uncomplimentary nature of the widely used words "treeless" and "semiarid." Why define this landscape in terms so negative and so obviously formed by outsiders? Why not stress instead the glories of low humidity, clear-blue skies, and lush grasslands . . .? The aesthetic of the Great Plains environment is also being rethought. Many long-term residents truly love the region's open spaces, but have lacked words to counter the outsider's frequent judgment of them as empty and lonely. New articulations now appear regularly to an enthusiastic audience.[71]

Asking "[h]ow about a little love for prairies?," editors of the *Lincoln Journal Star*, for example, assert that Nebraska has "something increasingly rare and valuable in today's crowded world — open spaces where a person can look across miles and miles of land without buildings, roads, power lines or fences."[72] Bloggers in rural Kansas, meanwhile, insist that "small towns have a beautiful story"[73] and that there's "no

Marmarth station

place like home."[74] Painters and photographers such as Wyoming's Linda Lillegraven strive to "capture the elemental, intolerable beauty [of the high plains] in [their] work."[75] There's even a website dedicated to documenting and preserving the poignant beauty of North Dakota's abandoned places: http://ghostsofnorthdakota.com.

It includes Marmarth.

Nothing blurs the dazzling white, shimmering light of the prairie . . . nothing disturbs the solitary silence. All noises seem to bound back from that silent, soft sea of grass over which rests an unexplainable, passive sadness.

—Alexandra Grippenberg. 1954. *A Half Year in the New World*[76]

In 2002, Senators Chuck Hagel (R-Nebraska) and Byron Dorgan (D-North Dakota) sponsored the "New Homestead Economic Opportunity Act" —a "bill to reward the hard work and risk of individuals who choose to live in and help preserve America's small, rural towns" through a mix of tax credits, loan forgiveness, and investment opportunities. Shortridge notes that "the word 'homestead' somehow caught the imagination of the [Great Plains] region," but did not inspire a flood of eager twenty-first century settlers. It's still nice to think, he writes, that "the unique environment of the Central Plains . . . [is] fertile and potentially rewarding, but also harsh enough to test people's character. Weak-willed settlers would leave the region. Those who stayed would be chastened and gain a clear-eyed, pragmatic approach to life."[77]

Yes, it's nice to rhapsodize, as does Kathleen Norris, that "[t]he large-ness of land and sky [in the Dakotas] is humbling, putting mankind in proper perspective."[78] But in truth, a daily dose of humility can erode away at the psyche. In practice, Bowden observes, "some people cash in on their property and move someplace warmer and easier. The rest grow old and die."[79]

As communities seek to stimulate socioeconomic growth—to lure tour-ists off the highway and into local shops and restaurants—they have to consider the fact that travel can either open people up to new places and new perspectives or it can reinforce stereotypes. When the tour-ism bureau for the state of Kansas unfurled its new slogan, "Kansas, As Big as You Think" in 2005, for example, reactions on online forums ranged from "People will think, 'It's probably as flat and brown as I think, too,' or 'It's as boring as I think,' or. . . 'It's probably as backward as I think'"[80] to "I like the new slogan. It's a hip kind of relativity. Each person gets to decide how big Kansas is to him or her."[81] When the company Kansas, Inc. conducted post-slogan surveys in the attempt to figure out why people had mostly negative reactions to the "Kansas

Image," they concluded: "While traditional stereotypes and clichés may never change, we must find a way to embrace who and what we are, and use that to our advantage. We must realize that we can change certain parts of our image, and certain parts we cannot—we are what we are."[82] (Shortridge notes that a reporter for the travel magazine *Holiday* once declared Kansas "'82,158 square miles of flat and cheerless prairie, producing little except wheat and tedium.'"[83] We are what we are. Wu-wei. Wheat.)

North Dakota is Legendary, Oklahoma just OK. Montana claims Big Sky Country, Wyoming is Forever West. South Dakota has *Great Faces. Great Places*, and in Nebraska, the Possibilities . . . Endless. Great Plains states are full of unexplored possibilities, Edmunds Bunkše observes, but they're not tourist destinations; rather, prairies and plains "favour *travellers*" (emphasis added) —people who perceive landscapes "through all the senses and with the mind"; people who want to know "What feeling of space is experienced in the trilling of skylarks over tilled fields in May? How does a path of cold clay feel to bare feet at sunrise?" That, argues Bunkše, is what these landscapes offer.[84]

It's a tricky cycle: try to convince people to visit plains so that they can fully experience them firsthand, but hope that when they do so, they see more than wheat and tedium. Hope they see more than highways and singing cowboys. Hope they don't feel hot and tired and bored. Hope that they're there with an open mind, that they're willing to do whatever their guidebook or daughter suggests. Hope they take the time to "feel the flat, gentle terrain swell into hills and valleys," as a brochure for the Sandhills Journey Scenic Byway urges; hope they "Turn down the radio. Notice the shapes in the clouds. . . . [Hope they] relax. Luxuriate in the scenic wonders . . . Tune in to the birds, the wind, the rivers: the symphony of the plains." Above all, hope they appreciate the "stretch of beauty" enough to, as Byway proponents hope, want to "Return every year."[85]

My mother liked the haybales; my father liked the bison staring us down from the middle of the road at Theodore Roosevelt, its breath steaming in the cool morning air. (Also the calves at Custer State Park, Mom insists, and the hike around the base of Devil's Tower, and a phenomenal meal for $7.95 in a small town near Jewel Cave . . .) We all enjoyed the thunderstorms and the ice cream. But would my parents have visited South Dakota if I hadn't been at Badlands? Would I have driven to North Dakota if they hadn't come? What convinces a person to travel?

Referring back to Tuan's "Life as a Field Trip," in which he writes of wandering forth "just to see what's out there, with no prior questions in mind," he questions the belief that "[a]n undertaking of this sort . . . [can] stimulate the imagination, leading one to ideas inspired by objects in the field rather than by words in a book." Does it? He asks, then responds, "Each geographer will no doubt want to give his or her own answer. Mine is no. I cannot say that casual outings have made me wiser, or even much more knowledgeable."[86]

But, dear Dr. Tuan, how would I have known of Medora, of Marmarth, if I hadn't gone? How would Mom have seen Montana (sort of) and Dad seen Sue if they hadn't been willing to travel at random, without any idea what they'd find over the next ridge? How would I have found the old dead juniper, or the road in Kansas, or Scottsbluff, if I'd just stayed at home or followed prescribed paths?

Go on a field trip!, I want to write a guidebook, "to real fields! To prairies, to parks, to grasslands!" Go without prior questions, especially without preconceptions. Simply wake at dawn, preferably while grumbles of thunder linger overhead or animals are stirring; walk—walk! Drive! Fly if you have to!—down the road or up to the overlook or the fencepost or the abandoned railroad depot or off into the middle of a big empty field, then open yourself to whatever surprises that big beautiful world has to offer.

(Watch out for rattlesnakes.)

2.4 Interpretation and Inspiration
Badlands National Park, South Dakota

As long as people—local residents and visitors, scientists and artists,
Park Rangers and you as a Junior Ranger—enjoy Badlands, they will help
protect this special place. Then it will be here for you and all of your family
and friends to come back to and enjoy again.

—"Being a Junior Ranger," *Badlands Junior Ranger Guidebook*

I've never liked the idea of getting in my car and driving to a trailhead
or making plans to go fossil-hunting or animal-watching with someone.
Maybe it's that I hate driving, or making plans in general—so much
fuss!—but really it's that doing so is a form of separation as well as confinement, a trammeling of curiosity and wonder. I like to feel free to dash
out the moment I feel like it, and return whenever it's dark or my legs
or tired or it's just time to return. I like to feel free to go as far as I like,
wherever I like, not out and back on a designated route at a designated
time. I like to feel like I am learning my backyard, not on an expedition
to some special foreign place. I like to walk and walk not for recreation,
re-creation, mere release from the pressures of daily life or renewal of
spirit, but rather for creation, life itself. Wandering—on foot, off-route—is
how I've learned to care for places.

At Badlands, I could step out my front door, stroll along a back road
past the maintenance yard and horse barn, and, within a matter of minutes, be standing somewhere between the open expanse of grassland and
the even bigger expanse of prairie sky. That was my route if I was in the
mood for contemplation (i.e. something fairly flat, fairly quiet). If I felt
like cool shade or the scent of pines (and didn't mind traffic and a bit of
a hill), I could huff halfway up the badlands wall, following the main park
road up to where the Cliff Shelf Trail winds through a grove of junipers
nestled in a geologic slump. I can count on my hands the number of

times I went hiking anywhere else, much less with other people. Early
in the season, a resource technician and I explored Castle Trail; we had
a grand time trying to clamber up to and around grassland "islands"—
clods of prairie held together by plants' strong, deep roots, isolated by
deep erosion of the clay soil—until we noticed that a thunderstorm was
approaching much more quickly than anticipated. (Lesson: it's hard to
judge motion against an infinite horizon.) Toward the end of the summer, I poked around the Old Northeast Road area with a volunteer who
wanted to show me a curious geologic formation he'd found years earlier;
we ended up crawling through the clay on hands and knees, looking for
scraps of bone. (Lesson: treasures everywhere, once you figure out what
you want to look for.) Sometime in the middle of the season, I headed
out to Buffalo Gap with my supervisor; we wanted to rockhound in an
area known for its agates, but the wind was howling, filling our eyelashes
and ears and teeth with grit and making it hard to stand upright, much
less look for rocks. (Lesson: sun, dirt, wind trump all.)

I never backpacked through the Sage Creek Wilderness, though; I don't
know what it's like to camp out with bison stomping and snorting nearby.
And I never spent time in the Stronghold Unit of the park; I don't know
much about it, except that it's managed by the Oglala Sioux in a unique
agreement with the Park Service. I never looked through a telescope at
the special Night Sky Program. I never spent an autumn at Badlands,
nor winter, nor spring—never saw the hills draped with snow or ravines
laced with ice; never rejoiced for the return of the birds. Every morning
or evening I hiked up that darn hill hoping to see the bobcat that lurked
in the brush; I never did.

What have I lost? What have I learned?

My official title at Badlands was "Junior Ranger Ambassador." Instead
of interacting with visitors firsthand, answering questions and giving talks, I worked behind the scenes to prepare an activity booklet

for children. Most Park Service units have Junior Ranger programs, in which younger visitors complete tasks—usually an assortment of drawing, writing, crossword puzzles, word searches, and treasure hunts—designed to help them learn more about the park. The programs are meant to spark interest and instill values of conservation, if not simply convince families to linger longer, giving each place a bit more time to work its magic.

"Explore. Learn. Protect," reads the Junior Ranger logo, assuming that people's experience naturally progresses from inherent curiosity to increased knowledge and, ultimately, to compassion. That is the standard mantra of "Interpretation," defined by the National Park Service as "the process of providing each visitor an opportunity to personally connect with a place. . . . The goal of all interpretive service is to increase each visitor's enjoyment and understanding of the parks, and to allow visitors to care about the parks on their own terms." The Park Service Interpretive Development Program (motto: "Aiming for the High Ground")—now a sophisticated system of training and development complete with curricula, national standards, certifications, and, most belovedly, an "interpretive equation" (KA + KR + AT = IO)—"encourages the stewardship of park resources by facilitating meaningful, memorable visitor experiences . . . based on the philosophy that people will *care for* what they first *care about*."[87]

This, then, is the challenge, for Park Service personnel and anyone who wants to protect a wild corner of the planet: *how* do you make a person care about a place? Freeman Tilden, the author of *Interpreting Our Heritage* and considered by many to be the father of interpretation, advises interpretation specialists to use "original objects" (i.e., rocks, flowers, homesteads, hawks), "firsthand experience" (talks, walks, wind, and that great blue sky), and "illustrative media" (newsletters, brochures, websites, and, yes, activity booklets) to "reveal . . . to such visitors as

desire the service, something of the beauty and wonder, the inspiration and spiritual meaning that lie behind what the visitor can with his
senses perceive."[88] Perhaps images do have the power to "bring about deep
emotional feeling . . . and to activate moral sentiments of care," as Karl
Benediktsson agrees[89], but can small, flat photographs truly "maximize
the visual beauty of the [Plains]," as Jerry Sheppard argues, "thereby
demonstrating that the Plains is a place whose Nature is worth saving"?[90]
Does experience and knowledge truly lead to connection and caring?

There are two important things to keep in mind. First, referring back
to Tilden, the process of interpretation can only inspire "such visitors as
desire the service." On the occasions when I led a gaggle of aspiring Junior
Rangers on naturalist-style expeditions out into the prairie, complete with
blank journals, writing/coloring utensils, and plenty of rocks, cacti, grass,
butterflies, birds, and ungulate tracks to learn and care about, some of
the participants were hyper-enthusiastic and others had to be dragged
along by their road-weary parents. The disgruntled ones probably didn't
learn much, and might forever think of Badlands as a hot, horrid place.
Moreover, for all of the families that agreed to go on the walk or just
stop by the visitor center to watch the movie and play with the exhibits,
many more missed out on the "illustrative media" and ranger-enhanced
"firsthand experience," preferring to slip through with just the official
map and maybe a glance at the newsletter.

This leads to the second point, articulated by Stan Godlovitch: "[t]
he fact is we perceive differences amongst things of a kind and have
preferences whether we like it or not."[91] Some visitors wanted to stay
out and wander empty creek beds all morning; others wanted to go
back immediately. Some kids thought the prairie was full of fun things
to draw; others saw it as boring, barren, empty of any beauty or delights.
Some parents perceived beauty in the rugged hills and oceans of grass
while others wanted to hurry on to the monumental scenery of Mount

Rushmore and Yellowstone. Not only do people see different details in a landscape, geographer D. W. Meinig observes, but people layer different meanings and different values on the scenery.[92] People may not, in the end, find more meaning much less value in a place after reading a book, seeing a picture, stopping at an overlook, or going on a hike.

That's okay. "[T]he tourist," Bunkše reminds us, "does not expect to be challenged with transformation of the self nor to induce transformation of the culture back home."[93] Philosophers who make judgments and issue moral imperatives—flinging out shoulds, oughts, and musts in the attempt to "bring our aesthetic appreciation of environments, both natural and human, in line with our environmental and moral responsibilities to maintain ecological health" (thank you, Allen Carlson[94])—can easily alienate audiences and/or propagate negative stereotypes. (Robert Fudge, for example, accuses people of "mistreating the unscenic" and being simply unable to see scientific beauty, then goes on to abuse prairies as "boring" and equate them with pesky insects and rotting elk carcasses.[95] Yuriko Saito, likewise, cites descriptions of the "tedious" and "scenically challenged" plains, then suggests that people who are not open to the aesthetics of "unscenic" nature are selfish and close-minded.[96]) "Does it make sense," I echo Marcia Eaton, "to say to someone, 'This is the way you ought to experience nature?'"[97]

The key word in Interpretation, then, is "opportunity"—providing visitors the *opportunity* to develop emotional and intellectual connections. Instead of insisting that people ought to or will experience nature in a certain way, interpretation acts on the hope that people *can* see places in a new light. Doing so need not take months, or miles. "For a relationship with landscape to be lasting," writes Barry Lopez, it merely need be reciprocal. "At the level at which landscape seems beautiful or frightening to us and leaves us affected, or at the level at which it furnishes us with the metaphors and symbols with which we pry into mystery, the nature of reciprocity is harder to define," he writes, then suggests, "[i]n approaching the land with an attitude of obligation. . . —perhaps only a gesture of the hands—one establishes a regard from which dignity can emerge."[98]

A gesture of the hands, a singing with the birds. A respect for the plains' quiet beauty and richness of life.

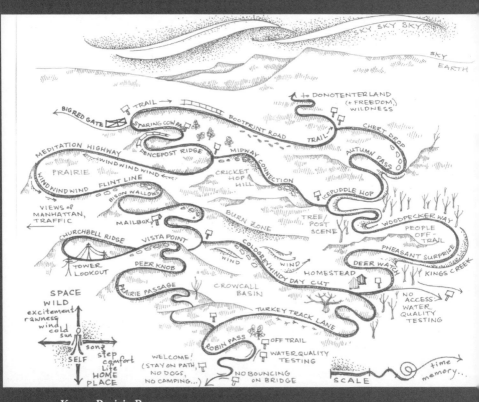

Konza Prairie Preserve

CHAPTER 3

Tallgrass

3.1 Experiment and Experience;
Or, How I Tried to Like a Prairie
Konza Prairie Preserve, Kansas

I didn't dare leave much out. I wanted to bear witness to the facts . . .

There's no cleverness to be found here, only rawness

—Rick Bass, *Book of Yaak*[1]

You cannot make yourself love a place. You can go again and again with different expectations, for different reasons, in different seasons, but you can't make yourself love a place. You can learn the names of the plants and the colors of the sky, make friends with the deer and come to terms with the wind, but you can't make yourself love a place. You can rationalize and rhapsodize, open your mind and narrow your field of vision, sit and watch, walk and think, think and try through rain snow sunrise sunset, but no. Know you cannot make yourself love a place.

When I moved to Manhattan, Kansas, late one summer, I was not dreading what journalists such as Stephen Darst denigrate as an "all-pervading flatness, moral, cultural, social, topographical, political."[2] Rather, I was eager for *Kansas!* The Heartland! Wide-Open America! As Big as I Thought! I thought it would be big. And beautiful. *Ad astra, per prairie!*

I was wrong. (*Aspera.*) Any self-respecting geographer should always remain conscious of scale, conscientious about place, and have the common sense to realize that abstract political and cultural concepts of "place" are very different from an all-too-real accumulation of sidewalks and streetlamps, apartment complexes and housing developments, bar district, Best Buy, and, of course, Super Wal-Mart that make up the micropolis of a specific, real world place. (I am not a city person.)

Right away, I felt lost, trapped, suffocated—how was I supposed to *think*, with all of the noise; how was I supposed to *sleep*, with all of the light; how was I supposed to *breathe*, so many people, so many cars, so much humidity, where was the sky?

Other people noted my anxiety and suggested I should go visit Konza Prairie Preserve, just down the road. Prairie? Preserve? Sanctuary!, I thought. So one beautiful day, mid-November, air an Indian-summer blue, grass a rich autumn gold, I drove the nine miles out to Konza, eagerly anticipating a wide open horizon, space (*space!*) to stretch the legs, the mind, to breathe.

Instead, I found a lined, captured, used, abused, tired little square of prairie lost under a big blue sky.

Konza is an 8600-acre remnant of tallgrass prairie nestled in the Flint Hills of Kansas. Having proved unfit for agricultural development (even plows made of steel can't cultivate ridges of stone), it now serves as a Biological Research Station jointly managed by Kansas State University and The Nature Conservancy. Though intended to promote understanding and

Trail, Konza Prairie Preserve

appreciation of grasslands, the preserve is quite clearly and unabashedly
not a park or pleasuring ground. School groups and visitors may attend
programs at the educational center and/or hike the facility's three recreational trails, but the site is, at heart, an object of science—an outdoor
laboratory in which botanists and biologists, climatologists and geomor-
phologists can conduct carefully controlled experiments on the flora, the
fauna, the rain and fire and grazing that make up a tallgrass ecosystem.

To facilitate this research, managers have systematically parceled the
prairie into tracts and monitor usage by means of gates, permits, and

strict regulations that say what grasses may grow, where bison may graze, and how people may interact with the place. Even the recreational trails are neatly mapped and marked to tell visitors where to go and what to look at: *Go here*, says the path. *Do not go here*, says the fence. *"No bouncing on bridge*," says the sign.

I'm not an avid bridge-bouncer; nor am I a fence-hopper. I have ambivalent opinions of paths, but dutifully obey them when they're there. I'm sometimes a scientist, sometimes an artist, always a walker. A prairie-walker, a plains person.

But I didn't want to walk at Konza.

Sunday morning, months after I'd first visited the Preserve, I was sitting in my little room in town, contemplating what to do with a whole beautiful day yawning ahead of me, empty empty, and suddenly remembered Konza. Oh, Konza. Perhaps I ought to give the place another chance?

The drive was longer and browner than I'd remembered; the light brighter, colder, sharper. *Frost*, I noted as I stepped onto the trail, trying to focus on simple pleasures, *Frost; grass; sun.* Then I came up over the hill and realized, *Sky.*

Sky. Could it be? Openness, freedom, beautiful blue infinity? The air was singing with birdcalls and churchbells; the earth was laughing with ripples of wind; the sun—oh that sun!—was beaming brilliantly down, illuminating woodpeckers and trees and grasses and me, beaming brilliantly back.

When the next Sunday dawned—cold; windy, too, and grey—I still packed up my boots, my camera, and my hopes and drove out to the trailhead. My enthusiasm paled slightly when I realized I had forgotten the law of the Wild ("Carry Kleenex," according to Annie Dillard[3]), but I wasn't about to let a runny nose sabotage Mission: Love Konza. I wrapped a scarf around my face and trudged off, glasses fogging with my breath.

Not long after I crossed the second bridge—before I even made it away from the wood-lined little creek and up to the actual prairie, really—my fingers had numbed and mind had frozen. Frozen solid; ceased to function; formed a cold hard lump in my skull. Crows stared at me from the fields, silent. I stared back, silent. *Forget it!* I decided, *Retreat!* Go home, curl up and cradle a warm mug of hot cocoa, curse the Kansas wind, curse Konza.

Before I could reverse my angry trudge, though, I happened to glance up. There they were—deer—four of them, five?—standing halfway up the big hill, calm and solid under the big watercolor sky. Time paused. Then more deer—four of them, three?—popped out of the tall grass next to me and everything came back to life. Deer! Deer everywhere! All around me, living, breathing, not complaining about the cold, just happy to be out there, out anywhere, Konza.

Well, I thought, *why not go a little farther, at least to the top of the hill?* Nod to the deer, the crows; feel cold, silent, free.

> [Deer] teach us new things about the landscape. They lead us into corners and crevices where we would never otherwise go, and teach us to notice, with senses inflamed, things we might never otherwise pay attention to— the direction of a stirring of breeze, the phase of the moon, a bent blade of grass, a faint odor, a funny feeling of being observed—and because of deer, we notice these things with an intensity that is both feral and comfortable.
> —Rick Bass, *The Wild Marsh: Four Seasons at Home in Montana*[4]

Perhaps, I began to wonder, I *can* learn to love Konza; I can *learn* to love Konza?

In order to "cultivate geophilic values"—to "heighten awareness, bring fresh insight," and "emotionally connect with a landscape"—according to Paul Faulstich, I need simply explore, symbolize, and take pleasure in the land.[5] Yi-Fu Tuan has postulated in his seminal *Space and Place*, "[w]hat begins as undifferentiated space becomes place when we get to know it better and endow it with value." It is possible to "extend the aesthetic experience," he continues in another essay, "through association, memory, and knowledge."[6]

Explore, symbolize, take pleasure. Form associations, cherish memories, cultivate knowledge. Experience + Knowledge = Value. Eventually, according to the experts, if I kept going to Konza, kept trying, I would no longer think of the place as just a prairie, but rather an amalgamation of scents, colors, and feels; no longer a preserve, but an accumulation of memories, moments, and lovely little experiences.

Konza! I would walk the paths each Sunday morning, I decided; wind or rain, I would skirt pastures and find vantage points. I would commune with the flint and *Andropogon* and meadowlarks. I would learn about, photograph, map, and derive great pleasure and aesthetic satisfaction from this parcel of prairie.

It worked at first.

Memory: the last week in January, a rustle in the grass inspired me to take a step, maybe two, off the path, and I scared a *quail* up! Then *another*! Then a *dozen*! My heart fluttered along with their wings as they flapped and squawked their way into the sky. (Holmes Rolston III: "[T]he bird in flight . . . constrain[s] the observer's appreciation to the moment—catch as catch can . . ."[7])

Association: the first week in February, a slight warmth to the air, mist in the fields, horsetails in the sky, footsteps soft on the rich, dark earth. Forget the telephone poles, ugh, and the radio tower; let the raucous caws of the crows drown out the airplane; give up the desire to take photographs—to frame images and steal memories—and instead settle into a sense of peace. Warm, sunny, fresh-air, big sky peace.

But knowledge. Reality. Oh. Mid-February, I went looking for inspiration or beauty or happiness and found only a pale, pale sky—weak, weary, barely a breeze stirring the emptiness. Turkey tracks. Deer. No magic. Even the frost seemed flat and heavy.

Hey, prairie? I asked, *Hey sky, hey grass—amaze me! Give me space to stretch, to walk, to think, to breathe!* Exhale. The prairie was silent.

Crunch crunch, I walked on. Walked the same three paths, over and over and over again, dulling any intimation of fresh adventure. Rather than adding to my appreciation of the place, each lap detracted from the excitement; each mile tarnished the novelty. Rather than becoming more deeply engaged, I just followed the path, going where it told me to go and seeing what it told me to see. There was no choice. Konza. A tired, old landscape; a tired, bored mindscape. Cold and grey.

Memory: mid-February, out on the farthest extent of the longest loop, I was limping in pain, flinching with every step. My socks had scootched down and left my skin exposed to the hard back of my boots, but I didn't bother to fix them or try to stop my heels from bleeding; blisters were the only thing that felt real, that felt raw, that felt at all.

Scholars and rangers, theorists and activists want to believe that people will fall in love with a place if they simply see it, understand it. Back to the Junior Ranger mantra: the more you learn, the more you appreciate the complex relationships between climate, soil, creeks, grass, insects, birds, grazers, fire, drought, fewer trees and more people; the longer you spend, the better you attune to the dramatic moments, the subtle rhythms. "Come to the Flint Hills!" brochures for Tallgrass Prairie National Preserve confidently exclaim, "experience the vast prairie landscape"![8] "The region's sweeping horizons enchant visitors!" says the Sandhills Journey Scenic Byway, "Careful scrutiny reveals the special beauty, wonder, and complexity of the prairie"![9] "[T]ake time and get closer," remember Rex Funk's tips to help people develop the skills, perspectives, and attitudes needed to discover the character and quality of open spaces: remain mindful of your tempo; focus on the scale; meditate on processes and cycles, continuity and change; and note the landscape's color, texture, pattern, line, form, movement, contrast, and light.[10]

Line, movement, light. Sounds lovely, no? But it doesn't work like that.

Back at Konza on a cold, wet, windy morning in early March, I drove in past a flock of turkeys who had been breakfasting on stubble next to the preserve road. My car sent them scurrying into the air, flapping with hungry displeasure. I parked at the trailhead, stepped out, and inhaled the rich scent of spring. Rain from the night before had left the sky clouded over and the earth saturated with color. I wanted to capture some sense of the scenery—grasses a rich bronze, trees a deep purple, and the horizons grey to the east and an off-blue, a distant blue to the west—but it was no use. The prairie was too subtle, too big, or too real for representations. I put away my camera and just walked. Added my bootprints to the muddy tracks of those who had traversed the same path. Sang with the birds, twee-oo, twee-oo; ta-tap tap tap.

A month later—a warm-air, cool-earth April morning—I drove in through waves of clouds and thickets of mist. The air was lifting, the grass greening, the peepers peeping, and the little creek was trickling and burbling and giggling as creeks should. I skipped along the path, over the bridge and out of the woods, through the field and up the hill, and along the ridge. Coming over a hill, I made a sudden discovery—a distinct line between last autumn's dry brown brush and a flat expanse of earth newly charred black. Burn! They had done the spring burn! The managers had set the dead grass on fire—torches mimicking lightning, scientists playing storm—and in so doing had exposed all sorts of secrets: outcrops of rocks ringing all the hills; little scraggly bushes and trees; *yucca?* There was *yucca* at Konza?

And a *mailbox?* What was a mailbox doing out at the top of a charred knob of prairie? Oh. Right. Biological Research Station. Prairie Preserve. Education program; environmental interpretation; brochures. The mailbox housed brochures. Brochures to tell me what I would learn as I walked the trail. Trail to tell me where to walk. Walk a thin pale line across the big black earth, under the big blue sky.

Envisioning "The Beholding Eye: Ten Versions of the Same Scene," D. W. Meinig suggests:

> take a small but varied company to any convenient viewing place . . . and have each, in turn, describe the "landscape". . .to detail what it is composed of and say something about the "meaning" of what can be seen. It will soon become apparent that even though we gather together and look in the same direction at the same instant, we will not—we cannot—see the same landscape.[11]

Physical scientists may look at Konza and see *Andropogon gerardii, Quercus macrocarpa, Odocoileus virginianus, Bos bison bison,* stream flows and climate cycles—a landscape of Nature, System, and maybe Problem waiting to be solved through experimentation and control. Social scientists may see a former Habitat—an Artifact, with a History that demonstrates different conceptions of Wealth. Artists may see Meinig's Aesthetic—the "color, texture, mass, line, position, symmetry, balance, tension" of wide open vistas, the grace of sun of wind of rain. No one of these perceptions is inaccurate, though all are wholly incorrect; Konza exists not just as biophysical phenomena or sociocultural values but as a Place and manifestation of Ideology that blends and even transcends compartmentalized conceptions.

How are we to understand this complexity? Many intellectuals have issued calls for synthesis among academic perspectives—a so-called "consilience" of ideas and approaches to learning that can birth more holistic understanding of places.[12] As defined by biologist and philosopher E. O. Wilson, consilience is "a jumping together of knowledge by the linking of facts and fact-based theory across disciplines to create a common groundwork for explanation."[13] In the manifesto subtitled *A Unity of Knowledge,* Wilson asserts that "[o]nly fluency across the boundaries [of the natural sciences, the social sciences, and the humanities] will provide a clear view of the world as it really is." An "unusual richness" of new knowledge, new understanding, and new opportunities exists not at the isolated centers but at the intersections of disciplines, agrees education professor Myra Strober.[14] Beyond academic consilience, Allen Carlson advocates rounding out "cognitive" knowledge about the origins, types, and properties of the environment with "noncognitive" emotional states and responses into a holistic understanding of a place. "When conjoined," he maintains, "they advocate bringing together feeling and knowing, which is the core of serious aesthetic experience."[15]

But are feelings acquired as easily as information? Can scientists think like artists, knowers like feelers? Yi-Fu Tuan believes "scientific knowledge can increase one's appreciation of landscape . . . but . . . scientific analysis leads to abstractions and removes us from any personal involvement."[16] Thomas Heyd too: "In many cases scientific knowledge may be neutral, or even harmful, to our aesthetic appreciation of nature, because it directs our attention to the theoretical level and the general case, diverting us from the personal level and particular case that we actually need to engage."[17] In another extended quote, sociologist Douglas Massey implored a room full of scholars to recognize an "*interplay* between rationality and emotionality":

> The [emotional and rational] brains are connected to one another, but operate in parallel to yield two different systems of perception and memory. While neural pathways between the emotional and the rational brain carry information in both directions, *the number of neural connections running from the limbic system to the cortex is far greater than the number connecting the cortex to the limbic system . . .* As a result, not only do unconscious

emotional feelings exist independently of rational appraisals of them, but . . . it is much more likely that emotional impulses will overwhelm rational cognition . . .

[S]timuli from the external world are perceived, evaluated, and acted upon by the emotional brain *before* the rational brain has received the pertinent information . . . By the time the rational brain receives incoming sensory stimuli about an event or object in the real world, the emotional brain has already swung into action and showered the neocortex with emotional messages that condition its perception.[18]

In other words, before we can *think* our way into happiness, much less beauty—before we can will ourselves to create neural pathways into what Aldo Leopold deemed the still unlovely human mind—first, we see, then we feel.

I tried to consciously analyze my emotional response to Konza and systematically construct an attachment to the place. But no matter how thoroughly I tried to conduct research or how objectively I tried to examine the details, I couldn't help but look at Konza and see rules reading "Trails open sunrise to sunset" (*No camping. No sleeping out under the stars, marveling at the universe above and the ground underneath*). I saw signs saying "No public access beyond this point." (*Important work is going on here—serious Science, real inquiry; we are busy learning, measuring, mapping, capturing Knowledge. There is no place here for love.*) Fences, paths, a parking lot; a trammeled facsimile of prairie.

The spring burn revealed a delicious puddle of sky-blue water. It looked so still, so refreshing that I wanted to dash off into it, to splash, to laugh, to feel the mud ooze between my toes. I wanted to wallow like a buffalo, to think like a buffalo, to "lay back, [roll] like a bison, [pause] as they do, looking upward," like William Least Heat-Moon's friend Venerable

Tashmoo, then to say, "'I don't see anything except sky. I feel the earth, but I don't see it.'"[19]

That's what it was—I wanted to *feel* the earth, to smell it, taste it, dark and rich and charred. But I could not. Please stay on the trail.

Konza might be an outstanding example of a functioning tallgrass ecosystem and an iconic Flint Hills landscape, but it doesn't *feel* like a prairie. "Whatever else prairie is," Least Heat-Moon writes of grass, sky, and wind, "it is most of all a paradigm of infinity, a clearing full of many things except boundaries, and its power comes from its apparent limitlessness."[20] As a biological research station, Konza is laced with boundaries, limits, and controls. ("The scientific process has two motives: one is to understand the natural world, the other is to control it," wrote C. P. Snow in his famous *Two Cultures*[21]; the Kansas State University motto reads "Rule by obeying nature's law.") The ecosystem may be preserved, but its spirit is not.

Maybe I'm just overly sensitive, or overly demanding. I know many people—scientists, artists, and outdoor enthusiasts alike—love the place. You don't need designated Wilderness Areas to discover a sense of wildness, to appreciate and love a natural environment, environmental historian William Cronon chides: "Wilderness gets us into trouble only if we imagine that this experience of wonder and otherness is limited to the remote corners of the planet."[22] Indeed, poet Gary Snyder reminds us, "[a] person with a clear heart and open mind can experience the wilderness anywhere on earth. It is a quality of one's own consciousness. The planet is a wild place and always will be."[23]

I must not have a clear heart and open mind, for I couldn't find the wildness; I couldn't appreciate the experience. When I drove the same drive, walked the same trails, the damn loops, each Sunday, past the fences, past the cattle, loop loop loop, I did not free, open, or infinite. I did not feel prairie.

Post-burn puddle

Except.

Memory: Sunday morning, early May. The weather service had issued tornado watches but I went to Konza anyway. Had to get out, go somewhere. The sky had a dark, curious glow; the earth was a dark, lively green. The wind whistled hollowly around my ears, whipping tears from my eyes, whirling through my nose and mouth and lungs. I stumbled along, crouching low to the ground, practically crawling to hold on against the gale. Kept getting blown off the path, off into the grassless prairie. Knew I should turn around, go back to my car, back to my apartment, spend the rest of the day (and spring and year) in town, but wanted to get to the top of the hill (just to the top of the hill!) so I could cling to the stone—the cold flint outcrops, smoothed by exposure to the cold gritty wind—and look out across the black-grey-green, half-burnt, half-budding landscape, just to see.

And there it was—in that storm, from that hill, in that moment before the wind tore my breath away, pause—

Konza.

Interim: In Which I Discover an Island and Fall in Love with a Forest
Tongass National Forest, Alaska

I look upon . . . the rise and fall of beliefs as but
traces left by the four seasons.

—Thirteenth-century Zen teacher Muju Shaseki-shu, *Collection of*
Stone and Sand[24]

This was not supposed to happen. I am a plains person. I like sunshine and bright open skies, not cold, soggy mist that perpetually condenses into rain. I like simplicity and emptiness, not scraggles of moss-draped

cedar lining the banks of limestone fjords. I have spent many years complaining about trees.

I don't know why I applied to be a "Cave Guide" in Southeast Alaska.
Pacific Coast; temperate rainforest; cold, dark, tight, perpetually drippy
cave—I have no idea. I just needed to get away from Konza, even if it
meant being chilled and wet and surely miserable for three months. (Did
I mention that I'm claustrophobic?)

The day I arrived in Ketchikan, it was, as expected, cold and rainy.
Though people talk of orcas and islands in the Inside Passage, I didn't see
much of anything on the ferry ride to Prince of Wales Island; everything
was grey. Not a leaden blanket like the winter skies over the plains, but
an all-around, suspended-in-a-cloud-of-resigned-cheerlessness grey. As
the ferry docked in Hollis, the shore loomed as a dense, dark mass of
green—forest. The first and only bright spot I saw all day was a splash
of yellow—skunk cabbage, my supervisor told me as we drove past a
giant, primeval-looking plant en route to Craig—one of the first things
to bloom in spring.

Rain pattered on the roof all night. When I woke the next morning,
though, I heard the splooshing of fish and squeaking of eagles and smelled
the air bright with the scent of pine. Everything was fresh and alive; I felt
fresh and alive. (And I began to get the sneaking suspicion that I might
like it there.)

My supervisor took me to Thorne Bay—my "base" for the season,
though I'd be spending weekdays living in a trailer a long drive down
muddy logging roads farther northwest. That evening, I joined others for
a bonfire at Sandy Beach, with views of snow-capped peaks rising over
a salty passage. Mergansers paddled smoothly along the shore. While
walking down the gravel road outside town two days later, I saw my first
black bear. The next morning, while hiking up to Water Lake, I saw my
first otter. And, oh!, heard a loon.

A loon! This was not supposed to happen.

Therefore the sage produces without possessing, / Acts without expectations

—Lao Tzu, *Tao Te Ching*[25]

Every morning, I woke in my damp but cozy trailer in the middle of nowhere (the beautiful, wild, peaceful, cold, wet Alaskan nowhere), slipped
on my boots and raincoat, stepped out into the misty air, and crunched
my way up the gravel track that winds through the forest and along the
shore. Some days I felt like walking all the way to the bridge by the main
road, moving quickly to get blood flowing to my fingers and toes. Other
days, I found myself poking along the water's edge, looking for shells and
listening to oysters spit. Sometimes I just stood still, pausing to watch
the fog lift and the world emerge.

After greeting the local heron and otter, I would return to the trailer
to make a pot of coffee and record the previous day's events in the Forest
Service logbook ("Heron," I would write, "otter. One tour, 2 people from
Craig. Rain.") I spent the remainder of each day lurking near the equip-
ment shed, ready to hand visitors a helmet and a headlamp and lead
them up a stairway and into the cave. When the weather was slightly less
drizzly, I strolled up and down the road, perhaps out to a peninsula about
a half-mile away, or around to the dock to watch for orcas. (I only saw
two, all season, but continually harbored hope.) When it was pouring,
I sat huddled in the shed, trying to get my stiff, mittened fingers to turn
the limp pages of Rick Bass's *Book of Yaak* ("This is not really a book.
This is instead an artifact of the woods, like a chunk of rhyolite, a shed
deer antler, a bear skull, a heron feather."[26]), Jim Harrison's *In Search of
Small Gods* ("get to where you're going, then walk like a heron or sandhill
crane"[27]) or the collected notebooks of Robert Frost ("In youth I looked
for flowers / Where now I look for trees"[28]).

At 4 or 5, I locked up the shed, tried to radio in to Thorne Bay to let
them know all was well, wolfed down a quick dinner, then headed out for
an evening walk, straying much farther at the end of the day—5 miles, 8,

10, sometimes not returning until well after the mottled grey of evening had begun transitioning to the opaque black of night. I hiked up old logging roads to fields of ghostly white stumps, out to mossy muskegs laced with small standing pools and ribbons of water, or along the rocky, weedy shore. Everywhere I went, there were signs of people—bottles, cans, tires, wire, not to mention the stumps and the roads themselves—but somehow that didn't matter. There were no other people out there with me then. Traces of use and abuse had begun to weather and the green of the forest had begun to reassert itself. It rained and rained and rained. I was happy.

Several times a day, I walked out to greet what I came to claim as my little island—a few rocks and a few trees that rose out of the water about ten yards away from the peninsula just down the road. I would bow "good morning" to it as the sky filled with a light grey-pink, wave "hello!" during the noon downpour, sing "good afternoon" as I headed out after dinner, and whisper "good night" into the darkness upon my return. My island. I saw it in the rain, in the sun, between clouds that caught on the crags and swirled along the shore. I saw it from the peninsula, from the mainland, from a little delta a mile or so east. I saw it populated with seagulls, with an eagle, alone. And, on the rare occasions when the moon's rhythm and my routine coincided, I could actually walk out to it across a slender isthmus that snaked from the main peninsula to the nameless knob at low tide. All I had to do was be there at the right time, tromp through green flats of glasswort, squish and squeak across slippery beds of kelp, and there I would be—a few rocks, a few trees, and me, floating together in the wild, misty world.

I never did figure out how to watch the tides, though. More than once, I became so engrossed in exploring my little island—crawling around on my hands and knees looking at moss, circling round and round the circumference, or just sitting on the outcrops, staring across the water, listening to loons—that I lost track of time and forgot to watch as the water rose back up. I would then have to wade through the cold, salty tide, ankle- or knee-deep in reality. (The mythic return.)

What does it matter? What does this have to do with the plains?

I can't praise the plains without admitting that I fell in love with a forest. I can't celebrate the steppe without dreaming of the seashore—the tides; the shells; a little island barely separated from a much bigger island along the rain-soaked, fjord-ridden, cedar-scented, grey-green coast of Southeast Alaska. There were thimbleberries! And fireweed! And fog! How could I *not* love it?

(Remember, *remember: anyone* can love the forest; it takes *soul* to love the prairie.)

(What does that mean?)

There was a wildlife biologist in Thorne Bay—an outdoorsman who taught me the names of the ferns and the routes to the peaks. On weekends, when I drove back into town and tried to remember how to carry on a conversation, we became entangled in conversations about the value of different landscapes. Put simply: he likes mountains; I like plains. He couldn't understand why I'm drawn to "flat, boring" (empty, desolate, et cetera, et cetera) space, and I can't understand how he could discriminate against any wild place. "I like mountains, too," I would insist (weakly), "and woods and lakes and all wild places." It did no good to cite Roderick Nash or William Cronon; Snyder, Leopold, Thoreau; any tomes tracing the evolution of Euro-American landscape perception. It did no good to remind him that I'd enjoyed splashing in lakes in Western New York, tromping through autumn woods in New England, and climbing mountains in Wyoming, or that I'd absolutely fallen in love with the forest, the ocean, my little island up there. ("Love"—a useless word, like saying the ocean was wet or the forest alive.) It did no good to show him photos, tell stories, insist over and over again that there's *something* wonderful

and entrancing about every wild open space—even plains! *Especially*
plains!—if he'd just give them a chance?

"Maybe," I struggled to articulate the mystique of grasslands, "it's that
you can't just hike through them or drive over them. There are no peaks
to 'conquer,' no panoramas to 'take.' You just have to be there. Wander.
Pause and look—*really* look, look hard, look long, get on your hands and
knees and crawl, sit, wait—or you won't get it. The smell of the sage, the
feel of the wind, the sound of the meadowlark—you have to experience
more than just the view. You have to like to walk, breathe, and *live* surrounded by space, not just look at calendar scenery or dash out on a hike
and drive back into town."

(Unspoken: "It takes *soul*.")

"Hmm," the unconvinced response.

Even while trying to champion the prairie aesthetic (and figure out what,
exactly, that means), I struggled to understand why I didn't like Konza;
why I hated it, even. Tallgrass Prairie, Preserved! I *should* love it, I *had*
to love it, I had *tried* to love it.

Oh good god, and I had to go back.

It was a great year for berries. Between stretches of rain, the sun peeked
through the clouds often enough to encourage riotous growth. Within a
few weeks of moving up to the cave, I encountered my first salmonberries—large, seedy, still a little tart, but delicious. Huckleberries started
ripening not long after that; the deer and I learned to tolerate one another's presence in the best patches. Ah, then the thick brush alongside
the road began sprouting soft, red thimbleberries. I had never eaten a
thimbleberry before, but as soon as I tasted one, I left the *Vaccinium* alone
and proceeded to graze my way through riots of *Rubus*—thimbleberries
with breakfast, lunch, dinner, dessert. I picked cupfuls and let them
mush into a sort of jam; I added them to pancakes, oatmeal, ice cream;

I ate them straight off the bushes, warm with sunshine or dripping with rain. "I'm stocking up," I excused myself for overindulging on their rich, velvety tang and staining my fingers and palms red; "I have to eat all I can this summer, here, now."

I gorged on the spoils of summer knowing that, come winter, I would be hungry—hungry for the taste of berries, hungry for the cries of birds and gruffs of bears, the rain pattering on my hood and seeping through the shoulders of my coat. Hungry for the freedom to walk. I had to stock up on enough wildness to sustain me upon my return to the buildings, sidewalks, and streetlamps in Kansas; I knew that even if I could find a pint of blueberries to pick up at the grocery store there, it would leave me hungry.

I began to accumulate shells, rocks, pieces of driftwood, curlings of bark—more permanent mementos. (Mementos: memories, moments, me.) They found their way into my palms and my pockets; they quietly followed me home.

I have always been a rock-collector, a gatherer of hard, cool things. Although I like river rocks best—I savor the feel of water-smoothed cobbles rolling neatly between my fingers—any rock will do if it catches my fancy or calls out "pick *me!* Take *me! I'll* help you remember this place, this moment." The same thing for driftwood, for bones, leaves, pinecones, deer antlers—some items simply seem pretty, others important; all add weight to my experiences in wild places. (But not wild*ernes*ses—no collecting in parks, preserves, or biological research stations. The ranger in me adheres fanatically to that rule.) Something about what I was gathering in Alaska, though—molluscs, twigs, white grey bluish brownish stones—was different. I wasn't gathering them for the innocent thrill of the discovery—the "aha!" I feel when I found small beauties. (Annie Dillard: "I cherish mental images I have of three perfectly happy people. One collects stones. Another . . . watches clouds. The third lives on a coast and collects drops of seawater"[29]). Rather, I began to feel as though I *needed* them. I couldn't take clouds and I couldn't take drops of seawater; I could take photos, but pixels have no weight, no depth, no reality. I had to take rocks so that they could remind me that this place was *real*, that I was there. It was a desperate sort of happy.

> Which is more painful, gain or loss?
> Therefore we always pay a great price for excessive love. / And suffer deep loss for great accumulation
> —Lao Tzu, *Tao Te Ching*[30]

Wildness, I decided; it's a matter of wildness. Once I had learned to wander freely, there was no going back. Up in Alaska, I could dash off anywhere I pleased almost anytime. No one was there to judge me; no one to think me crazy for slipping out of bed in the middle of the night and returning sopping wet. No one to ask why I greeted islands and lamented with loons. It was so *easy* to love that place—that place of peacefulness, of serenity, of mist with a little magic stirred in; so *easy* to love that place of heron, of otter, of sweet wild strawberries and salmon jumping sploosh from the water.

It was *too* easy. I could just sit and let the beauty roll over me, soft and grey and cool. My feet were perpetually wet; my pockets full of wonders. Every day, I wanted to drift off into the water or nestle into a crook of cedar; wind my toes into the rock or my fingers up into the clouds—the low grey clouds.

But Konza? Kansas? There, I was as fenced in as the bison, as regulated as the burn.

And yet, I began to realize (still searching for soul), there was always the sun. And the wind. The weather. Fences, trails, and signs can't trammel the sky.

Maybe that's what it was? Plains are *exposed*! It's all about the *sky*! I *like* to feel exposed, to see the sky! I like to know I'm *alive*. Rocks, shells, trees—these things remind me the world is real; clouds, wind, birds—these things remind me *I* am real. Cold, wet; sunburned, surprised . . . *alive.*

"That's why I'm always out walking," I tried to explain to the wildlife biologist once, "because I don't want to miss anything." Mist!, I meant, Rain! Sunlight dripping off boughs, salmon spawning up creeks. Eagles! Bears! The bright fat moon! "And that's why I like living on the plains," I continued, "It makes me feel alive *all the time.* I don't have to scale a mountain or apply for a backpacking permit; I can step out my back door and be in the middle of it all." Air!, I meant, Light! Dust whirling down dry washes and grasses rippling before dawn. Ravens. Coyotes. The bright fat moon.

Unsaid: Don't you see, don't you see? I fall in love with wild places, with their rocks and their plants and their animals and their skies, with their cycles and their moods. Some people develop a sense of place or are drawn to a particular type of landscape; others fall into and out of relationships with friends, family, lovers. I am one for wild places. I carry them with me. They become part of me.

Before that summer, I believed that, like Terry Tempest Williams, I "belong[ed] to a particular landscape . . . [that it] inform[ed] who [I am], carrie[d my] history, [my] dreams"[31]—the Painted Desert was, like Abbey's Arches, my ideal place, my one true home. [32]I thought that, to borrow a phrase from Tuan, the plains were "my geographical double—the objective correlative of the sort of human being I am when the shallow, social layers are stripped away."[33] I am part sandstone in Angels Garden!, I wanted to tell the biologist, part mud in Lithodendron Wash! I am the smell of sage, the moment of sunrise, an old dead juniper winding up toward the stars. Semi-desert sagebrush steppe is what I breathe, what I dream.

But then I breathed in mist swirling through the forest and along the shore. I became part cedar, part otter. I became an island off the coast of a larger island—a few rocks, a few trees, a few birds sometimes there, sometimes not.

"We cannot choose the past or the places that create us any more than we can choose our biological grandparents, our genetic heritage," John Price reminds us in *Not Just Any Land*.[34] When the time came, I gathered up all of my rocks and shells and sweeps of driftwood, put them in a box, and mailed them back to Kansas. I set off on my last walk, bid the birds and the bears farewell, and, finally, sat out by my island, letting waves of

My little island, off the coast of a larger island off the coast of southeast Alaska

sadness and desire—a sense of rootedness, of belonging and longing—wash over me, then pass. The mist swirled around me. I inhaled deeply, deeply, let the cool rich air permeate the space in all of my cells, pause. Then I exhaled. I left.

In time, I knew, I would see and maybe fall in love with another place. Meanwhile, in Alaska, salmon would stop spawning and bear would stop eating. Nights would get longer and wind colder. Snow would fall. The rocks, the trees, the islands, and the paths would be buried in white. In spring, the rain would fall and the snow would melt. Rivulets would run into rivers then into the channel and into the sea. Skunk cabbage would bloom. The little island will be there, even when the heron and I are gone.

3.2 Conversations with Konza
Konza Prairie Preserve, Kansas

"Ask me why a person should walk cross-country."
"Tell me."
"It frees you from wanting to own it. It liberates you."

—the Venerable Tashmoo, quoted in
William Least Heat-Moon's *PrairyErth*[35]

The first Sunday in October featured a leaden sky rent by bitter wind; rumors of snow swirled in the air. Perfect. I zipped on a jacket, laced up my boots, and drove out to Konza Prairie Preserve, curious (and, admittedly, somewhat anxious) to see how I would react. *I will not compare, I will not complain,* I told myself, trying to internalize lessons the rainforest had taught me, *I will not demand wilderness. Instead I will celebrate wildness, whatever little happinesses I can find.*

When I stepped out of my car, I breathed in the fresh air, delighted to have a place to walk. "You can't walk unconsciously for long," William

Least Heat-Moon's friend the Venerable Tashmoo attests, "things thrust themselves right into your ears, up your nose. When you're on foot, life vibrates."[134] Walking, I thought, who cares if I have to follow a path? I'm moving at my own pace, saying hello to the crows and the grass and the wind tearing sprinkles from the sky. Who cares if I'm not allowed to head cross-country, dip into the woody ravines, climb along the flinty ridges, or lie down in the middle of a field and watch the clouds dance? Walking! At least there is a place to walk, this little patch of tallgrass prairie nestled in the otherwise privatized hills.

It felt comfortable to greet familiar places, old friends. The path led me back to the spots where I saw the deer, the birds, and the burn, each loop full of memories. Oh!, I realized with delight, grass in the burned area had grown back just as tall. Oh! The mailbox, how could I ever have missed that? Oh! That old tree, this old ridge, oh! Wind and rain, path crunching underfoot. Crunch.

Instead of reaching a soothing rhythm, the crunching started to grate on my mind. Fences and signs commanded my attention and crowded my thoughts. Don't go here. Don't do that. Somewhere out around the back loop, sadness—hatred almost; ambivalence—again began to throb. Although I enjoyed the pure sensation of walking out under the big grey prairie sky, I couldn't appreciate the Biological Research Station as a place, no matter what aesthetic experience it afforded. By the time I got back to the bridge (no bouncing), I felt so alienated and so lonely that I swore I would never return.

Konza. Was that really all I had? Was that really all I could do?

(*No expectations,* remember; *no demands. Soul.*)

Take Two. Halloween. The sun was shining, wind whooshing, crickets chirping and turkeys glarbeling, what was I to do? Konza. I went and sat. Drove all the way out there, hiked out on the trail, one mile, two, then plunked down in the middle of the dry, rocky four-point-four trail and stared at the ground. Konza. I gave up trying to challenge the prairie (*Hey, Konza, show me something new! Amaze me! Tell me why I should care*) and sank into a disinterested, disengaged reverie. Thoughtless. Empty, hopeless, demandless.

If you sit anywhere long enough, though, something is bound to happen. That day, it came in the form a grasshopper. Insects had been chirping all morning, but weren't more than ambient effect to me until a little brown something leaped into sight. It balanced on a blade of dry, rustly grass and stared at me. I stared at it. An hour later, I was still crawling around on my hands and knees in an attempt to photograph grasshoppers. Big blue skies overhead, sun rippling through the bluestem all around; somewhere turkeys, somewhere cows, somewhere traffic, talk, a bright beautiful world, and I was living through the macro lens on my camera.

Konza?

Celastrina (neglecta?) – an azure butterfly, one of the prairie's little wonders

Konza. No more pretending to make sense of experience, no more attempts to fit sensations and perceptions into theories. I am none the wiser. Yes, John Fraser Hart, I am one of those geographers who "thoroughly enjoy the thrill of exploration and discovery." I too

> derive great pleasure and aesthetic satisfaction from wandering down narrow roads and lanes, stumbling across the countryside, bashing through underbrush, tearing [my] clothes on barbed wire fences, skirting pastures where bulls are grazing, talking to farmers, finding vantage points that command superb views across the land, having the wind and the rain in [my] hair, and communing with nature.[36]

All I want, Konza, is great pleasure and aesthetic satisfaction. I won't slip under fences or skirt pastures, but at least at least I can have the wind and rain in my hair? Konza?

Mid-November. After a soft, sunny Indian summer, autumn decided to return—cold, windy, sprinkles of rain on the roof and rumors of snow on the radio. I zipped up my fleece, added an extra pair of socks, pulled on my mitten-capped-gloves, and headed to out to Konza. It was still early when I got there (and cold and wet), so I was surprised to see another car in the parking lot. I felt an instant camaraderie with whatever other intrepid soul and/or desperate fool had come to trod the trail.

For whatever reason, I decided to loop counter-clockwise, taking the right-hand fork in the path with a delicious sense of spontaneity. (Little things). What did I see? Well, sparrows, deer, trees, path—same old same old, no? No, completely different views. I was so excited to see a particular tree— really see it, from a whole new angle, with a single branch stretched out to hold the horizon—that I completely forgot to turn onto the first loop. I didn't realize it until a mile later, when my fingers were stiff and purpley-blue and I was beginning to wonder why the route seemed longer from this direction. (You'd think I'd have been able to manage not to get lost. Three trails, for goodness' sake.) (Then again, I wouldn't have felt lost at all if I had been wandering freely, fully engaged in the landscape.)

Meanwhile, I crossed paths with the other hiker. It turned out that he was not a hiker at all, but some spandex-clad, ear-bud-equipped jogger. I think he saw me first, as I was flapping my mitten-tops in a ridiculous attempt to get blood circulating through my fingers. I blushed as he passed, embarrassed to think I must have resembled a turkey shaking its feathers. Oh. (That's why I prefer to have places to myself: I can flap my arms or clap my hands, sing and dance and crawl around and hunt for crickets without worrying about looking like an idiot. The birds and the grasses and the stones either understand or don't care.)

Later, though, after I'd found the turn for the second loop, climbed the big hill up to the grassy ridge / fenceline, and been refreshed by a little burst of rain, I encountered another person—a red-cheeked, grey-haired, flannel-wearing and hiking-stick-bearing man who was clearly delighted to be out in the inclement weather too. We smiled at one another and murmured something to the effect of "great day to be out, eh?" before continuing onward.

Onward. It *was* a great day to be out. Konza.

Late November, on another sunny day (prairie weather in autumn is as fickle as my moods), I went "backwards" again, winding alongside the wooded creek and saving the prairie for later. That way, I realized, rather than start off eager and inspired only to lose interest and have to plod through the last few miles, I would get to warm up my legs and mind a little before walking out onto (into?) the cool bright gusty landscape. It seemed to work—when I got out of the woods and climbed to the top of the back ridge, I was rewarded with views of grass, sky, sun, mmmm, clouds and grasshoppers and . . . a fence. Cattle.

Mooless Konza cattle

My first encounter with the cattle, a few weeks earlier, had been a bit surreal: they'd been mooing merrily away until they saw or sensed me approaching, at which point they stopped mooing, stopped eating, and just stood there, cows in a field. Silent. Staring.

This week, though, they ignored me and continued to happily munch away at the forbs by the fence. Did they recognize me as an old friend?

After I'd nodded hello and begun to continue on my way, I heard a nonchalant "mooooo" emanating from the bushes and grasses alongside the trail. Umm? There it was—a rogue cow! (I don't know why "rogue" sprang to mind, but it was free, defying the fence, feasting on the ungrazed vegetation. Hooray for the audacity of the rogue cow!) I couldn't help but attribute some sort of symbolism to the scene—a tamed beast yearning to be free! The streak of wildness that lurks in all living creatures!

When I got back to the bridge by the beginning/end of the trail, however, my pleasant walk was interrupted by a family standing down by the creek bed, throwing rocks into the water. Dad, kids, mom watching from above—how that annoyed me! They weren't rogues; they were rule-breakers, sign-ignorers. "Stream monitoring project," I wanted to point out, "Please stay on trail." Please return to the trail, I wanted to tell them. (Oh how I wanted to splash in the water too.)

Is it the same instinct as that of the rogue cow?, I wondered, a primeval turn toward wildness, delight? Do layers of culture inhibit deeper, rawer appreciation of natural places?

No conclusions. Just Konza. Trails, signs, rules. Experiments. Experience.

Two weeks later, it was cold. Cold and grey. I didn't really want to drive anywhere, but had been sitting in town for too long and needed some fresh air. Besides, there'd been a blizzard mid-week and I was curious to see Konza in winter. (Real winter—none of that sunshine-and-blue sky nonsense that Kansas gets in January. *Winter.* Cold and grey.)

The prairie in winter, then—aside from being cold and grey, it was icy. Most of the path was glazed over; I had to concentrate on where and how I stepped, sometimes boot-shuffling across slippery patches. Someone had been out skiing and someone else snowshoeing, though both activities are against the rules. *I should be skiing right now,* I thought, as I slid cautiously across the ice, *swooshing through the tall grass and across that big horizon. I should* have been out skiing, skiing away from a comfortable little apartment and a nondescript little micropolis; away from a computer

Trail in winter

and a tired, tamed lifestyle. I should have been out somewhere between white earth and white sky, breathe. No skiing at Konza.

Konza did have something to offer that day, though. The cold grey wintry prairie was a study in noises. Not so much landscapes—the snow had decided to sublime; a thick mist hovered in every hollow, mystery, beauty—but soundscapes abounded: Twinklings of grass! (The breeze was relatively calm, but if I paused and listened carefully, I swear I could hear frost-coated blades tinging together—acres and acres of tiny windchimes.) Tweeterings of robins! (I think every red-breasted little bird in the state had decided to come to Konza to sing of the snow; the air vibrated with notes and wingflaps, joy.) And, of course, my own breathing and crunching. *Real* crunches—loud crunches—not gravely or sidewalk-style crunches, but cold crystal-breaking crunches. I huffed and puffed and crunched around to the first loop, then skipped and hopped and twirled and stomped—Cr-crunch! Crunchcrunchcrunch! Crrrrrrrrrunch! CRUNCH!—out across the path. Must have looked silly, sounded silly, but who can resist fresh snow, leaving dizzy tracks all the way down the trail? Besides, there was no one else there. No one else wanted to go to a cold, grey, icy, misty, crunchy prairie. I wasn't disturbing anyone's peacefulness.

Peacefulness. Pause.

So it went: hate, then love; desire, then despair. Autumn, winter, into spring. Sun, then snow; snow, then rain. Grass, cattle, burn. Wind. Always wind. Prairie.

Each time I returned, I had to revise my perceptions—not totally erase and rewrite, but add layers, depth, and dimension. I alternated between exhilaration and abhorrence, making frenetic attempts to understand why I couldn't just enjoy the place. Was it because the Biological Research Station is subject to so many rules and scientific regimes? Because I had to follow the path? Because I had to drive out to the site, turn each Sunday into an expedition rather than simply step out my back door whenever I felt the need to wander? Questions unanswered, unanswerable.

No matter how delightful and stimulating they can be—subtle, rhythmic, secretive—plains cannot simply be seen or visited. I want to live the prairie, to step outside and forever be in the middle of a bright beautiful world. But Konza, Konza—to me, Konza became and always will be a string of separate experiences, historic events. Even though memories and places pooled together, overlapping and intertwining, each walk was separated by a week and nine miles there and back. Each involved a beginning, an end, and a set route (or three) in between. Each involved waking up Sunday morning, checking the weather, lacing on my boots, turning on my car, driving out to the parking lot / trailhead, traipsing through the sun or the wind or the rain, happy until I got to the end of the trail, had to get back in my car, return to town, and unlace my boots.

Life bursting forth after burn

I was a visitor, who did not remain; a questor with a prescribed journey; a novitiate reciting someone else's surpriseless koan.

Finally, one beautiful May day, I left. For good, I hoped. Forever leaving, leaving, but this time—when I left this place—I left nothing of me behind. No soul. I took nothing from it. Let it be.

Grasses grow back; I leave

Fossil Butte, Wyoming

CHAPTER 4

Shortgrass /
Semi-Desert Shrub-Steppe

4.1 The Return to the Plains
Fossil Butte National Monument, Wyoming

He who pursues learning will increase every day; /
He who pursues Tao will decrease every day.

—Lao Tzu, *Tao Te Ching*[1]

I could tell you about how I'd seen the place a year earlier, when traveling through on the way to somewhere from somewhere else, and thought, *hmmm, I could live here.* I could tell you about how circumstances obliged and I moved to southwestern Wyoming—Fossil Butte National Monument—late one spring to start work as a physical science technician (paleontology). I could tell you about the months I spent perched halfway up the side of a tawny bluff, peeling up layers of limestone in search of 52-million-year-old fossil fish, or the hundreds of walks I took up and down old ranching roads and off into the scraggly steppe, looking for wonders. In short, I could review the process of getting to know a place—exploration, exhilaration, familiarity; flowers, marmots, cattle; sunrise, sunset, storms—and *Look*, I could sing, *how beautiful the plains are!*

But by now you know how that goes—the rhythms, the routines, the exclamation points. Seasons changed; people came and went; skies darkened and cleared.

But wait! Something different! Instead of just a single season—a few months of learning and leaving, accumulating more memories and musings, questions without answers—I stayed at Fossil Butte for the winter. Wyoming's semi-desert sagebrush steppe had something to teach me, or rather it swept all expectations and desires away.

Before winter, autumn—that season of remembering and yearning that rises between summer's exuberance and winter's austerity.

Summer ended when I shut down the paleontological quarry and retreated inside to work on interpretive publications. After that came a pronounced emptying: visitation slowed, seasonal employees and interns returned to life elsewhere, and birds flew south, pausing to rest in puddles or stock ponds along the way. Next, a change in routine: by early October, I could no longer cut cross-country to get from living quarters to the office—out my back door, up over a ridge, down into a slight drainage, up a much higher ridge, and down to the spot where the visitor center nestles above Chicken Creek in full view of the butte. Instead, with the sun rising later and setting earlier, I began walking about a mile east down the county road, then another mile northwest up the park road. Though it was farther distance-wise, it was easier to trust the pavement than to trip over brush in the predawn light. (Oh, how well I would come to know every rise and turn of that pavement!—by mid-winter, I could find my way through the cold, crystalline darkness based on nothing but memory and the crunch of snow, ice, or asphalt beneath my boots.) On the weekends, too,

I couldn't go rambling about wherever I pleased, slipping under the fences that separate Fossil Butte from adjoining BLM land. Instead, I had to pay attention to border lines and wear bright orange—hunting season had begun.

In a curious man-made migration pattern, game animals began to flock inside the monument's protective borders as soon as they felt threatened on public land outside. (No exaggeration. Wildlife biologists have been using radio collars to track elk for years; data shows a pronounced movement of herds into Fossil Butte, managed by a "preservation of wild life" policy, around the start of hunting season.) Soon, my morning walks were filled with a new magic, a new timbre: bugling.

There is nothing like the sound of elk bugle. There is no way to describe it. If you have never heard an elk bugle, I'm sorry—try to imagine something hollow, something haunting, something desperate but powerful and primeval; imagine what autumn would sound like if you could distill it to a single sound. If you have heard an elk bugle, I'm happy for you. You know. You remember. John Price describes the experience best: "[It is] not about factual knowledge, not about appreciation or empathy . . ."

> It [is], instead, a moment of crystalline clarity, of cohesion, and yet also a dispersion of self, a negation of consciousness. I was consumed [by my encounter with elk at Wind Cave National Park] . . . [W]hen I try to describe it to others, I not only want to verbalize I want to embody: the shivering fury of the bulls, their urgency, their heat. My voice rises in the telling, I exaggerate, I gesture wildly. I make a fool of myself. And when the conversation moves on to other subjects I want to interrupt and say: "Wait! I've seen the elk—*remember?*"[2]

Remember? Remember the elk? Remember the cranes? The color of cottonwoods, gold in the sun? Autumn is a poignant season, each minute tinged with urgency as well as nostalgia—you know the leaves will

Road alongside Fossil Butte; autumn sky rolling in

fall, the darkness descend, and all you will have left to wield against the emptiness and desolation and depression of winter are the tracings of memories. Happy moments—sunsets, like salmonberries. You struggle to accumulate as many as possible.

But then what do you do with them?

Interim : The Mapmaker's Discipline
Fossil Butte National Monument, Wyoming
and Petrified Forest, Arizona

The writer's discipline lies in steeping oneself in landscape and subject, and then in making oneself present enough for the story to rise, for the words, like things one might find in a landscape, to present themselves.

—Mark Tredinnick, *The Land's Wild Music*[3]

The tao that can be told is not the eternal Tao. /
The name that can be named is not the eternal name.
The unnamable is the eternally real

— Lao Tzu, *Tao Te Ching*[4]

I began to write. As the skies grew cold and grey and the animals readied themselves for winter, I found myself spending long hours sitting and thinking, thinking and writing, writing and walking, trying to bring order and meaning to years of scattered experiences and observations. I wanted to share what I'd seen—wanted others to acknowledge the beauty and complexity of grasslands; wanted others to know what it means to fall in love with a wild, open place; wanted anyone to understand. But I still didn't understand, myself.

Surely each place has taught me something?, I would doodle, stretched out on the porch of my quarters at Fossil Butte, trying to soak in the last few weak rays of autumn sunlight and letting the rumble of passing trains purr in my bones, *Surely life progresses; or does it whirl forever in spirals?*

I had gone back to Petrified Forest National Park. The story was supposed to end there, with the first semi-desert sagebrush steppe that had filled my soul. Having applied for and been accepted to a short position as "Artist-In-Residence," I intended to use my time there to revisit old friends (Pintado Point! The Old Dead Juniper! Yes, even Pilot Rock), explore new territory, take plenty of photographs, and, ultimately, nestle into a little cabin across from the Painted Desert Inn and figure out what, exactly, it was about the place that haunted me; what it had taught me; what I had left to learn.

Technically, I was there to make hand-drawn maps—that's my "specialty," I'd written for the application. Mapping is a good way to figure out your relationship with a place; in choosing what elements to include and how to arrange them, you're forced to decide what locations are most important and what memories are most meaningful: what is "home"? What is "horizon"? Where, exactly, does the sun rise and set?

I was fairly pleased with the results. The Painted Desert was just as wild and wonderful as I'd remembered—the skies just as big, the colors just as rich. Within a few days, I discovered new washes, new glyphs, and new bones. I relocated the solstice marker and resummitted Pilot Rock. (I got entirely, unsurprisingly, happily lost on the way back.) In short, I recalibrated to the place and reaffirmed my relationship with it. I was ready to map it.

But then, when my residency was up and I returned to Wyoming, I found myself struggling to articulate my experiences. How was I supposed to describe the color of the air or smell of the rain or the sound a hawk's wings makes as it glides by? Who cares what it feels like to sit alone at Puerco Pueblo or stand scared on Chinde Mesa? More importantly, why had I left? And what was I seeking, that I had not found again at Badlands or Konza? Once again, I was consumed by what Zen sages refer to as "word-drunkenness" and "mind wandering." Sitting and thinking, thinking and writing did no good; adjectives, adverbs, and academic theories all failed me.

"The more I write about [a place]," warns Paul Gruchow, "the less I [can] remember of it. To write about something is to take leave of it."[5] His method, when he has written himself away from a place, is to take a break—step back out in the real world, explore, and feel.

"So I went down to the waters of one of the springs that feeds it," he explains an attempt to recover his sense of a lake, "expecting to find some sign of fresh life to color over my own grayness." Ah, but what happened then? "As I was standing there," he learned, "the bank of snow gave way, and I was plunged in . . .

"It was not the thing I had imagined I might find."

Late one afternoon—one of those restless, can't-concentrate-can't-function-can't-for-the-life-of-me-sit-still afternoons in which mid-October specializes—I went looking for inspiration, for insight, for yet another good, long walk. It had been, for the most part, an unremarkable day. When I'd stepped out that morning, a bright, crisp hunter's moon cast the landscape in sharp shades of black and white, à la Ansel Adams; a few clouds danced around Orion and a few more lurked on the eastern horizon, ready to absorb the sun as it rose. By noon, vapor stretched gauzily across the upper atmosphere, leaving the sky a flimsy, filtered blue. A cold front began lumbering through mid-afternoon, bringing with it a low, lumpy blanket of clouds and a heavy, palpable exhaustion. The earth was turning over, tucking in, tired and ready for winter.

I needed to get away from the table and computer and mug half-full of cold coffee, so headed out down the road to the east, toward the butte. Wrapped entirely in my own thoughts (or entirely empty of thoughts), I walked without noticing the color of the sky (grey), the temperature of the air (grey), the skitterings of little animals (grey, grey, all grey). Finally, I decided I'd gone far enough, wasn't going anywhere, wasn't fully engaged anyway, so turned for home. In so doing, I caught a whiff of something on the wind. Something new. On the way out, the wind had been at my back, broken by my tight coat and flapping hood, but when I turned, the taste of the air filled my nose and mouth. What *was* that smell? More sharp than dull, bitter than sweet. Not rain, not snow. Nor sage, aspen, sunlight; frost, dirt, rock—nothing that I knew. It struck me, though—stopped me in my tracks. As I stood and struggled to identify it or at least describe it, something by the side of the road caught my eye—something small, round, dull grey with splotches of russet . . . a rock!

I picked it up, heavy and cold and smooth. It fit perfectly in my palm, that rock. My rock. My autumn rock, my shrub-steppe rock; my hold-in-my-hand-feel-the-weight-of-the-world rock.

I know that, like Edward Abbey, I cannot fit the plains into a book "any more than a fisherman can haul up the sea with his net."[6] But, unlike Abbey, who had to throw a stone at a rabbit in order to feel a part of the wildness around him, I decided to hold on to my rock. With it heavy in my hand or pocket, I thought, or sitting quiet and grey by my side, maybe I would be able to write something that read less like a book and, to reword Rick Bass, more like an artifact of the plains, "like a chunk of rhyolite, a shed [elk] antler, a [coyote] skull, a [raven] feather."[7]

I sat and thought, thought and walked, walked and turned over my rock in my hand. While I did so, the earth kept whirling around its orbit, tilting me away from the sun. The rain outside turned to snow; land and sky were erased. Icy banks accumulated and I was plunged in.

Winter. It was not the thing I had imagined I might find.

The first blizzard sweeps in, with 30 mph winds, dangerously bitter temperatures, and breathtakingly beautiful skies

4.2: Winter
Fossil Butte National Monument, Wyoming

You can only make yourself present...
watch earnestly, listen attentively...
[I]n due time, perhaps, you will absorb something of the land.
What you absorb will eventually change you.
This change is the only real measure of a place.

— Paul Gruchow, *Journal of a Prairie Year*[8]

In Zen practice, Buddhists strive for Enlightenment—an end to desire; freedom from want; clarity, lightness, and bliss. True Bodhisattvas achieve *satori*—a state of deep understanding and compassion, marked by full engagement in the present moment and harmony between the external and internal worlds. On the path to Enlightenment, novices may momentarily experience what is referred to as *kensho*—a glimpse of Beauty or Truth, when, in the words of Nyogen Senzaki and Paul Reps, "[i]n a flashing moment something opens. You are new all through. You see the same unsame world with new fresh eyes."[9] Western aesthetes might use the term "epiphany," or refer to the same phenomenon simply as an "oh!-" or "aha!-" moment—that euphoria-filled, adrenaline-laced flash of surprise and delight in which an individual feels connected with the universe. Remember sunrise and sunset at Petrified Forest?

Ah, but then there's winter. Winter, you see, winter on the plains.

If you listen carefully enough to the bitter winter wind blowing across the prairie, you can, as Willa Cather promises, hear it singing out, "'[t]his is reality, whether you like it or not. All those frivolities of summer, the light and shadow, the living mask of green that trembled over everything, they were lies, and this is what was underneath. This is the truth.'"[10]

Winter comes to Fossil Butte

Truth. The truth is wind, the truth is cold. The truth is emptiness, exposure, disorientation, fear. So too is it sparkle, delight, sharp bright sunshine; a thousand shades of white. Winter, Aldo Leopold knows, excels in purity and simplicity; the rest of the year, then, is "a geometric progression in the abundance of distractions."[11]

Simple, unabashed, raw—you can pay attention to every crystalline detail. Open, extreme, unrelenting—you must admit your own vulnerability. As Barry Lopez observed in the Arctic, vulnerability, in turn, begets intimacy.[12] Full exposure, as the Venerable Tashmoo explains the experience to William Least Heat-Moon, makes a person feel "insignificant, but never nonexistent: my point is that [you feel] *more* existent."[13] You find yourself shedding frivolities, intentions, expectations; you have to open yourself up to the world, proceed nakedly, palms open, eyes wide. You have to feel the loneliness, the longing, the fear, the cold. It may hurt to inhale.

Dawn at -5 degrees; air raw with light

Ah, then exhale, winter scours your soul, sweeps it clean, leaves it as sparkling white as a snow-covered field. Empty of desire, you realize that, through your years of wandering and wanting, *this* is what you sought.

Winter. You can feel the sun before it rises. It gets cold, colder, coldest, until your eyelashes freeze and breathing burns and you fear that the stars will shatter and fall from the sky. (Sometimes they do, cutting sharp, bright streaks across the pre-dawn darkness.) Then you begin to sense a flush to the east—a pinkishness, a pale rose, maybe champagne; all the color you'll get that day. Eventually you realize you can *see* your breath, you can see! You must be breathing! It must be day! Coyote howl.

Winter. Know, as does Rick Bass, that "it's going to snow, whether you want it to or not. And it's going to be beautiful, whether you want it to snow hard or not."[14] You can feel the snow before it falls, as if the sky is aching to expand, divide, and drift to earth. If the wind's howling (which it likely is), you know when the first flakes go tearing by that millions more will be quick to follow; you'll soon be swept up a maelstrom of crystals—snow in your eyes, your ears, your nose, on your tongue, sharp, stinging, real. If, somehow, the air has fallen still, then you can watch sparkles float down; listen as they come to rest on the rocks, on the sage, on the coats of the jackrabbits, now silvery-white.

Sparkling world of snow, sky, and rabbit

Winter. You can feel the blizzard before it hits. A peculiar silence descends—the atmosphere inhaling—and everything stands still, watching, waiting; rabbits' ears twitch and birds call nervously, fluffing their feathers and huddling together for warmth. Then, *wham!* A wall of wind—a three-day long howl of wind and ice and wind and snow and wind and your power goes out and you clutch your empty mug and you feel vulnerable and alone and truly afraid then, there, in that darkness, with that wind, afraid that wolves may come to carry you away.

Then, too, you can feel when the storm is ready to end, when it has grown sad, weary, ready to move on. Its cry takes on a different tone, a different timbre and you wake in the night, aware of the imminent calm. You know that when you step outside—the first fresh air in days!—the

Post-blizzard stillness

world will be shimmering, draped in blue-white drifts. You will believe, like Paul Gruchow, that "[t]here [is] something of bliss in this stillness, and something ominous in it too. It [is] the kind of stillness that beckons us to turn inward, toward the beginnings of our existence."[15]

Winter. You can feel the trains before they rumble by, rectangles of red so bright that you're startled to remember that the world has color. (Barry Lopez knows, "[t]he browns and blacks and whites [are] so rich [you can] feel them. The beauty here is a beauty you feel in your flesh. You feel it physically, and that is why it is sometimes terrifying to approach. Other beauty takes only the heart, or the mind."[16]) You can feel the moose bedding down beneath the aspen, and plan to curl into the depressions they've left in the snow. (Rick Bass: "[W]e become tempered to the very shape of the land itself . . . our bellies spooned against each curve and hummock of soil, each swell of stone, and the snow above pressing down, kneading and pressing and sculpting us physically."[17]) You can feel the crest of the hill as you huff up and anticipate the whoosh of the skis as you glide back down. You can feel the hollowness of the drifts and fear you will fall into the creek. You know that whenever you step out your door, your fingers will turn purple and your nose will freeze; you will see the hoofprints of pronghorn, the hoppings of rabbits, the twitterings of birds. You will add your happy, crooked bootprints, then return home, wrap your fingers around a warm mug of hot chocolate, and dream of the world out there.

Early one morning, deep into winter, long before dawn, while I was trudging up to the visitor center through sculpted drifts of snow and across invisible patches of ice, I had a sudden realization or a brief glimpse of enlightenment—*kensho*, aha! Looking out over the moon-lit landscape, I kept thinking, *what am I supposed to* do *with all of this beauty*? This smooth, cold, white, bright beauty? This sparkling, glimmering, laughing,

Train cutting through the late morning canvas

crying beauty? This full, clean, pure, true beauty? *It's too much*, I wanted to burst, *I can feel it, it hurts, I ache, may I* always always *walk in such beauty. In beauty may I walk.*

Oh, then, I gasped, sending a little puff of breath out to freeze and fall from the air, *in beauty may I walk!* It is not a hope or a demand; it's not just needing a beautiful place in which to walk. "In beauty may I walk" is "may I walk in beauty"—with beauty, in a beautiful manner. May I learn from the land and honor it in my walking, my being. May I walk with the wild, open wisdom of winter on the plains.

Zen

A Brief Meditation on Expectation and Emptiness

I discovered that it is necessary, absolutely necessary, to believe in nothing.

—Shunryu Suzuki Roshi, speaking of his Zen training[1]

Let the snow fall. Let it cleanse all color, leaving the world sparkling in shades of white. Let it erase all texture, burying the bluestem, burying the sage, burying the rocks the ridges, leaving all swept smooth. Let it negate forms, inverting the play of light and dark, the sense of near and far, any idea of self and shadow. Finally, let it remove lines. No more fences, no more roads, even that horizon—gone, meaningless. No difference between the land and the sky.

Then there is space. Space there in the wide white world. Not emptiness, nor a lack of things, much less a memory of what was once there and desire for what could be. No, in that space, there's a rich possibility, an anything, an everything.

Within that space, pause.

Breathe.

Feel.

Zen of the Plains.

Endnotes

Notes to Prologue

1. Whitman, Walt. 1892. *Specimen Days*. Philadelphia: David McKay.
2. Cather, Willa. 1918. *My Ántonia*. Boston: Houghton Mifflin.
3. Childs, Craig. 2002. *Soul of Nowhere*. Seattle: Sasquatch Books.
4. Scanlan, Tom. 1990. "The Prairie as Perennial Symbol." *Proceedings of the Twelfth North American Prairie Conference*, eds. Daryl D. Smith and Carol A Jacobs, 201–204. Cedar Falls: University of Northern Iowa. See also Kinsey, Joni L. 1995. "Not So Plain—Art of the American Prairies." *Great Plains Quarterly* 15 (3): 185–200. Kinsey, Joni L., R. Roberts, and R. Sayr. 1996. "Prairie Prospects: The Aesthetics of Plainness." *Prospects* 21: 261–297.
5. Bailey, Robert G. 1983. "Delineation of Ecosystem Regions." *Environmental Management* 7(4):365–373. ––––. 1980. "Ecoregions of the United States." Washington, D.C.: USDA Forest Service Miscellaneous Publication No. 1391. Accessed 09 November 2011. http://www.fs.fed.us/land/ecosysmgmt/index. html. The Nature Conservancy. 2011. "Grasslands and Prairies." Accessed 3 November 2011. http://www.nature.org/ourinitiatives/habitats/grasslands/index.htm ––––. 2008. "Grassland Types of the Great Plains [Map]." Minneapolis: Central Division GIS Lab. Accessed 9 November 2011. http://dsc.discovery. com/earth/im–interview/grasslands–map–pg.html
6. Rossum, Sonja and Stephen Lavin. 2000. "Where Are the Great Plains? A Cartographic Analysis." *Professional Geographer* 52 (3): 543–552. See also Sheppard, Jerry G. 1995. *Singing out of Tune: Cultural Perceptions and National Park History on the American Great Plains*. PhD diss., Texas Tech University.
7. Quoted in Norris, Kathleen. 1993. *Dakota: A Spiritual Geography*. New York: Houghton Mifflin. See also: "Scottsbluff National Monument." Accessed 29 September 2011. http://www.nps.gov/scot/index.htm ––––. 2005. *Oregon Trail National Historic Trail* bulletin.
8. Quoted in Retzinger, Jean 1998. "Framing the Tourist Gaze: Railway Journeys across Nebraska 1866–1906." *Great Plains Quarterly* 18 (3): 213–226. See also Wycoff, William and Lary M. Dilsaver. 1997. "Promotional Imagery of Glacier

National Park." *The Geographical Review* 87 (1): 1–26. Shaffer, M. S. 1996. "See America First: Re-Envisioning Nation and Region through Western Tourism." *Pacific Historical Review* 65 (4): 559–581.

9. Retzinger 1998. See above.

10. Norris 1993. See above.

11. Evernden, Neil. 1983. "Beauty and Nothingness: Prairie as Failed Resource." *Landscape* 23 (3): 1–9.

12. Leopold, Aldo. 1966. *A Sand County Almanac: With Essays on Conservation from Round River.* New York: Ballantine Books. See also Callicott, J. Baird. 1984. "The Land Aesthetic." *Orion Nature Quarterly* 3: 16–22. Saito, Yuriko. 1998. "The Aesthetics of Unscenic Nature." *The Journal of Aesthetics and Art Criticism* 56(2): 101–111.

13. Blake, Kevin. 2006. "First View." *Trail & Timberline Quarterly* 993: 10–12.

Notes to Chapter 1: Shortgrass / Semi–Desert Shrub–Steppe

1. Reps, Paul and Nyogen Senzaki, eds. 1957 (1985). *Zen Flesh Zen Bones: A Collection of Zen and Pre–Zen Writings.* Rutland: Tuttle Publishing.

2. National Park Service. 2011. "Petrified Forest National Park." Accessed 29 September 2011. http://www.nps.gov/pefo/index.htm

3. Wright, John K. 1947. "Terrae Incognitae: The Place of the Imagination in Geography." *Annals of the Association of American Geographers* 37(1): 1–16.

4. Bunkše, Edmunds V. 2007. "Feeling is Believing, or Landscape as a Way of Being in the World." *Geografiska Annaler* 89B (3): 219–231.

5. Lopez, Barry. 1986 (1987). *Arctic Dreams: Imagination and Desire in a Northern Landscape.* New York: Bantam Books.

6. Souman, Jan L., Ilja Frissen, Manish N. Sreenivasa, and Marc O. Ernst. 2009. "Walking Straight into Circles." *Current Biology* 19: 1538–1542.

7. Philbeck, John W. and Shannon O'Leary. 2005. "Remembered Landmarks Enhance the Precision of Path Integration." *Psicologica* 26: 7–24. See also: Wolbers, Thomas, and Mary Hegarty. 2010. "What Determines Our Navigational Abilities?" *Trends in Cognitive Sciences* 14: 138–146.

8. Wang, Ranxiao F., and Elizabeth S. Spelke. 2002. "Human Spatial Representation: Insights from Animals." *Trends in Cognitive Science* 6: 376–382

9. Philbeck and O'Leary 1995. See above.

10. Appleton, Jay. 1975. *The Experience of Landscape.* London: John Wiley & Sons. See also Aoki, Yoji. 1999. "Review Article: Trends in the Study of the Psychological Evaluation of Landscape." *Landscape Research* 24 (1): 85–94. Cosgrove, Denis. 1985. "Perspective and Evolution of the Landscape Idea." *Transactions of the Institute of British Geographers* 10 (1): 45–62.

11. Kaplan, Stephen. 1979. "Perception and Landscape: Conception and Misconception." In *Proceedings of Our National Landscape*, USDA Forest Service General Technical Report PSW–35: 241–248. ––––. 1987. "Aesthetics, Affect, and Cognition: Environmental Preference from an Evolutionary Perspective." *Environment and Behavior* 19 (1): 3–32. ––––. 2001. "Meditation, Restoration, and the Management of Mental Fatigue." *Environment and Behavior* 33: 480–506. See also Herzog, Thomas R. and Gregory J. Barnes. 1999. "Tranquility and Preference Revisited." *Journal of Environmental Psychology* 19 (2): 171–181.

12. Least Heat-Moon, William. 1991. *PrairyErth: A Deep Map* Boston: Houghton Mifflin.

13. USDA Forest Service. 2010. "The Lone Tree Exhibit." Accessed 28 October 2011. http://www.fs.fed.us/grasslands/lonetree/index.shtml See also Gardner, R. 2009. "Constructing a Technological Forest: Nature, Culture, and Tree-Planting in the Nebraska Sand Hills." *Environmental History* 14 (2): 275–298.

14. Cited in Sheppard 1995. See above.

15. Cited in Scanlan, Tom. 1994. "The Prairie Eye." Proceedings of the 14th Annual North American Prairie Conference : 247–250.

16. Cited in Sheppard 1995. See above.

17. Harrison, Jim and Ted Kooser. 2003. *Braided Creek: A Conversation in Poetry.* Port Townsend: Copper Canyon Press.

18. Heyd, Thomas. 2003. "Basho and the Aesthetics of Wandering: Recuperating Space, Recognizing Place, and Following the Ways of the Universe." *Philosophy East & West* 53(3): 291–307.

19. Lopez 1986. See above.

20. See also Adams, Paul. 2001. "Peripatetic Imagery and Peripatetic Sense of Place." In *Textures of Place: Exploring Humanist Geographies*, edited by Paul Adams, Steven Helscher, and Karen Till. Minneapolis: University of Minnesota Press, 186–206.

21. Childs, Craig. 2006. *House of Rain: Tracking a Vanished Civilization across the American Southwest.* New York: Little, Brown and Company.

22. Tuan, Yi–Fu. 2004. "Life as a Field Trip." *The Geographical Review* 94(1–2): 41–45.

23. United States Department of the Interior Bureau of Land Management. 1984. *BLM Manual Handbook H–8400, Rel. 8–24. Visual Resource Management* and *BLM Manual Handbook H–8401. Visual Resource Inventory:* Washington, D.C. Accessed 18 April 2002. http://www.blm.gov/nstc/VRM/Sitemahtml

24. Olivia, Aude, Soojin Park, and Talia Konkle. 2011. "Representing, Perceiving, and Remembering the Shape of Visual Space." In *Vision in 3D Environments*, edited by L. R. Harris and M. Jenkin. Cambridge: Cambridge University Press.

25. Casey, Edward S. 2001. "Between Geography and Philosophy: What Does It Mean to Be in the Place-World?" *Annals of the Association of American Geographers* 91 (4): 683–693.

26. Tredinnick, Mark. 2005. *The Land's Wild Music: Encounters with Barry Lopez, Peter Matthiessen, Terry Tempest Williams, and James Galvin*. San Antonio: Trinity University Press.

27. Thacker, Robert. 1989. *The Great Prairie Fact and the Literary Imagination*. Albuquerque: University of New Mexico Press.

28. Bowden, Charles. 2006. *Inferno*. Austin: University of Texas Press.

29. Fudge, Robert. 2001 "Imagination and the Science–Based Aesthetic Appreciation of Unscenic Nature." *Journal of Aesthetics and Art Criticism* 59: 275–285.

30. Cather, Willa. 1927 (1990). *Death Comes for the Archbishop*. New York: Vintage Books.

31. Frost, Robert. 1996. *The Collected Notebooks of Robert Frost*. Edited by Robert Faggan. Cambridge: Belknap Press of Harvard University Press.

32. Cohen, Erik. 1979. "A Phenomenology of Tourist Experiences." Sociology 13 (2): 179–201.

33. O'Brien, Dan. 2001. *Buffalo for the Broken Heart: Restoring Life to a Black Hills Ranch*. New York: Random House.

34. Least Heat-Moon 1991. See above.

35. Gruchow, Paul. 1985 (1990). *Journal of a Prairie Year*. Minneapolis: Milkweed Editions.

36. Bunkše, Edmunds V. 2007. "Beyond Images: The Phenomenology of Travel *Versus* Tourism and Implications for Rural Landscapes." In *European Landscapes and Lifestyles: The Mediterranean and Beyond*. Lisbon: Edições Universitárias Lusófonas, 1–12.

37. Childs 2002. See above.

38. Retzinger 1998. See above.

39. Scanlan 1990. See above.

40. Appleton 1975. See above.

41. Lopez 1986. See above.

42. Lao Tzu. 1991 (2005). *Tao Te Ching*. Translated by Charles Muller. New York: Barnes & Noble Classics.

43. Tempest Williams, Terry. 2002. *Red: Passion and Patience in the Desert*. New York : Vintage Books.

44. National Park Service. 2011. "Tallgrass Prairie Preserve." Accessed 29 September 2011. http://www.nps.gov/tapr/index.htm

45. Audubon of Kansas. 2005. "Tallgrass Prairie Parkway Wildlife and Natural Heritage Trail Guide."

46. *Sandhills Journey Scenic Byway*. 2010. Custer County Chief: Broken Bow, NE.

47. Funk, Rex. 1996. "Experiencing Albuquerque's Open Space: Aesthetics and Ethics." Accessed 21 October 2010. http://www.cabq.gov/aes/s10pnspc.html

48. Savage, Candace. 2004. *Prairie: A Natural History*. Vancouver: Greystone Books.

49. Reps 1957. See above.

50. Cather 1927. See above.

51. Olivia, Aude, Soojin Park, and Talia Konkle. See above.

52. Least Heat-Moon 1991. See above.

53. Crang, Michael. 1997. "Picturing Practices: Research through the Tourist Gaze." *Progress in Human Geography* 21 (3): 359–373.

54. Goin, Peter. 2001. "Visual Literacy." *Geographical Review* 91 (1–2): 363–369.

55. Gifford, Don. 1993. "The Touch of Landscape." In *Landscape, Natural Beauty and the Arts*, edited by Salim Kemal and Ivan Gaskell, 127–138. New York: Cambridge University Press.

56. Tuan 2004. See above.

57. Quoted in Giblett, Rod. 2007. "Shooting the Sunburnt Country, the Land of Sweeping Plains, the Rugged Mountain Ranges: Australian Landscape and Wilderness Photography." *Continuum: Journal of Media & Cultural Studies* 21 (3): 335–346.

58. Urry, John. 1992. "The Tourist Gaze 'Revisited.'" *American Behavioural Scientist* 36: 172–186.

59. Garrod, Brian. 2009. "Understanding the Relationship between Tourism Destination Imagery and Tourist Photography." *Journal of Travel Research* 47: 346–358.

60. Bunkse 2007. See above.

61. Giblett, 2007. See above.

62. Gruchow 1985. See above.

63. Abbey, Edward. 1968 (1990). *Desert Solitaire: A Season in the Wilderness.* New York: Simon &Schuster.

64. Gobster, Paul. 1999. "An Ecological Aesthetic for Forest Landscape Management." *Landscape Journal* 18 (1):54–64.

65. McMurtry, Larry. 2006. In *Home Ground: Language for an American Landscape.* Edited by Barry Lopez and Debra Gwartney. San Antonio: Trinity University Press.

66. Norris 1993. See above.

67. Baylor, Byrd. 1986 (1995). *I'm in Charge of Celebrations.* New York: Aladdin Paperbacks.

68. Malotki, Ekkehart and Donald E. Weaver, Jr. 2002. *Stone Chisel and Yucca Brush: Colorado Plateau Rock Art.* Illustrations by Patricia McCreery. Walnut: Kiva Publishing.

69. Childs 2006. See above.

70. Baylor, Byrd. 1978 (1998). *The Way to Start a Day.* New York: Aladdin Paperbacks.

71. Reps 1957, See above.

72. Childs 2006. See above.

73. Tempest Williams 2002. See above.

74. Sofaer, Anna, Volker Zinser, and Rolf M. Sinclair. 1979. "A Unique Solar Marking Construct." *Science* 206 (4416): 283–291.

75. Least Heat-Moon 1991 and Childs 2006, See above.

76. Bowden, Charles.2008. "The Emptied Prairie." *National Geographic Magazine.* Accessed 29 September 2011 http://ngm.nationalgeographic.com/2008/01/ emptied–north–dakota/bowden–text

77. Baylor, Byrd. 1978 (1997). *The Other Way to Listen.* New York: Aladdin Paperbacks.

78. Dillard, Annie. 1974 (1999.) *Pilgrim at Tinker Creek.* New York: Harper Collins.

79. Momaday, N. Scott. 1968 (1999). *House Made of Dawn.* New York: Harper Collins.

80. Flores, Dan. 2001. *The Natural West: Environmental History in the Great Plains and Rocky Mountains.* Norman: University of Oklahoma Press. National Park Service. 2011.

81. Gruchow 1985. See above.

82. Stegner, Wallace. 1955. *Wolf Willow: A History, a Story, and a Memory of the Last Plains Frontier.* New York: Viking Press.

83. Norris 1993. See above.

84. Reps and Senzaki 1957. See above.

85. Lopez 1986. See above.

86. Quayle, William. 1905. *The Prairie and the Sea.* Cincinnati: Jennings and Graham.

87. In Hamill, Sam and J. P. Seaton, eds. 2004. *The Poetry of Zen.* Boston: Shambhala.

88. "Awe." 1971. *The Compact Edition of the Oxford English Dictionary.* Oxford, U.K.: Oxford University Press.

89. Konečni, Vladimir J. 2010. "Aesthetic Trinity Theory and the Sublime." In *Proceedings of the European Society for Aesthetics, Vol. 2,* edited by A. Bertinetto, F. Dorsch, and C. Todd, 244–264.

90. Keltner, Dacher and Jonathan Haidt. 2003. "Approaching Awe, a Moral, Spiritual, and Aesthetic Emotion." *Cognition and Emotion* 17 (2): 297–314.

91. Momaday 1968. See above.

92. Burke, Edmund. 1757 (1990). *A Philosophical Inquiry into the Origin of Our Ideas of the Sublime and Beautiful.* Oxford, U.K.: Oxford University Press.

93. Carlson, Allen. 2010. "Environmental Aesthetics." In *The Stanford Encyclopedia of Philosophy (Fall 2010 Edition),* edited by Edward N. Zalta. Accessed 21 October 2010. http://plato.stanford.edu/archives/fall2010/entries/ environmental–aesthetics/

94. Kant, Immanuel. Described in Forsey, Jane. 2007. "Is a Theory of the Sublime Possible?" *The Journal of Aesthetics and Art Criticism* 65 (4): 381–389.

95. Freud, Sigmund. Cited in Konečni, Vladimir J. 2010. See above.

96. Cited in Benediktsson, Karl. 2007. "'Scenophobia,' Geography and the Aesthetic Politics of Landscape." *Geografiska Annaler* 89 B (3): 203–217.

97. Harrison, Jim and Ted Kooser. 2003. See above.

98. Godlovitch, Stan.1998. "Evaluating Nature Aesthetically."*The Journal of Aesthetics and Art Criticism* 56 (2):113–125.

99. Chenowith, Richard E., and Paul Gobster. 1990. "The Nature and Ecology of Aesthetic Experiences in the Landscape." *Landscape Journal* 9 (1): 1–9.
100. Benediktsson, Karl. 2007. See above.
101. Translated by Paul Reps. Edited by Paul Reps and Nyogen Senzaki. 1957. See above.
102. Suzuki-Roshi, Shunryu. 1970. *Zen Mind, Beginner's Mind.* New York: Weatherhill.
103. Tuan, Yi-Fu. 1977. *Space and Place: The Perspective of Experience.* Minneapolis: University of Minnesota Press.
104. Abbey 1968. See above.
105. Bass, Rick. 1996. *The Book of Yaak.* New York: Houghton Mifflin.
106. Lao Tzu. Translated by Muller. See above.
107. Lopez 1986. See above.
108. Lao Tzu. Translated by Muller. See above.
109. Tuan 1977. See above.
110. Tuan, Yi-Fu. 1974. *Topophilia: A Study of Environmental Perception, Attitudes, and Values.* New York: Columbia University Press.
111. Faulstich, Paul. 1998. "Geophilia: Landscape and Humanity." *Wild Earth* Spring 1998: 82–89.
112. See, for example, Altman, Irwin, and S. Low. 1992. *Place Attachment.* New York: Plenum. Davenport, Mae A. and Dorothy H. Anderson. 2005. "Getting from Sense of Place to Place-Based Management: An Interpretive Investigation of Place Meanings and Perceptions of Landscape Change." *Society and Natural Resources.* 18: 625–641. Shumaker, S. A. and R. B. Taylor. 1983. "Toward a Classification of People-Place Relationships: A Model of Attachment to Place." In *Environmental Psychology: Directions and Perspectives*, edited by N. R. Feimer and E. S. Geller, 219–256. New York: Praeger. Stedman, Richard C. 2003. "Is It Really Just a Social Construction? The Contribution of the Physical Environment to a Sense of Place." *Society and Natural Resources* 16:671–685.
113. Cheng, Antony, Linda Kruger, and Steven Daniels. 2003. "'Place' as an Integrating Concept in Natural Resource Politics: Propositions for a Social Science Research Agenda." *Society and Natural Resources* 16:87–104.
114. Buttimer, Anne. 1976. "Grasping the Dynamism of Lifeworld." *Annals of the Association of American Geographers* 66 (2): 277–292.
115. Olstad, Tyra. 2007. "Desert Dimensions: Attachment to a Place of Space." Masters Thesis, University of Wyoming.
116. See Ferguson, Charles. 2008. "Geology of the Red Desert." In *Red Desert: History of a Place*, edited by Annie Proulx, 85–105. Austin: University of Texas Press. McNab, W. H. and E. Avers. 1994. "Ecological Subregions of the United States." USDA Forest Service WO-WSA-5. Accessed 20 November 2009. http://www.fs.fed.us/land/pubs/ecoregions. Thompson, Craig. 2008. "Water in the Red." In *Red Desert: History of a Place*, edited by Annie Proulx, 107–119. Austin: University of Texas Press.

117. Jones, George 2008. "Sagebrush." In *Red Desert: History of a* Place, edited by Annie Proulx, 201–215. Austin: University of Texas Press.

118. Beauvais, Gary 2008. "Vertebrate Wildlife of the Red Desert." In *Red Desert: History of a* Place, edited by Annie Proulx, 143–170. Austin: University of Texas Press. Lockwood, Jeffrey A. 2008. "Insects of the Red Desert: An Exercise in Scientific Humility." In *Red Desert: History of a* Place, edited by Annie Proulx, 189–199. Austin: University of Texas Press. Orabona, Andrea. 2008. "Birds of the Red Desert." In *Red Desert: History of a Place,* edited by Annie Proulx, 171–180. Austin: University of Texas Press.

119. Dakin, Susan. 2003. "There's More to Landscape than Meets the Eye: Towards Inclusive Landscape Assessment in Resource and Environmental Management." *Canadian Geographer* 47(2): 185–200.

120. Brady, Emily. 2002. "Interpreting Environments." *Essays in Philosophy* 3 (1). Accessed 28 October 2011. http://commons.pacificu.edu/eip/vol3/iss1/16

121. Proulx, Annie. 2008. *Red Desert: History of a Place.* Austin: University of Texas Press.

122. Friends of the Red Desert. 2009. "Desert Values." 30 October 2009. http://www.reddesert.org/values/index.php

123. Clifford, Hal. 2002. "The last lonesome place." *OnEarth.* Accessed 2 November 2011 http://www.nrdc.org/onearth/o2fal/desert1.asp

124. Biodiversity Conservation Alliance. 2009. "Red Desert." Accessed 30 October 2009 http://www.voiceforthewild.org/l

125. Forman, Richard T. T. 2000. "Estimate of the Area Affected Ecologically by the Road System in the United States." *Conservation Biology* 14: 31–35.

126. Friends of the Red Desert. See above.

127. See, for example, Jones, D. 2005. "Don't Sacrifice the Northern Red Desert for One Use." *Casper Star–Tribune,* October 24.

128. See, for example, Wyoming Wilderness Association. 2006. *Wyoming Wilderness Roundup.* Summer/Fall. Wyoming State Office of Travel and Tourism. 2005. *Wyoming Vacation Guide.*

129. Molvar, Erik. 2010. *Wyoming's Red Desert: A Photographic Journey.* Laguna Beach, CA: Laguna Wilderness Press.

130. Bureau of Land Management, Rawlins Field Office. 1996. Green River Resource Area Resource Management Plan and Final Environmental Impact Statement.

131. Olstad 2007. See above.

132. Biodiversity Conservation Alliance. 2009. See above.

133. See also Trimble, Stephen and Terry Tempest Williams. 1996. "An Act of Faith." In *Testimony: Writers of the West Speak on Behalf of Utah Wilderness,* edited by S. Trimble and T. Tempest Williams. Minneapolis: Milkweed Editions.

134. Olstad 2007. See above.

135. Brown, Thomas C. 1984. "The Concept of Value in Resource Allocation." *Land Economics.* 60 (3): 231–246.

136. Massey, Douglas S. 2002. "A Brief History of Human Society: The Origin and Role of Emotion in Social Life." *American Sociological Review* 67: 1–29.
137. Eisenhauer, Brian, Richard Krannich, and Dale Blahna. 2000. "Attachments to Special Places on Public Lands : An Analysis of Activities, Reason for Attachments, and Community Connections." *Society & Natural Resources* 13(5): 421–441.
138. Appleton 1975. See above.
139. Wright 1947. See above.
140. Bunkse 2007. See above.
141. Summary information available online at http://www.nps.gov/history/history/online_books/pefo/wilderness_recommendations.pdf
142. Williams, Daniel, Michael Patterson, Joseph W. Roggenbuck, and Alan E. Watson. 1992. "Beyond the Commodity Metaphor: Examining Emotional and Symbolic Attachment to Place." *Leisure Sciences* 14: 29–46.
143. Foreman, Dave. 1994. "Where Man Is a Visitor." In *Place of the Wild*, edited by David Clarke Burks. Washington, D. C.: Island Press.
144. Snyder, Gary. 1990. *Practice of the Wild*. Berkeley: North Point Press. See also Stokols, D., and Shumaker, S. A. 1981. "People in Places: A Transactional View of Settings." In *Cognition, social behavior, and the environment*, edited by J. H. Harvey, 441–488. Hillsdale: Erlbaum.
145. Olstad, Tyra A. 2013. "Personal Experience and Public Place Creation." In *Place-Based Conservation: Perspectives from the Social Sciences*, edited by Daniel Williams, William Stewart and Linda Kruger. New York: Springer.
146. Wallach, Bret. 1985. "The Return of the Prairie." *Landscape* 28 (3): 1–6.
147. Quoted in Lopez 1986. See above.
148. Dillard 1974. See above.
149. Turner, Jack. 1997. *The Abstract Wild*. Tucson: University of Arizona Press.
150. Norris 1993. See above.
151. Lopez 1986. See above.
152. Emerson, Ralph Waldo. 1909. *Nature*. New York: Duffield & Company.
153. Gruchow 1985. See above.
154. Bass, Rick. 2009. *The Wild Marsh: Four Seasons at Home in Montana*. Boston: Houghton Mifflin Harcourt.
155. Meloy, Ellen. 2003. The Anthropology of Turquoise: Reflections on Desert, Sea, Stone, and Sky. New York: Vintage Books.
156. Abbey 1968. See above.
157. Abbey 1968. See above.
158. Tempest Williams, Terry. 1991. *Refuge: An Unnatural History of Family and Place*. New York: Vintage Books.
159. Childs 2002. See above.
160. Gruchow 1985. See above.
161. Abbey, Edward. 1975 (2000). *The Monkey Wrench Gang*. New York: Perennial Classics.

162. Translated by Reps. Reps and Senzaki 1957. See above.
163. Skidmore, Lorimer, quoted in Laura S. Harrison. 1986. *Architecture in the Parks A National Historic Landmark Theme Study.* National Park Service. Accessed 2 November 2011. http://www.cr.nps.gov/history/online_books/harrison/harrison28.htm
164. Harrison 1986. See above.
165. Campbell, Joseph. 1949 (2008). *The Hero with a Thousand Faces.* New York: Pantheon Books.
166. Nash, Roderick. 1967. *Wilderness and the American Mind.* New Haven: Yale University Press.
167. Eliade, Mircea. 1967. *Myths, Dreams and Mysteries.* Translated by Philip Mairet. New York: Harper & Row.
168. Jung, Carl G. and M.-L. von Franz. 1964. *Man and His Symbols.* New York City: Dell.
169. Translated by Reps. Reps and Senzaki 1957. See above.
170. Norris 1993. See above.
171. Snyder 1990. See above.
172. Trimble, Stephen. 1996. "Our Gardens, Our Canyons." In *Testimony: Writers of the West Speak on Behalf of Utah Wilderness,* edited by S. Trimble and T. Tempest Williams, 19–22. Minneapolis: Milkweed Editions.
173. Gruchow 1985. See above.
174. Tempest Williams 1991. See above.
175. Meine, Curt. 1988. *Aldo Leopold: His Life and Work.* Madison: University of Wisconsin Press.
176. Least Heat-Moon 1991. See above.
177. Shortridge, James R. 1988. "The Heart of the Prairie: Culture Areas in the Central and Northern Great Plains." *Great Plains Quarterly* 8: 206–221.
178. Pichaske, David. 2006. "Where Now 'Midwestern Literature'?" *Midwest Quarterly* 48 (1): 100–119.
179. Sanders, Scott Russell. 2009. "Foreword." In *Journal of a Prairie Year,* Paul Gruchow. Minneapolis: Milkweed Editions.
180. Irving, Washington. 1832. Quoted in Price, John. 2004. *Not Just Any Land: A Personal and Literary Journey into the American Grasslands.* Lincoln: University of Nebraska Press.
181. Quayle 1905. See above.
182. Scanlan 1990. See above.
183. Quoted in Bowden 2008. See above.
184. Abbey 1975. See above.
185. Lopez 1986. See above.
186. Tempest Williams 1991. See above.
187. Momaday 1968. See above.
188. Pichaske 2006. See above.
189. Lopez 1986. See above.

190. Dillard 1974. See above.
191. Spirn, Anne Whiston. 1988. "The Poetics of City and Nature: Towards a New Aesthetic for Urban Design." *Landscape Journal* 7 (2): 108–126.
192. Oliver, Mary. 1986. *Dream Work.* New York: Atlantic Monthly Press.
193. Sanders 2009. See above.
194. Cather 1927. See above.
195. Tolstoy, Leo. 1966. *War and Peace (Norton Critical Editions).* Translated by Louse Maude and Aylmer Maude. New York: W W Norton & Co Inc.

Notes to Chapter 2: Mixedgrass

1. Cather 1918. See above.
2. Cather 1918. See above.
3. Bryce, S. A., J. M. Omernik, D. A. Pater, M. Ulmer, J. Schaar, J. Freeouf, R. Johnson, P. Kuck, and S. H. Azevedo. 1996. *Ecoregions of North Dakota and South Dakota, (Color Poster with Map, Descriptive Text, Summary Tables, and Photographs).* Reston: U.S. Geological Survey.
4. National Park Service. 2011. "Badlands National Park." Accessed 29 September 2011. http://www.nps.gov/badl/index.htm
5. Leidy, Joseph. 1869. "On the Extinct Mammalian Fauna of Dakota and Nebraska, Including an Account of Some Allied Forms from Other Localities, Together with a Synopsis of the Mammalian Remains of North America." *Journal of the Academy of Natural Sciences of Philadelphia* (7): 1–472.
6. Kieley, James F. 1940. *A Brief History of the National Park Service.* US Department of the Interior National Park Service. Accessed 30 September 2011. http://www.cr.nps.gov/history/online_books/kieley/index.htm
7. Haines, Aubrey L. 1974. *Yellowstone National Park: Its Exploration and Establishment.* U.S. Department of the Interior National Park Service. Accessed 30 September 2011 http://www.cr.nps.gov/history/online_books/haines1/iee3a.htm
8. Sheppard 1995. See above.
9. Cited in Mattison, Ray H., Robert A. Grom, and Joanne W. Stockert, eds. 1968. *History of Badlands National Monument and the White River (Big) Badlands of South Dakota.* Badlands Natural History Association. Accessed 31 Aug 2011. http://www.cr.nps.gov/history/online_books/badl/index.htm
10. Quoted in Mattison et al. 1968. See above.
11. Cited in Mattison et al. 1968. See above.
12. Quayle 1905. See above.
13. Cited in Sheppard 1995. See above.
14. Cited in Sheppard 1995. See above.
15. National Park Service. 2011. "Tallgrass Prairie Preserve." See above.

16. Conard, R., and S. Hess. 1998. *Tallgrass Prairie National Preserve Legislative History, 1920–1996*. Iowa City: Tallgrass Historians L.C.

17. Olson, Eric. 1997. *National Grasslands Management: A Primer*. Washington, D.C.: USDA Forest Service. And West, Terry.1990. USDA Forest Service Management of the National Grasslands. *Agricultural History* 64 (2): 86–98.

18. Hurt, R. Douglas. 1985. "The National Grasslands: Origin and Development in the Dust Bowl." *Agricultural History* 59 (2): 246–259.

19. USDA Forest Service. 2011. "National Grasslands." Accessed 2 November 2011. http://www.fs.fed.us/grasslands

20. Moul, Francis. 2006. The National Grasslands: A Guide to America's Undiscovered Treasures. Lincoln: University of Nebraska Press.

21. USFS National Grasslands Management Review Team. 1996. Included in West 1990, Appendix A. (See Below)

22. Collins, Sally, and Elizabeth Larry. 2007. *Caring for Our Natural Assets: An Ecosystem Services Perspective*. Portland: USDA Forest Service Pacific Northwest Research Station.

23. Millenium Ecosystem Assessment. 2005. *Ecosystems and Human Well-Being: Synthesis*. Washington, DC.: Island Press.

24. USDA Forest Service. 1995. *Landscape Aesthetics: A Handbook for Scenery Management*. Agriculture Handbook Number 701. Washington, D.C.: USDA Forest Service.

25. Evernden 1983. See above.

26. USDA Forest Service. 2007. "Valuing Ecosystem Services: Capturing the true value of nature's capital." Accessed 21 February 2009 http://www.fs.fed.us/ecosystemservices

27. Henry, Thomas. 2009. "Trails and Grasslands." Accessed 13 January 2009. http://www.trailsandgrasslands.com

28. Williams, Daniel R. and Susan I. Stewart. 1998. "Sense of Place: An Elusive Concept that is Finding a Home in Ecosystem Management." *Forest Science* 96(5): 18–23.

29. Cheng et al. 2003. See above.

30. Snyder, Gary. 1980. *The Real Work: Interviews and Talks 1964–1979*. New York: New Directions.

31. Forrest, Steve, Holly Strand, William H. Haskins, Curt Freese, Jonathan Proctor, and Eric Dinerstein. 2004. *Ocean of Grass: A Conservation Assessment for the Northern Great Plains*. Bozeman: Northern Plains Conservation Network and Northern Great Plains Ecoregion, WWF-US.

32. Kirby, Don. 2009. *Grasslands*. Portland: Nazraeli Press.

33. Price 2004. See above.

34. Translated by Hamill. *The Poetry of Zen*, edited by Sam Hamill and J. Seaton, 1–7. Boston: Shambhala.

35. Baylor 1986. See above.

36. National Park Service. 2011. "Badlands National Park." See above.

37. Leopold, Aldo. 1949 (1989). *A Sand County Almanac and Sketches Here and There*. Oxford: Oxford University Press.

38. Tempest Williams 1991. See above.

39. Beletsky, Les, and Jon L. Dunn. 2006. *Bird Songs: 250 North American Birds in Song*. San Francisco: Chronicle Books.

40. Rolston, Holmes III. 1987. "Beauty and the Beast: Aesthetic Experience of Wildlife." In *Valuing Wildlife: Economic and Social Perspectives*, edited by Daniel J. Decker and Gary R. Goff, 187–1986. Boulder: Westview Press.

41. Ballantyne, Roy, Jan Packer, and Lucy A. Sutherland. 2011. "Visitors' Memories of Wildlife Tourism: Implications for the Design of Powerful Interpretive Experiences." *Tourism Management* 32: 770–779.

42. Rolston 1987. See above.

43. Rolston 1987. See above.

44. Cited in Mattison et al. 1968. See above. See also Redington, Paul G. 1929. "Policy of the U.S. Biological Survey in Regard to Predatory Mammal Control." *Journal of Mammology* 10 (3): 276–279.

45. Askins, R. A., F. Chavez–Ramirez, B. C. Dale, C. A. Haas, J. R. Herkert, F. L. Knopf, and D. Vickery. 2007. "Conservation of Grassland Birds in North America: Understanding Ecological Processes in Different Regions." *Ornithological Monographs* 64: 1–46.

46. A question explored in Samson, Fred. B. and Fritz L. Knopf. 1994. "Prairie Conservation in North America." *BioScience* 44: 418–421. Samson, Fred B., Fritz L. Knopf, and Wayne R. Ostlie. 2004. "Great Plains Ecosystems: Past, Present, and Future." *Wildlife Society Bulletin* 32: 6–15. Samson, Fred B., Fritz L. Knopf, C. W. McCarthy, B. R. Noon, Wayne R. Ostlie, S. M. Rinehart, S. Larson, G. E. Plumb, G. L. Schenbeck, D. N. Svingen, and T. W. Byer. 2003. "Planning for Population Viability on Northern Great Plains National Grasslands." *Wildlife Society Bulletin* 31 (4): 986–999. Fuhlendorf, S. D. and D. M. Engle 2001. "Restoring Heterogeneity on Rangelands: Ecosystem Management Based on Evolutionary Grazing Patterns." *BioScience* 51: 626–632.

47. Popper, Deborah and Frank Popper. 1987. "The Great Plains: From Dust to Dust." *Planning* 53(2): 12–18.

48. Popper, Deborah and Frank Popper. 1993. "The Buffalo Commons: Then and Now." *FOCUS on Geography* 43(4): 17–25.

49. Shortridge, James R. 2005. "Regional Image and Sense of Place in Kansas." *Kansas History: A Journal of the Central Plains* 28: 202–219.

50. De Bres, Karen J., David E. Kromm, and Steven E. White. 1993. "Comment on the Future of the Great Plains: Not a Buffalo Commons." *FOCUS on Geography* 43 (4): 16.

51. Popper and Popper 1993. See above. Roebuck, Paul. 1993. "The Great Plains: from Bust to Bust." *FOCUS on Geography* 43 (4): 16.

52. Popper and Popper. 1999. "The Buffalo Commons: Metaphor as Method." *Geographical Review* 89(4): 491–510.

53. Wild Idea Buffalo. 2011. "Wild Idea Buffalo." Accessed 21 September 2011. http://wildideabuffalo.com

54. The Nature Conservancy. 2011. "The Nature Conservancy" Accessed 21 September 2011 http://www.nature.org/

55. Smith, Brooke. 2011. *Tatanka: The 2011 Guide to Custer State Park.* S.D. Department of Game, Fish and Parks. Accessed 6 September 2011. http://gfp.sd.gov/state-parks/directory/custer/docs/tatanka.pdf

56. National Park Service. 2011. "Wind Cave National Park. Accessed 29 September 2011. http://www.nps.gov/wica/index.htm

57. Sanderson,Eric W., Kent H. Redford, Bill Weber, Keith Aune, Dick Baldes, Joel Berger, Dave Carter, Charles Curtin, James Derr, Steve Dobrott, Eva Fearn, Craig Fleener, Steve Forrest, Craig Gerlach, C. Cormack Gates, John E. Gross, Peter Gogan, Shaun Grassel, Jodi A. Hilty, Marv Jensen, Kyran Kunkel, Duane Lammers, Rurik List, Karen Minkowski, Tom Olson, Chris Pague, Paul B. Robertson, and Bob Stephenson. 2008. "The Ecological Future of the North American Bison: Conceiving Long-Term, Large-Scale Conservation of Wildlife." *Conservation Biology* 22 (2): 252–266.

58. Catlin, George. 1841. *Letters and Notes on the Manners, Customs, and Condition of the North American Indians, Vol. 1.* Picadilly: Tosswill and Myers. Cited in Sheppard 1995.

59. National Park Service. 2011. Badlands National Park: "Restoration of Native Animals". Accessed 29 September 2011. http://www.nps.gov/wica/index.htm

60. Price 2004. See above.

61. Bowden 2008. See above.

62. Bowden 2008. See above.

63. See, for example, Cromartie, John B. 1998. "Net Migration in the Great Plains Increasingly Linked to Natural Amenities and Suburbanization." *Rural Development Perspectives* 13 (1): 27–34. Fuguitt, Glenn V. and Calvin L. Beale. 1996. "Recent Trends in Nonmetropolitan Migration: Toward a New Turnaround?" *Growth and Change* 27: 156–174. Johnson, Kenneth. 1993. "When Deaths Exceed Births: Natural Decrease in the United States." *International Regional Science Review* 15 (2): 179–198. Johnson, Kenneth and John B. Cromartie. 2006. "The Rural Rebound and Its Aftermath: Changing Demographic Dynamics and Regional Contrasts." In *Population Change and Rural Society*, edited by W. Kandel and D. Brown, 25–49. The Netherlands: Springer. Stauber, Karl. 2001. "Why Invest in Rural America—And How? A Critical Public Policy Question for the 21st Century." *Economic Review* 86 (2): 57–74. Woods, Michael. 2005. *Rural Geography: Processes, Responses and Experiences in Rural Restructuring.* London: Sage Publications.

64. Bunkše 2007. See above.

65. Wood, Richard E. 2008. *Survival of Rural America: Small Victories and Bitter Harvests.* Lawrence: University Press of Kansas.

66. Theodore Roosevelt Medora Foundation . 2009. "Medora: North Dakota's #1 Vacation" Accessed 10 March 2009. http://www.medora.com/
67. Garstka, Katharine. 2011. "Welcome to Historic Marmarth." Accessed 18 September 2011. http://www.marmarth.org/index.htm See also Nelson, Annika. 2009. "Tyler Lyson & 'Dakota' the Dinomummy: Two 'Rock Stars' from the Hell Creek Formation." North Dakota Horizons Spring 2009. Accessed 02 November 2011. http://www.ndhorizons.com/horizons/featured/index.asp?ID=47
68. Popper and Popper 1993. See above.
69. Hoeven, John. 2008. Response. National Geographic Magazine Editor's Blog January 2008. Accessed 04 November 2011. http://blogs.ngm.com/blog_central/2008/01/in-response-to-north-dakota-governor-hoeven.html
70. *National Geographic Magazine Editor's Blog* January 2008. See above.
71. Shortridge 2005. See above.
72. Lincoln Journal Star Editorial. 11 March 2008. "Nature Is Just Out the Door, Down the Road." *The Lincoln Journal Star.* Accessed 10 March 2009. http://www.grasslandfoundation.org/resources ––––. 21 April 2007. "How About a Little Love for Prairies?" *The Lincoln Journal Star.* Accessed 10 March 2009. http://www.grasslandfoundation.org/resources
73. Kansas Sampler Foundation. 2009. "Small Towns Have a Beautiful Story." Accessed 4 November 2011. http://kansassampler.blogspot.com/2009/04/small–towns–have–beautiful–story.html
74. Lowry, Andrea. 2011. "No Place Like Home—Western Kansas." *Discover Phillips County Economic Development (Blog).* Accessed 04 November 2011. http://www.discoverpced.com/blog/no–place–like–home–western–kansas/ See also Toll, Dennis. 24 Dec 2008. "No Place Like Home" *Flint Hills, Tall Grass.* Accessed 04 November 2011. http://flinthillstallgrass.org/2008/12/24/no–place–like–home/
75. Lillegraven, Linda. 2010. "Artist statement." *Kneeland Gallery.* Accessed 10 Oct 2010. http://www.kneelandgallery.com/Artist/Lillegraven%20–%20Linda/bio.htm
76. Quoted in Retzinger1998. See above.
77. Shortridge, James. 2004. "A Cry for Help: Kansasfreeland.com." *Geographical Review* 94(4). See also Lu, Max and Darci A. Paull. 2007. "Assessing the Free Land Programs for Reversing Rural Depopulation." *Great Plains Research* 17 (1):73–86.
78. Norris 1993. See above.
79. Bowden 2008. See above.
80. Lawrence Journal-World. 2005. "What Do You Think of Our New State Slogan, 'Kansas: As Big as You Think'?" Accessed 17 Sept 2011. http://www2.ljworld.com/onthestreet/2005/jan/08/kansasbig/
81. Benedict, Simone. 15 July 2011. "Is Kansas as Big as You Think?" Accessed 17 September 2011 http://simonebenedict.wordpress.com/2011/07/15/is–kansas–as–big–as–you–think/.

82. Kansas, Inc. 2007. *The Kansas Image: Overview and Analysis.* Accessed 9 Sept 2011 http://www.kansasinc.org/pubs/working/ImageRpt6.30.07.pdf

83. Shortridge 2005. See above.

84. Bunkse 2007. See above.

85. Sandhills Journey Scenic Byway. 2010. See above.

86. Tuan 2004. See above.

87. National Park Service. 2011. "Interpretive Development Program." Accessed 29 September 2011 http://www.nps.gov/idp/interp/

88. Tilden, Freeman. 1957 (2007). *Interpreting Our Heritage.* Chapel Hill: University of North Carolina Press.

89. Benediktsson 2007. See above

90. Sheppard 1995. See above.

91. Godlovitch 1998. See above.

92. Meinig, D. W. 1979. "Introduction." In *The Interpretation of Ordinary Landscapes: Geographical Essays,* edited by D. W. Meinig, 1–7. New York: Oxford University Press.

93. Bunkše 2007. See above.

94. Carlson, Allen. 1979. "Appreciation and the Natural Environment." *The Journal of Aesthetics and Art Criticism* 37 (3): 267–275.

95. Fudge 2001. See above.

96. Saito, Yuriko. 1984. "Is There a Correct Aesthetic Appreciation of Nature?" *Journal of Aesthetic Education* 18 (4): 35–46.

97. Eaton, Marcia Muelder. 1998. "Fact and Fiction in the Aesthetic Appreciation of Nature." *The Journal of Aesthetics and Art Criticism* 56 (2): 149–156.

98. Lopez 1986. See above.

Notes to Chapter 3: Tallgrass

1. Bass 1996. See above.

2. Cited in Shortridge 2005. See above.

3. Dillard, Annie. 1999. "Afterword to the Twenty–fifth Anniversary Edition." In *Pilgrim at Tinker Creek.* New York: Harper Collins.

4. Bass 2009. See above.

5. Faulstich 1998. See above.

6. Tuan 1977. See above.

7. Rolston 1987. See above.

8. National Park Service 2011. "Tallgrass Prairie Preserve." See above.

9. *Sandhills Journey Scenic Byway* 2010. See above.

10. Funk 1996. See above.

11. Meinig, D. W. 1979. "The Beholding Eye: Ten Versions of the Same Scene." In *The Interpretation of Ordinary Landscapes: Geographical Essays*, edited by D. W. Meinig, 33–48. New York: Oxford University Press.

12. See, for example, Gober, Patricia. 2000. "In Search of Synthesis." *Annals of the Association of American Geographers* 90 (1): 1–11. Kinzig, Ann P. 2001. "Bridging Disciplinary Divides to Address Environmental and Intellectual Challenges." *Ecosystems* 4 (8) : 709–715. Swanson Frederick J, Charles Goodrich, and Kathleen Dean Moore. 2008. "Bridging Boundaries: Scientists, Creative Writers, and the Long View of the Forest." *Frontiers in Ecology and the Environment* 6(9):499–504. Taylor, Peter ed. 2009. *Integrative Science for Society and Environment: A Strategic Research Plan*. Research Initiatives Subcommittee of the LTER Planning Process Conference Committee and the Cyberinfrastructure Core Team. Accessed 29 December 2009. http://www.lternet.edu/decadalplan/

13. Wilson, Edward O. 1998. *Consilience: The Unity of Knowledge*. New York: Alfred A. Knopf.

14. Strober, Myra H. Forthcoming. "Habits of the Mind: Challenges for Multidisciplinarity." *Social Epistemology*. Accessed 20 November 2009 http://www.stanford.edu/~myras/Publications.htm

15. Carlson 2010. See above.

16. Tuan, Yi–Fu. 1979. "Thought and Landscape: The Eye and the Mind's Eye." In *The Interpretation of Ordinary Landscapes: Geographical Essays*, edited by D. W. Meinig, 89–102. New York: Oxford University Press.

17. Heyd, Thomas. 2001. "Aesthetic appreciation and the many stories about nature." *British Journal of Aesthetics* 41 (2): 125–137.

18. Massey 2002. See above.

19. Least Heat-Moon 1991. See above.

20. Least Heat-Moon 1991. See above.

21. Snow, C. P. 1963. *The Two Cultures: And a Second Look*. New York: Cambridge University Press.

22. Cronon, William. 1995. "The Trouble with Wilderness; or, Getting Back to the Wrong Nature." In *Uncommon Ground*, edited by William Cronon. New York: W. W. Norton & Co., 69–90.

23. Cited in Cronon 1995. See above.

24. Reps, Paul and Nyogen Senzaki, eds. 1957. See above.

25. Lao Tzu. Translated by Muller. See above.

26. Bass 1996. See above.

27. Harrison, Jim. *In Search of Small Gods*. Port Townsend, WA : Copper Canyon Press. 2009.

28. Frost, Robert. 1996. *The Collected Notebooks of Robert Frost*. Edited by Robert Faggan. Cambridge: Belknap Press of Harvard University Press.

29. Dillard 1974. See above.

30. Lao Tzu. Translated by Muller. See above.
31. Tempest Williams 2002. See above.
32. Abbey 1968. See above.
33. Tuan, Yi–Fu. 2001. "The Desert and I: A Study in Affinity." *Michigan Quarterly Review.* 40(1): 7–18.
34. Price 2004. See above.
35. Least Heat-Moon 1991. See above.
36. Least Heat-Moon 1991. See above.
37. Hart, John F. 1982. "The Highest Form of the Geographer's Art." *Annals of the Association of American Geographers* 72: 1–29.

Notes to Chapter 4: Shortgrass / Semi-Desert Shrub-Steppe

1. Lao Tzu. Cited in Capra, Fritjof. 1976 (1989). *The Tao of Physics (Second Edition).* New York: Bantam Books.
2. Price 2004. See above.
3. Tredinnick 2005. See above.
4. Lao Tzu. Translated by Muller.. See above.
5. Gruchow 1985. See above.
6. Abbey 1968. See above.
7. Bass 1996. See above.
8. Gruchow 1985. See above.
9. Reps and Senzaki 1957. See above.
10. Cather 1918. See above.
11. Leopold 1949. See above.
12. Lopez, Barry. 2007. Coldscapes. *National Geographic Magazine*: 142–145.
13. Least Heat-Moon 1991. See above.
14. Bass 2009. See above.
15. Gruchow 1985. See above.
16. Lopez 1986. See above.
17. Bass 2009. See above.

Notes to Conclusion

1. Suzuki-Roshi 1970. See above.

Bibliography

Abbey, Edward. 1975 (2000). *The Monkey Wrench Gang*. New York: Perennial Classics.
———. 1968 (1990). *Desert Solitaire: A Season in the Wilderness*. New York: Simon & Schuster.
Adams, Paul. 2001. "Peripatetic Imagery and Peripatetic Sense of Place." In *Textures of Place: Exploring Humanist Geographies*, edited by Paul Adams, Steven Helscher, and Karen Till. Minneapolis: University of Minnesota Press, 186–206.
Altman, Irwin, and S. Low, eds. 1992. *Place Attachment*. New York: Plenum.
Aoki, Yoji. 1999. "Review Article: Trends in the Study of the Psychological Evaluation of Landscape." *Landscape Research* 24 (1): 85–94.
Appleton, Jay. 1975. *The Experience of Landscape*. London: John Wiley & Sons.
Askins, R. A., F. Chavez-Ramirez, B. C. Dale, C. A. Haas, J. R. Herkert, F. L. Knopf, and D. Vickery. 2007. "Conservation of Grassland Birds in North America: Understanding Ecological Processes in Different Regions." *Ornithological Monographs* 64: 1–46.
Audubon of Kansas. 2005. "Tallgrass Prairie Parkway Wildlife and Natural Heritage Trail Guide."
Bailey, Robert G. 1983. "Delineation of Ecosystem Regions." *Environmental Management* 7 (4):365–373.
———. 1980. "Ecoregions of the United States." Washington, D.C.: USDA Forest Service Miscellaneous Publication No. 1391. Accessed 09 November 2011. http://www.fs.fed.us/land/ecosysmgmt/index.html.
Ballantyne, Roy, Jan Packer, and Lucy A. Sutherland. 2011. "Visitors' Memories of Wildlife Tourism: Implications for the Design of Powerful Interpretive Experiences." *Tourism Management* 32: 770–779.
Bass, Rick. 2009. *The Wild Marsh: Four Seasons at Home in Montana*. Boston: Houghton Mifflin Harcourt.
———. 1996. *The Book of Yaak*. New York: Houghton Mifflin.
Baylor, Byrd. 1986 (1995). *I'm in Charge of Celebrations*. New York: Aladdin Paperbacks.
———. 1978 (1998). *The Way to Start a Day*. New York: Aladdin Paperbacks.
———. 1978 (1997). *The Other Way to Listen*. New York: Aladdin Paperbacks.

Beauvais, Gary 2008. "Vertebrate Wildlife of the Red Desert." In *Red Desert: History of a* Place, edited by Annie Proulx, 143–170. Austin: University of Texas Press.

Beletsky, Les, and Jon L. Dunn. 2006. *Bird Songs: 250 North American Birds in Song.* San Francisco: Chronicle Books.

Benediktsson, Karl. 2007. "'Scenophobia,' Geography and the Aesthetic Politics of Landscape." *Geografiska Annaler* 89 B (3): 203–217.

Biodiversity Conservation Alliance. 2009. "Red Desert." Accessed 30 October 2009 http://www.voiceforthewild.org/l

Blake, Kevin. 2006. "First View." *Trail & Timberline Quarterly* 993: 10–12.

Bowden, Charles.2008. "The Emptied Prairie." *National Geographic Magazine.* Accessed 29 September 2011 http://ngm.nationalgeographic.com/2008/01/emptied–north–dakota/bowden–text

Bowden, Charles. 2006. *Inferno.* Austin: University of Texas Press.

Brady, Emily. 2002. "Interpreting Environments." *Essays in Philosophy* 3 (1). Accessed 28 October 2011. http://commons.pacificu.edu/eip/vol3/iss1/16

Brown, Thomas C. 1984. "The Concept of Value in Resource Allocation." *Land Economics.* 60 (3): 231–246.

Bryce, S.A., J.M. Omernik, D.A. Pater, M. Ulmer, J. Schaar, J. Freeouf, R. Johnson, P. Kuck, and S.H. Azevedo. 1996. *Ecoregions of North Dakota and South Dakota, (color poster with map, descriptive text, summary tables, and photographs).* Reston: U.S. Geological Survey.

Bunkše, Edmunds V. 2007. "Feeling Is Believing, or Landscape as a Way of Being in the World." *Geografiska Annaler* 89B (3): 219–231.

——. 2007. "Beyond Images: The Phenomenology of Travel *Versus* Tourism and Implications for Rural Landscapes." In *European Landscapes and Lifestyles: The Mediterranean and Beyond.* Lisbon: Edições Universitárias Lusófonas,1–12.

Burke, Edmund. 1757 (1990). A Philosophical Inquiry into the Origin of Our Ideas of the Sublime and Beautiful. Oxford, U.K.: Oxford University Press.

Buttimer, Anne. 1976. "Grasping the Dynamism of Lifeworld." *Annals of the Association of American Geographers* 66 (2): 277–292.

Callicott, J. Baird. 1984. "The Land Aesthetic." *Orion Nature Quarterly* 3: 16–22.

Campbell, Joseph. 1949 (2008). *The Hero with a Thousand Faces.* New York: Pantheon Books.

Capra, Fritjof. 1976 (1989). *The Tao of Physics (Second Edition).* New York: Bantam Books.

Carlson, Allen. 2010. "Environmental Aesthetics." In *The Stanford Encyclopedia of Philosophy (Fall 2010 Edition),* edited by Edward N. Zalta. Accessed 21 October 2010. http://plato.stanford.edu/archives/fall2010/entries/environmental–aesthetics/

——. 1979. "Appreciation and the Natural Environment." *The Journal of Aesthetics and Art Criticism* 37 (3): 267–275.

Casey, Edward S. 2001. "Between Geography and Philosophy: What Does It Mean to Be in the Place–World?" *Annals of the Association of American Geographers* 91 (4): 683–693.

Cather, Willa. 1918. *My Ántonia*. Boston: Houghton Mifflin.

———. 1927 (1990). *Death Comes for the Archbishop*. New York: Vintage Books.

Catlin, George. 1841. *Letters and Notes on the Manners, Customs, and Condition of the North American Indians, Vol. 1*. Picadilly: Tosswill and Myers. Cites in Sheppard 1995.

Cheng, Antony, Linda Kruger, and Steven Daniels. 2003. "'Place' as an Integrating Concept in Natural Resource Politics: Propositions for a Social Science Research Agenda." *Society and Natural Resources* 16:87–104.

Chenowith, Richard E., and Paul Gobster. 1990. "The Nature and Ecology of Aesthetic Experiences in the Landscape." *Landscape Journal* 9 (1): 1–9.

Childs, Craig. 2006. *House of Rain: Tracking a Vanished Civilization across the American Southwest*. New York: Little, Brown and Company.

———. 2002. *Soul of Nowhere*. Seattle: Sasquatch Books.

Clifford, Hal. 2002. "The Last Lonesome Place." *OnEarth*. Accessed 2 November 2011 http://www.nrdc.org/onearth/o2fal/desert1.asp

Cohen, Erik. 1979. "A Phenomenology of Tourist Experiences." *Sociology* 13 (2): 179–201.

Collins, Sally, and Elizabeth Larry. 2007. *Caring for Our Natural Assets: An Ecosystem Services Perspective*. Portland: USDA Forest Service Pacific Northwest Research Station.

Conard, R., and S. Hess. 1998. *Tallgrass Prairie National Preserve Legislative History, 1920–1996*. Iowa City: Tallgrass Historians L.C.

Cosgrove, Denis. 1985. "Perspective and Evolution of the Landscape Idea." *Transactions of the Institute of British Geographers* 10 (1): 45–62.

Crang, Michael. 1997. "Picturing Practices: Research through the Tourist Gaze." *Progress in Human Geography* 21 (3): 359–373.

Cromartie, John B. 1998. "Net Migration in the Great Plains Increasingly Linked to Natural Amenities and Suburbanization." *Rural Development Perspectives* 13 (1): 27–34.

Cronon, William. 1995. "The Trouble with Wilderness; or, Getting Back to the Wrong Nature." In *Uncommon Ground*, edited by William Cronon. New York: W. W. Norton & Co., 69–90.

Dakin, Susan. 2003. "There's More to Landscape than Meets the Eye: Towards Inclusive Landscape Assessment in Resource and Environmental Management." *Canadian Geographer* 47 (2): 185–200.

Davenport, Mae A. and Dorothy H. Anderson. 2005. "Getting from Sense of Place to Place-Based Management: An Interpretive Investigation of Place Meanings and Perceptions of Landscape Change." *Society and Natural Resources*. 18: 625–641.

De Bres, Karen J., David E. Kromm, and Steven E. White. 1993. "Comment on the Future of the Great Plains: Not a Buffalo Commons." *FOCUS on Geography* 43 (4): 16.

Dillard, Annie. 1974 (1999.) *Pilgrim at Tinker Creek.* New York: Harper Collins.

Eaton, Marcia Muelder. 1998. "Fact and Fiction in the Aesthetic Appreciation of Nature." *The Journal of Aesthetics and Art Criticism* 56 (2): 149–156.

Eisenhauer, Brian, Richard Krannich, and Dale Blahna. 2000. "Attachments to Special Places on Public Lands : An Analysis of Activities, Reason for Attachments, and Community Connections." *Society & Natural Resources* 13 (5): 421–441.

Eliade, Mircea. 1967. *Myths, Dreams and Mysteries.* Translated by Philip Mairet. New York: Harper & Row.

Emerson, Ralph Waldo. 1909. *Nature.* New York: Duffield & Company.

Evernden, Neil. 1983. "Beauty and Nothingness: Prairie as Failed Resource." *Landscape* 23 (3): 1–9.

Faulstich, Paul. 1998. "Geophilia: Landscape and Humanity." *Wild Earth* Spring 1998: 82–89.

Ferguson, Charles. 2008. "Geology of the Red Desert." In *Red Desert: History of a Place,* edited by Annie Proulx, 85–105. Austin: University of Texas Press.

Flores, Dan. 2001. *The Natural West: Environmental History in the Great Plains and Rocky Mountains.* Norman: University of Oklahoma Press. National Park Service. 2011.

Foreman, Dave. 1994. "Where Man Is a Visitor." In *Place of the Wild,* edited by David Clarke Burks. Washington, D. C.: Island Press.

Forman, Richard T. T. 2000. "Estimate of the Area Affected Ecologically by the Road System in the United States." *Conservation Biology* 14: 31–35.

Forrest, Steve, Holly Strand, William H. Haskins, Curt Freese, Jonathan Proctor , and Eric Dinerstein. 2004. *Ocean of Grass: A Conservation Assessment for the Northern Great Plains.* Bozeman: Northern Plains Conservation Network and Northern Great Plains Ecoregion, WWF–US.

Friends of the Red Desert. 2009. "Desert Values." 30 October 2009. http://www.reddesert.org/values/index.php

Frost, Robert. 1996. *The Collected Notebooks of Robert Frost.* Edited by Robert Faggan. Cambridge: Belknap Press of Harvard University Press.

Fudge, Robert. 2001 "Imagination and the Science–Based Aesthetic Appreciation of Unscenic Nature." *Journal of Aesthetics and Art Criticism* 59: 275–285.

Fuguitt, Glenn V. and Calvin L. Beale. 1996. "Recent Trends in Nonmetropolitan Migration: Toward a New Turnaround?" *Growth and Change* 27: 156–174.

Fuhlendorf, S. D. and D. M. Engle 2001. "Restoring Heterogeneity on Rangelands: Ecosystem Management Based on Evolutionary Grazing Patterns." *BioScience* 51: 626–632.

Funk, Rex. 1996. "Experiencing Albuquerque's Open Space: Aesthetics and Ethics." Accessed 21 October 2010. http://www.cabq.gov/aes/s10pnspc.html

Gardner, R. 2009. "Constructing a Technological Forest: Nature, Culture, and Tree–Planting in the Nebraska Sand Hills." *Environmental History* 14 (2): 275–298.

Garrod, Brian. 2009. "Understanding the Relationship between Tourism Destination Imagery and Tourist Photography." *Journal of Travel Research* 47: 346–358.

Garstka, Katharine. 2011. "Welcome to Historic Marmarth." Accessed 18 September 2011. http://www.marmarth.org/index.htm

Giblett, Rod. 2007. "Shooting the Sunburnt Country, the Land of Sweeping Plains, the Rugged Mountain Ranges: Australian Landscape and Wilderness Photography." *Continuum: Journal of Media & Cultural Studies* 21 (3): 335–346.

Gifford, Don. 1993. "The Touch of Landscape." In *Landscape, Natural Beauty and the Arts,* edited by Salim Kemal and Ivan Gaskell, 127–138. New York: Cambridge University Press.

Gober, Patricia. 2000. "In Search of Synthesis." *Annals of the Association of American Geographers* 90 (1): 1–11.

Gobster, Paul. 1999. "An Ecological Aesthetic for Forest Landscape Management." *Landscape Journal* 18(1):54–64.

Godlovitch, Stan.1998. "Evaluating Nature Aesthetically." *The Journal of Aesthetics and Art Criticism* 56 (2):113–125.

Goin, Peter. 2001. "Visual Literacy." *Geographical Review* 91 (1–2): 363–369.

Gruchow, Paul. 1985 (1990). *Journal of a Prairie Year.* Minneapolis: Milkweed Editions.

Haines, Aubrey L. 1974. *Yellowstone National Park: Its Exploration and Establishment.* U.S. Department of the Interior National Park Service. Accessed 30 September 2011 http://www.cr.nps.gov/history/online_books/haines1/iee3a.htm

Hamill, Sam and J. P. Seaton, eds. 2004. *The Poetry of Zen.* Boston: Shambhala.

Harrison, Jim. *In Search of Small Gods.* Port Townsend, WA : Copper Canyon Press. 2009.

Harrison, Jim and Ted Kooser. 2003. *Braided Creek: A Conversation in Poetry.* Port Townsend: Copper Canyon Press.

Hart, John F. 1982. "The Highest Form of the Geographer's Art." *Annals of the Association of American Geographers* 72: 1–29.

Henry, Thomas. 2009. "Trails and Grasslands." Accessed 13 January 2009. http://www.trailsandgrasslands.com

Herzog, Thomas R. and Gregory J. Barnes. 1999. "Tranquility and Preference Revisited." *Journal of Environmental Psychology* 19 (2): 171–181.

Heyd, Thomas. 2003. "Basho and the Aesthetics of Wandering: Recuperating Space, Recognizing Place, and Following the Ways of the Universe." *Philosophy East & West* 53(3): 291–307.

———. 2001. "Aesthetic Appreciation and the Many Stories about Nature." *British Journal of Aesthetics* 41 (2): 125–137.

Hurt, R. Douglas. 1985. "The National Grasslands: Origin and Development in the Dust Bowl." *Agricultural History* 59 (2): 246–259.

Johnson, Kenneth. 1993. "When Deaths Exceed Births: Natural Decrease in the United States." *International Regional Science Review* 15 (2): 179–198.

Johnson, Kenneth and John B. Cromartie. 2006. "The Rural Rebound and Its Aftermath: Changing Demographic Dynamics and Regional Contrasts." In *Population Change and Rural Society*, edited by W. Kandel and D. Brown, 25–49. The Netherlands: Springer.

Jones, D. 2005. "Don't sacrifice the Northern Red Desert for one use." *Casper Star–Tribune*, October 24.

Jones, George 2008. "Sagebrush." In *Red Desert: History of a Place*, edited by Annie Proulx, 201–215. Austin: University of Texas Press.

Kant, Immanuel. Described in Forsey, Jane. 2007. "Is a Theory of the Sublime Possible?" *The Journal of Aesthetics and Art Criticism* 65 (4): 381–389.

Kaplan, Stephen. 1979. "Perception and Landscape: Conception and Misconception." In *Proceedings of Our National Landscape*, USDA Forest Service General Technical Report PSW–35: 241–248.

———. 1987. "Aesthetics, Affect, and Cognition: Environmental Preference from an Evolutionary Perspective." *Environment and Behavior* 19 (1): 3–32.

———. 2001. "Meditation, Restoration, and the Management of Mental Fatigue." *Environment and Behavior* 33: 480–506.

Keltner, Dacher and Jonathan Haidt. 2003. "Approaching Awe, a Moral, Spiritual, and Aesthetic Emotion." *Cognition and Emotion* 17 (2): 297–314.

Kieley, James F. 1940. *A Brief History of the National Park Service*. US Department of the Interior National Park Service. Accessed 30 September 2011. http://www.cr.nps.gov/history/online_books/kieley/index.htm

Kinsey, Joni L. 1995. "Not So Plain: Art of the American Prairies." *Great Plains Quarterly* 15 (3): 185–200.

Kinsey, Joni L., R. Roberts, and R. Sayr. 1996. "Prairie Prospects: The Aesthetics of Plainness." *Prospects* 21: 261–297.

Kinzig, Ann P. 2001. "Bridging Disciplinary Divides to Address Environmental and Intellectual Challenges." *Ecosystems* 4 (8) : 709–715.

Kirby, Don. 2009. *Grasslands*. Portland: Nazraeli Press.

Konečni, Vladimir J. 2010. "Aesthetic Trinity Theory and the Sublime." In *Proceedings of the European Society for Aesthetics, Vol. 2*, edited by A. Bertinetto, F. Dorsch, and C. Todd, 244–264.

Least Heat-Moon, William. 1991. *PrairyErth: A Deep Map*. Boston: Houghton Mifflin.

Lao Tzu. 1991 (2005). *Tao Te Ching*. Translated by Charles Muller. New York: Barnes & Noble Classics.

Leidy, Joseph. 1869. "On the Extinct Mammalian Fauna of Dakota and Nebraska, Including an Account of Some Allied Forms from Other Localities, Together with a Synopsis of the Mammalian Remains of North America." *Journal of the Academy of Natural Sciences of Philadelphia* (7): 1–472.

Leopold, Aldo. 1966. *A Sand County Almanac: With Essays on Conservation from Round River*. New York: Ballantine Books.

———. 1949 (1989). *A Sand County Almanac and Sketches Here and There*. Oxford: Oxford University Press.

Lockwood, Jeffrey A. 2008. "Insects of the Red Desert: An Exercise in Scientific Humility." In *Red Desert: History of a* Place, edited by Annie Proulx, 189–199. Austin: University of Texas Press.

Lopez, Barry. 2007. Coldscapes. *National Geographic Magazine*: 142–145.

———. 1986 (1987). *Arctic Dreams: Imagination and Desire in a Northern Landscape*. New York: Bantam Books.

Lu, Max and Darci A. Paull. 2007. "Assessing the Free Land Programs for Reversing Rural Depopulation." *Great Plains Research* 17(1):73–86.

Malotki, Ekkehart and Donald E. Weaver, Jr. 2002. *Stone Chisel and Yucca Brush: Colorado Plateau Rock Art*. Illustrations by Patricia McCreery. Walnut: Kiva Publishing.

Massey, Douglas S. 2002. "A Brief History of Human Society: The Origin and Role of Emotion in Social Life." *American Sociological Review* 67: 1–29.

Mattison, Ray H., Robert A. Grom, and Joanne W. Stockert, eds. 1968. *History of Badlands National Monument and the White River (Big) Badlands of South Dakota*. Badlands Natural History Association. Accessed 31 Aug 2011. http://www.cr.nps.gov/history/online_books/badl/index.htm

McMurtry, Larry. 2006. In *Home Ground: Language for an American Landscape*. Edited by Barry Lopez and Debra Gwartney San Antonio: Trinity University Press.

McNab, W. H. and E. Avers. 1994. "Ecological Subregions of the United States." USDA Forest Service WO-WSA-5. Accessed 20 November 2009. http://www.fs.fed.us/land/pubs/ecoregions.

Meine, Curt. 1988. *Aldo Leopold: His Life and Work*. Madison: University of Wisconsin Press.

Meinig, D. W. 1979. "The Beholding Eye: Ten Versions of the Same Scene." In *The Interpretation of Ordinary Landscapes: Geographical Essays*, edited by D. W. Meinig, 33–48. New York: Oxford University Press.

Meloy, Ellen. 2003. *The Anthropology of Turquoise: Reflections on Desert, Sea, Stone, and Sky*. New York: Vintage Books.

Millenium Ecosystem Assessment. 2005. *Ecosystems and Human Well-Being: Synthesis*. Washington, DC.: Island Press.

Molvar, Erik. 2010. *Wyoming's Red Desert: A Photographic Journey*. Laguna Beach, CA: Laguna Wilderness Press.

Momaday, N. Scott. 1968 (1999). *House Made of Dawn*. New York: Harper Collins.

Moul, Francis. 2006. The National Grasslands: A Guide to America's Undiscovered Treasures. Lincoln: University of Nebraska Press.

Nash, Roderick. 1967. *Wilderness and the American Mind*. New Haven: Yale University Press.

National Park Service. 2005. *Oregon Trail National Historic Trail* bulletin.

The Nature Conservancy. 2011. "Grasslands and Prairies." Accessed 3 November 2011. http://www.nature.org/ourinitiatives/habitats/grasslands/index.htm

———. 2008. "Grassland Types of the Great Plains [Map]." Minneapolis: Central Division GIS Lab. Accessed 9 November 2011. http://dsc.discovery.com/earth/im–interview/grasslands–map–pg.html

Norris, Kathleen. 1993. *Dakota: A Spiritual Geography.* New York: Houghton Mifflin.

O'Brien, Dan. 2001. *Buffalo for the Broken Heart: Restoring Life to a Black Hills Ranch.* New York: Random House.

Oliver, Mary. 1986. *Dream Work.* New York: Atlantic Monthly Press.

Olivia, Aude, Soojin Park, and Talia Konkle. 2011. "Representing, Perceiving, and Remembering the Shape of Visual Space." In *Vision in 3D Environments,* edited by L. R. Harris and M. Jenkin. Cambridge: Cambridge University Press.

Olson, Eric. 1997. *National Grasslands Management: A Primer.* Washington, D.C.: USDA Forest Service.

Olstad, Tyra A. 2013. "Personal Experience and Public Place Creation." In *Place-Based Conservation: Perspectives from the Social Sciences,* edited by Daniel Williams, William Stewart and Linda Kruger. New York: Springer.

———. 2007. "Desert Dimensions: Attachment to a Place of Space." Masters Thesis, University of Wyoming.

Orabona, Andrea. 2008. "Birds of the Red Desert." In *Red Desert: History of a Place,* edited by Annie Proulx, 171–180. Austin: University of Texas Press.

Philbeck, John W. and Shannon O'Leary. 2005. "Remembered Landmarks Enhance the Precision of Path Integration." *Psicologica* 26: 7–24.

Pichaske, David. 2006. "Where Now 'Midwestern Literature'?" *Midwest Quarterly* 48 (1): 100–119.

Popper, Deborah and Frank Popper. 1999. "The Buffalo Commons: Metaphor as Method." *Geographical Review* 89(4): 491–510.

———. 1993. "The Buffalo Commons: Then and Now." *FOCUS on Geography* 43(4): 17–25.

———. 1987. "The Great Plains: From Dust to Dust." *Planning* 53(2): 12–18.

Price, John. 2004. *Not Just Any Land: A Personal and Literary Journey into the American Grasslands.* Lincoln: University of Nebraska Press.

Proulx, Annie, ed. 2008. *Red Desert: History of a Place.* Austin: University of Texas Press.

Quayle, William. 1905. *The Prairie and the Sea.* Cincinnati: Jennings and Graham.

Redington, Paul G. 1929. "Policy of the U.S. Biological Survey in Regard to Predatory Mammal Control." *Journal of Mammology* 10 (3): 276–279.

Reps, Paul and Nyogen Senzaki, eds. 1957 (1985). *Zen Flesh Zen Bones: A Collection of Zen and Pre-Zen Writings.* Rutland: Tuttle Publishing.

Retzinger, Jean 1998. "Framing the Tourist Gaze: Railway Journeys across Nebraska 1866–1906." *Great Plains Quarterly* 18 (3): 213–226.

Roebuck, Paul. 1993. "The Great Plains: from Bust to Bust." *FOCUS on Geography* 43 (4): 16.

Rolston, Holmes III. 1987. "Beauty and the Beast: Aesthetic Experience of Wildlife." In *Valuing Wildlife: Economic and Social Perspectives*, edited by Daniel J. Decker and Gary R. Goff, 187–1986. Boulder: Westview Press.

Rossum, Sonja and Stephen Lavin. 2000. "Where Are the Great Plains? A Cartographic Analysis." *Professional Geographer* 52 (3): 543–552.

Saito, Yuriko. 1998. "The Aesthetics of Unscenic Nature." *The Journal of Aesthetics and Art Criticism* 56(2): 101–111.

———. 1984. "Is There a Correct Aesthetic Appreciation of Nature?" *Journal of Aesthetic Education* 18 (4): 35–46.

Samson, Fred. B. and Fritz L. Knopf. 1994. "Prairie Conservation in North America." *BioScience* 44: 418–421.

Samson, Fred B., Fritz L. Knopf, and Wayne R. Ostlie. 2004. "Great Plains Ecosystems: Past, Present, and Future." *Wildlife Society Bulletin* 32: 6–15.

Samson, Fred B., Fritz L. Knopf, C. W. McCarthy, et al. 2008. "The Ecological Future of the North American Bison: Conceiving Long-Term, Large-Scale Conservation of Wildlife." *Conservation Biology* 22 (2): 252–266.

Schenbeck, D. N. Svingen, and T. W. Byer. 2003. "Planning for Population Viability on Northern Great Plains National Grasslands." *Wildlife Society Bulletin* 31 (4): 986–999.

Sanders, Scott Russell. 2009. "Foreword." In *Journal of a Prairie Year*, Paul Gruchow. Minneapolis: Milkweed Editions.

Sandhills Journey Scenic Byway. 2010. Custer County Chief: Broken Bow, NE.

Savage, Candace. 2004. *Prairie: A Natural History.* Vancouver: Greystone Books.

Scanlan, Tom. 1994. "The Prairie Eye." Proceedings of the 14th Annual North American Prairie Conference : 247–250.

———. 1990. "The Prairie as Perennial Symbol." *Proceedings of the Twelfth North American Prairie Conference*, eds. Daryl D. Smith and Carol A Jacobs, 201–204. Cedar Falls: University of Northern Iowa.

Shaffer, M. S. 1996. "'See America First': Re-Envisioning Nation and Region through Western Tourism." *Pacific Historical Review* 65 (4): 559–581.

Sheppard, Jerry G. 1995. "Singing Out of Tune: Cultural Perceptions and National Park History on the American Great Plains." PhD diss., Texas Tech University.

Shortridge, James R. 2005. "Regional Image and Sense of Place in Kansas." *Kansas History: A Journal of the Central Plains* 28: 202–219.

———. 2004. "A Cry for Help: Kansasfreeland.com." *Geographical Review* 94(4).

———. 1988. "The Heart of the Prairie: Culture Areas in the Central and Northern Great Plains." *Great Plains Quarterly* 8: 206–221.

Shumaker, S. A. and R. B. Taylor. 1983. "Toward a Classification of People-Place Relationships: A Model of Attachment to Place." In *Environmental Psychology: Directions and Perspectives*, edited by N. R. Feimer and E. S. Geller, 219–256. New York: Praeger.

Skidmore, Lorimer, quoted in Laura S. Harrison. 1986. *Architecture in the Parks A National Historic Landmark Theme Study.* National Park Service. Accessed 2

November 2011. http://www.cr.nps.gov/history/online_books/harrison/harrison28.htm

Smith, Brooke, ed. 2011. *Tatanka: The 2011 Guide to Custer State Park*. S. D. Department of Game, Fish and Parks. Accessed 6 September 2011. http://gfp.sd.gov/state-parks/directory/custer/docs/tatanka.pdf

Snow, C. P. 1963. *The Two Cultures: And a Second Look*. New York: Cambridge University Press.

Snyder, Gary. 1990. *Practice of the Wild*. Berkeley: North Point Press.

——. 1980. *The Real Work: Interviews and Talks 1964–1979*. New York: New Directions.

Sofaer, Anna, Volker Zinser, and Rolf M. Sinclair. 1979. "A Unique Solar Marking Construct." *Science* 206 (4416): 283–291.

Souman, Jan L., Ilja Frissen, Manish N. Sreenivasa, and Marc O. Ernst. 2009. "Walking Straight into Circles." *Current Biology* 19: 1538–1542.

Spirn, Anne Whiston. 1988. "The Poetics of City and Nature: Towards a New Aesthetic for Urban Design." *Landscape Journal* 7 (2): 108–126.

Stauber, Karl. 2001. "Why Invest in Rural America—And How? A Critical Public Policy Question for the 21st Century." *Economic Review* 86 (2): 57–74.

Stedman, Richard C. 2003. "Is It Really Just a Social Construction? The Contribution of the Physical Environment to a Sense of Place." *Society and Natural Resources* 16:671–685.

Stegner, Wallace. 1955. *Wolf Willow: A History, a Story, and a Memory of the Last Plains Frontier*. New York: Viking Press.

Stokols, D., and Shumaker, S. A. 1981. "People in Places: A Transactional View of Settings." In *Cognition, Social Behavior, and the Environment*, edited by J. H. Harvey, 441–488. Hillsdale, NJ: Erlbaum.

Strober, Myra H. Forthcoming. "Habits of the Mind: Challenges for Multidisciplinarity." *Social Epistemology*. Accessed 20 November 2009 http://www.stanford.edu/~myras/Publications.htm

Suzuki-Roshi, Shunryu. 1970. *Zen Mind, Beginner's Mind*. New York: Weatherhill.

Swanson Frederick J., Charles Goodrich, and Kathleen Dean Moore. 2008. "Bridging Boundaries: Scientists, Creative Writers, and the Long View of the Forest." *Frontiers in Ecology and the Environment* 6(9):499–504.

Tempest Williams, Terry. 2002. *Red: Passion and Patience in the Desert*. New York :Vintage Books.

——. 1991. *Refuge: An Unnatural History of Family and Place*. New York: Vintage Books.

Thacker, Robert. 1989. *The Great Prairie Fact and the Literary Imagination*. Albuquerque: University of New Mexico Press.

Thompson, Craig. 2008. "Water in the Red." In *Red Desert: History of a Place*, edited by Annie Proulx, 107–119. Austin: University of Texas Press.

Tilden, Freeman. 1957 (2007). *Interpreting our Heritage*. Chapel Hill: University of North Carolina Press.

Tolstoy, Leo. 1966. *War and Peace (Norton Critical Editions)*. Translated by Louse Maude and Aylmer Maude. New York: W W Norton & Co Inc.

Tredinnick, Mark. 2005. *The Land's Wild Music: Encounters with Barry Lopez, Peter Matthiessen, Terry Tempest Williams, and James Galvin*. San Antonio: Trinity University Press.

Trimble, Stephen. 1996. "Our Gardens, Our Canyons." In *Testimony: Writers of the West Speak on Behalf of Utah Wilderness*, edited by S. Trimble and T. Tempest Williams, 19–22. Minneapolis: Milkweed Editions.

Trimble, Stephen and Terry Tempest Williams. 1996. "An Act of Faith." In *Testimony: Writers of the West Speak on Behalf of Utah Wilderness*, edited by S. Trimble and T. Tempest Williams. Minneapolis: Milkweed Editions.

Tuan, Yi-Fu. 2004. "Life as a Field Trip." *The Geographical Review* 94 (1–2): 41–45.

——. 2001. "The Desert and I: A Study in Affinity." *Michigan Quarterly Review*. 40 (1): 7–18.

——. 1979. "Thought and Landscape: The Eye and the Mind's Eye." In *The Interpretation of Ordinary Landscapes: Geographical Essays*, edited by D. W. Meinig, 89–102. New York: Oxford University Press.

——. 1977. *Space and Place: The Perspective of Experience*. Minneapolis: University of Minnesota Press.

——. 1974. *Topophilia: A Study of Environmental Perception, Attitudes, and Values*. New York: Columbia University Press.

Turner, Jack. 1997. *The Abstract Wild*. Tucson: University of Arizona Press.

United States Department of the Interior Bureau of Land Management. 1984. *BLM Manual Handbook H-8400, Rel. 8-24. Visual Resource Management* and *BLM Manual Handbook H-8401. Visual Resource Inventory:* Washington, D.C. Accessed 18 April 2002. http://www.blm.gov/nstc/VRM/Sitemahtml

——. Rawlins Field Office. 1996. Green River Resource Area Resource Management Plan and Final Environmental Impact Statement.

USDA Forest Service. 2010. "The Lone Tree Exhibit." Accessed 28 October 2011. http://www.fs.fed.us/grasslands/lonetree/index.shtml

——. 2007. "Valuing Ecosystem Services: Capturing the True Value of Nature's Capital." Accessed 21 February 2009 http://www.fs.fed.us/ecosystemservices

——. National Grasslands Management Review Team. 1996. Included in West 1990, Appendix A. (See Below)

——. 1995. *Landscape Aesthetics: A Handbook for Scenery Management*. Agriculture Handbook Number 701. Washington, D.C.: USDA Forest Service.

Urry, John. 1992. "The Tourist Gaze 'Revisited.'" *American Behavioural Scientist* 36: 172–186.

Wallach, Bret. 1985. "The Return of the Prairie." *Landscape* 28 (3): 1–6.

Wang, Ranxiao F., and Elizabeth S. Spelke. 2002. "Human Spatial Representation: Insights from Animals." *Trends in Cognitive Science* 6: 376–382.

West, Terry.1990. USDA Forest Service Management of the National Grasslands. *Agricultural History* 64(2): 86–98.

Whitman, Walt. 1892. *Specimen Days.* Philadelphia: David McKay.

Williams, Daniel R. and Susan I. Stewart. 1998. "Sense of Place: An Elusive Concept that is Finding a Home in Ecosystem Management." *Forest Science* 96(5): 18–23.

Williams, Daniel, Michael Patterson, Joseph W. Roggenbuck, and Alan E. Watson. 1992. "Beyond the Commodity Metaphor: Examining Emotional and Symbolic Attachment to Place." *Leisure Sciences* 14: 29–46.

Wilson, Edward O. 1998. *Consilience: The Unity of Knowledge.* New York: Alfred A. Knopf.

Wolbers, Thomas, and Mary Hegarty. 2010. "What Determines Our Navigational Abilities?" *Trends in Cognitive Sciences* 14: 138–146.

Wood, Richard E. 2008. *Survival of Rural America: Small Victories and Bitter Harvests.* Lawrence: University Press of Kansas.

Woods, Michael. 2005. *Rural Geography: Processes, Responses and Experiences in Rural Restructuring.* London: Sage Publications.

Wright, John K. 1947. "Terrae Incognitae: The Place of the Imagination in Geography." *Annals of the Association of American Geographers* 37 (1): 1–16.

Wycoff, William and Lary M. Dilsaver. 1997. "Promotional Imagery of Glacier National Park." *The Geographical Review* 87 (1): 1–26.

Wyoming State Office of Travel and Tourism. 2005. *Wyoming Vacation Guide.*

Wyoming Wilderness Association. 2006. *Wyoming Wilderness Roundup.* Summer/Fall.

Index

A

aesthetic experience, 32, 73-74, 152, 159, 188, 192

wildlife, 159-160

Alaska (Southeast), 196-206

Ancestral Puebloan, 12, 40, 52-53, 54, 58

archaeoastronomy, 58

archaeology, 40, 100-107

awe, 71

B

Badlands (geologic formation), 80, 97, 115, 139-140

Badlands National Park, 136, 137-145, 156, 160, 161, 164, 176, 179

beauty, 9, 14, 38, 41, 45, 71-72, 74, 78, 90, 130-131, 146, 148, 152, 164, 171, 172, 174, 179, 193, 227, 230, 232-233

Bennett, Lyle, 115

bird-watching, 156-159

bison, 161-164, 174, 191

black-footed ferret, 161, 164-165

Buffalo Commons, 162

Buffalo Gap National Grassland, 145, 148, 152, 165

Bureau of Land Management, 49, 83, 147, 150

C

cartography, 223-224

Cather, Willa, 33

cattle, 210-211

Chinde Mesa, 17, 21, 38, 102-104

Colter, Mary Jane, 115-116, 119

consilience, 191-192

Coronado, Francisco, 10-11

coyote, 28-29, 155, 161, 165

D

dawn, 62, 87, 134, 142, 166, 175, 229-230

disturbance regime, 161

Dust Bowl, 5, 145, 148

E

ecosystem services, 151

elk, 221

emptiness, 2, 6, 16, 28, 33, 36, 50, 69, 83, 85, 88, 111, 112, 128-129, 168, 171, 228-229, 235

enchantment, 72

enlightenment, 227

exposure, 111, 203, 228

F

Faith, South Dakota, 168

Flint Hills, Kansas, 184

Fossil Butte National Monument, 219-222, 225, 227

Fred Harvey Company, 116

G

grassland, 4, 47, 146-147, 161, 171, 185, 201, 223

Great Plains, 2, 5, 162, 167, 170-171

H
Hayden, Ferdinand, 140, 141
homestead, 5, 34, 36, 143, 145, 148, 173
Hopi, 12, 115-117
horizon, 4, 6, 16, 23, 51, 57, 63, 71-72, 88,
    99-103, 106, 166, 177, 184, 189, 209,
    224

I
interpretation, 178-180

J
Junior Ranger, 178

K
Kabotie, Fred, 116-118, 119
Kansas, 32, 34-35, 173-174, 184, 194
Kensho, 37, 227, 232
keystone species, 161
Konza Prairie Preserve, 184-191, 194-196,
    206-214

L
Lacey, John Fletcher, 38
landmark, 16, 18, 22-23, 46, 71, 112
landscape design, 6, 27
landscape perception, 2, 4-6, 19-20, 35,
    36, 47, 63, 64, 71-74, 77, 78, 132, 142,
    150-152, 159, 163, 171-174, 179, 180,
    189-191, 200-201
Leidy, Joseph, 140
Leopold, Aldo, 77, 126-127
loneliness, 6, 36, 90, 128, 129, 130, 168, 228
Lore, Herbert, 114-115

M
Marmarth, North Dakota, 170
Medora, North Dakota, 168, 169
"Mission 66," 118
monsoon, 65
mountains, 2, 7, 159
Muir, John, 11-12, 77, 104

N
National Grasslands, 22, 49, 147, 148-151,
    152, 153
National Park Service, 3, 6, 51, 65, 93, 142,
    143, 147, 164, 178
Navajo (Diné), 12
Nebraska, 1, 3, 6, 33, 171, 174
nighthawk, 157-158

P
Painted Desert, 10, 12-13, 16, 20, 26, 32,
    43, 76, 80-85, 90, 92, 99, 104, 125, 131
Painted Desert Inn, 16, 105, 114-116,
    118-119
paleontology, 140
Petrified Forest National Park, 9, 12, 38,
    42, 51-52, 58, 76, 93, 99, 114, 131, 156,
    223
petroglyph, 26, 54-56
photography, 22, 34, 46, 47, 86, 141, 148,
    154, 167, 172, 188, 203
Pilot Rock, 17, 32, 43, 44, 50, 70, 94, 95,
    96-99, 106, 107, 110, 121, 124
place, 14, 16, 19, 23, 25, 27-28, 31, 46, 47,
    74, 78, 79, 82, 86-89, 91, 101, 124,
    188, 204
place attachment, 78, 79, 91, 126, 183
place identity, 78, 79, 88, 126, 204
sense of place 46, 89, 152, 153, 206
plains, 5, 7, 16, 17, 33, 35, 40, 42, 50, 56, 58,
    63, 69, 78, 93, 95, 111, 132, 133, 180,
    201, 203, 204
Popper, Deborah and Frank, 146, 152
prairie, 1, 4, 5, 7, 10, 42, 47, 51, 111, 123,
    133, 138, 146, 152, 160, 161, 163, 164,
    174, 175, 177, 184, 188, 189, 194, 200,
    212-214
prairie dog, 82, 148, 160, 161, 162, 165
prairie madness, 129
Prospect-Refuge Theory, 19
Puerco Pueblo, 52
Puerco River, 40

Q
quest 117, 119-120

R
Red Desert, 80-88, 92
Rocky Mountain National Park, 2, 7
Roosevelt, Theodore, 12
"Route 66," 61

S
Sandhills Journey Scenic Byway, 41, 174, 189
Scottsbluff National Monument, 3, 8
sky, 3, 5, 15, 21, 22, 33, 66, 68, 69, 72, 101, 114, 119, 132-133, 134, 152, 171, 176, 186, 188, 203, 222, 225, 229, 230, 235
solitude, 6, 59, 62, 76, 129, 136
space, 3, 6, 8, 10, 12, 20, 27-28,40-42, 45, 47, 48, 70, 71, 75, 76, 78, 85, 88-90, 105, 110, 127, 128-129, 132, 171, 174, 188, 200-201, 235
sublime, 71-72, 77, 213
sunset, 4, 35, 36, 41, 70-71, 74, 193, 222, 227
swift fox, 161, 164, 165

T
Tallgrass Prairie National Preserve, 41, 147, 189
Tallgrass Prairie Parkway, 41
Tao, 78, 219, 223
Theodore Roosevelt National Park, 147, 166, 169, 175
Tongass National Forest, 196-206
tourism, 6, 7, 35, 46, 47, 48, 114, 167-169, 174-175, 180

travel, 35-36, 41, 95, 116, 128, 152, 163, 170, 173, 174, 175
trees, 22-23, 100, 197, 209

V
vacation, 34, 46
Visual Resource Inventory, 27
vulnerability, 22, 111, 228, 231

W
walking, 22, 25, 37, 42, 51, 60-62, 76-77, 90, 96,121, 128, 131-132, 158, 176, 186, 188, 189, 191,198, 201, 206-207, 210, 219, 220, 223, 225-226, 233
wandering, 16, 25, 96, 175-176, 229
Whipple, Amiel Weeks, 11
Wilderness (idea), 12, 15, 46, 91, 98, 110, 119-120, 122, 133, 194
Wilderness Area (land management classification), 12, 14, 17-18, 26, 43, 90, 99, 104
wildlife reintroduction, 164
wind, 9, 15, 18, 20, 25, 28, 40, 42, 52, 83, 87, 91, 92, 112, 124, 129, 130, 133, 152, 174, 167, 177, 178, 186, 187, 194, 196, 201, 203, 206, 207, 209, 214, 225, 227, 228, 230, 231
winter, 57, 157, 202, 212, 220, 228-234
writing, 107, 146, 222-224

Y
Yellowstone National Park, 1, 141, 163, 180

Z
Zazen, 42, 51